Living Without Free Will

In *Living Without Free Will*, Derk Pereboom contends that given our best scientific theories, factors beyond our control ultimately produce all of our actions, and that we are therefore not morally responsible for them. His stance is similar to traditional hard determinism, although he maintains that if our actions exhibit the sort of indeterminacy attributed to quantum mechanical events, they would still be produced by factors beyond our control, and we would not be responsible for them.

Pereboom defends the view that morality, meaning, and value remain intact even if we lack moral responsibility, and moreover, he argues that adopting his position could even be significantly beneficial for our lives.

Living Without Free Will brings an original perspective to the topic of free will that compels us to reevaluate many of our most deeply entrenched ideas about ourselves. It will interest professionals and students in philosophy, psychology, and criminology.

Derk Pereboom is a professor of philosophy at the University of Vermont.

RECENT TITLES:

For my parents, Jan Dirk and Maria Elisabeth

Living Without Free Will

DERK PEREBOOM

University of Vermont

CAMBRIDGE
UNIVERSITY PRESS

PUBLISHED BY THE PRESS SYNDICATE OF THE UNIVERSITY OF CAMBRIDGE
The Pitt Building, Trumpington Street, Cambridge, United Kingdom

CAMBRIDGE UNIVERSITY PRESS
The Edinburgh Building, Cambridge CB2 2RU, UK
40 West 20th Street, New York, NY 10011-4211, USA
10 Stamford Road, Oakleigh, VIC 3166, Australia
Ruiz de Alarcón 13, 28014 Madrid, Spain
Dock House, The Waterfront, Cape Town 8001, South Africa

http://www.cambridge.org

First published 2001

Printed in the United States of America

Typeface Bembo 10.5/13 pt.   *System* QuarkXPress [BTS]

A catalog record for this book is available from the British Library.

Library of Congress Cataloging in Publication Data

Pereboom, Derk, 1957–
Living without free will / Derk Pereboom.
p.   cm. – (Cambridge studies in philosophy)
Includes bibliographical references.
ISBN 0-521-79198-7 (hardcover)
1. Free will and determinism.   I. Title.   II. Series.
BJ1461 .P47 2001
123'.5 – dc21   00-059877

ISBN   0 521 79198 7   hardback

[|7ﬧ|12]

Contents

Acknowledgments

Many people have provided helpful comments on the material in this book. For conversations and other exchanges about the issues raised here, I want to thank Marilyn Adams, Robert Adams, Lynne Rudder Baker, Robert Card, Emily Fleschner, Ken Gemes, Bernard Gert, Timothy Hall, Isaac Levi, Stephanie Menner, Amanda Mikkel, Dana Nelkin, Michael Otsuka, Cranston Paull, Carol Rovane, Seana Schiffren, George Sher, Walter Sinnott-Armstrong, Rachel Wertheimer, and many students I have taught over the past decade.

A number of philosophers who work on free will have provided splendid comments on some or all of the manuscript – Robert Bishop, Randolph Clarke, Keith De Rose, Richard Double, John Fischer, Carl Ginet, Ishtiyaque Haji, Robert Kane, Michael McKenna, Alfred Mele, Saul Smilansky, Linda Zagzebski, and the anonymous referees. Their acute and insightful challenges have very much helped to make the book what it became, and for this I thank them.

I acknowledge my colleagues at the University of Vermont for their contributions. Kathy Fox in Sociology gave me valuable assistance with the material on criminology. Fellow philosophers Sin yee Chan, Charles Guignon, Arthur Kuflik, Don Loeb, William Mann, and Alan Wertheimer all provided perceptive discussion and criticism. Leslie Weiger helped correct the page proofs. I would like to thank in particular David Christensen and Hilary Kornblith, each of whom read and commented on the entire manuscript at least twice, and with whom I discussed many issues for countless hours. They made invaluable contributions to the shape and content of the book.

I thank especially my wife, Nancy, for many enlightening conversations about these issues, and for her support in bringing this project to completion.

Finally, I wish to thank Cambridge University Press, and in particular, Ronald Cohen, whose editorial work was superb, and Robyn Wainner, whose efforts on behalf of the book were first-rate.

I have used previously published articles of mine in this book. "Determinism Al Dente," *Noûs* 29 (1995), provides the book's general conception, and "Alternative Possibilities and Causal Histories," *Philosophical Perspectives* 14 (2000), with revisions, constitutes part of Chapter 1. In addition, I draw upon my "Review of Robert Kane, The Significance of Free Will," *Ethics* 111 (2000) in Chapter 2, and upon my introduction to the anthology *Free Will* (Indianapolis: Hackett, 1997), pp. vii–x, in the Introduction to this book. I thank the publishers for permission to incorporate this material here.

Introduction: Hard Incompatibilism

In recent decades, with advances in psychology, sociology, and neuro-science, the notion that certain patterns of human behavior may ultimately be due to factors beyond our control has become a serious cultural concern. In our society, the possibility that criminal behavior, for example, may be caused by influences in upbringing or by abnormal features of the brain is very much a live hypothesis. Furthermore, many people agree that criminals cannot be blameworthy for actions and tendencies produced in this way. At the same time, most assume that even if criminal actions frequently have this sort of causal history, ordinary actions are not similarly generated, but rather are freely chosen, and we can be praiseworthy or blameworthy for them.

A less popular and more radical claim is that factors beyond our control produce all of our actions. Since the first appearance of strate-gies for comprehensive explanation in ancient times, philosophers have been aware that our theories about the world can challenge our com-monplace assumptions about agency in this more general way. One reaction to this stronger claim is that it would leave morality as it is, or that if any revisions must occur, they are insubstantial. But another is that we would not then be blameworthy or praiseworthy for our actions – in the philosophical idiom, we would not be morally respon-sible for them. I shall argue that our best scientific theories indeed have the consequence that we are not morally responsible for our actions. A common objection to this position is that if it were correct, morality would have no place, and human life would be meaningless and without value. I shall defend the view that morality, meaning, and value remain intact even if we are not morally responsible, and that adopting this perspective could provide significant benefits for our lives.[1]

The problem about moral responsibility arises from a conflict between two powerful considerations. On the one hand, we human beings feel that we are the source of our actions in a particularly weighty sense. We feel that the way in which we are the source of our actions is very different from the way a machine is the source of what it produces. We express this sense of difference by attributing moral responsibility to human beings but not to machines. Traditionally, it has been assumed that moral responsibility requires us to have some type of free will in producing our actions, and hence we assume that human beings, but not machines, have this sort of free will. At the same time, there are reasons for regarding human beings as more like machines than we ordinarily suppose. These reasons stem from various sources: most prominently, from scientific views that consider human beings to be parts of nature and therefore governed by natural laws, and from theological concerns that require everything that happens to be causally determined by God. For many contemporary philosophers, the first of these is especially compelling, and as a result, they accept determinism or claims about the universe that are similarly threatening to moral responsibility.

The history of philosophy records three types of reaction to this dilemma. Some philosophers maintain that determinism is not compatible with the free will required for moral responsibility – they are *incompatibilists*. But they resist the reasons for determinism, and claim that we have free will of this kind – this is the *libertarian* position. *Hard determinists* (William James's term[2]) are also incompatibilists, but they accept determinism and deny that we have the sort of free will required for moral responsibility. *Compatibilists* contend that we may have the free will required for moral responsibility even if determinism is true. In this book, I argue that there are strong reasons to reject both libertarianism and compatibilism and to accept a view akin to hard determinism instead.

According to the libertarian, we can choose to act without being causally determined by factors beyond our control, and we can therefore be morally responsible for our actions. Arguably, this is the

---

1. In this book, I develop ideas that I presented in the article "Determinism *Al Dente*," *Noûs* 29 (1995), pp. 21–45.
2. William James, "The Dilemma of Determinism," in *The Will to Believe* (New York: Dover, 1956), pp. 145–83.

common-sense position. Libertarian views can be divided into two categories. In *agent-causal libertarianism*, free will is explained by the existence of agents who can cause actions not by virtue of any state they are in, such as a belief or a desire, but just by themselves – as substances. Such agents are capable of causing actions in this way without being causally determined to do so. In an attractive version of agent-causal theory, when such an agent acts freely, she can be inclined but not causally determined to act by factors such as her desires and beliefs. But such factors will not exhaust the causal account of the action. The agent herself, independently of these factors, provides a fundamental element. Agent-causal libertarianism has been advocated by Thomas Reid, Roderick Chisholm, Richard Taylor, Randolph Clarke, and Timothy O'Connor. Perhaps the views of William of Ockham and Immanuel Kant also count as agent-causal libertarianism. In the second category, which I call *event-causal libertarianism*, only causation involving states or events is permitted. Required for moral responsibility is not agent causation, but production of actions that crucially involves indeterministic causal relations between events. The Epicurean philosopher Lucretius provides a rudimentary version of such a position when he claims that free actions are accounted for by uncaused swerves in the downward paths of atoms. Sophisticated variants of this type of libertarianism have been developed by Robert Kane and Carl Ginet.

Libertarianism and incompatibilism more generally are the main concerns of the first chapter of this book. There I examine Frankfurt-style arguments against incompatibilism, which aim to show that moral responsibility does not require alternative possibilities for action. I contend that such arguments are largely successful, and in the process I present a new type of Frankfurt-style argument that I believe will resist objections to earlier versions. However, I also argue that such arguments do not threaten what I consider to be the core incompatibilist claim – that moral responsibility requires actions to have indeterministic actual causal histories, or more fundamentally, to have causal histories that make agents ultimate sources of their actions. This discussion plays two important roles in my argument. On the one hand, it serves to capture what I consider to be the most significant requirements for moral responsibility. And further, it thereby provides a way to ascertain what sort of libertarianism might secure agents that are morally responsible.

Accordingly, in the second chapter, I argue that libertarians of the event-causal variety are mistaken to think that agents can be morally responsible for the sorts of indeterminist events they envision human actions to be, for the reason that this kind of indeterminism does not allow agents to be the sources of their actions in the way required. There I also contend that agent-causal libertarianism might well satisfy this requirement. In the third chapter, I develop the claim that agent-causal theory is nevertheless seriously challenged by empirical considerations. The main problem for this position is that our choices produce physical events in the brain and in the rest of the body, and these events seem to be governed by physical laws. The agent-causal libertarian must make it credible that our actions can be freely willed in the sense it advocates given the evidence we have about these physical laws. I argue that given this evidence, it is doubtful that our actions can be freely willed in the sense that the agent-causal view proposes.

Beginning students typically recoil at the compatibilist response to the problem of moral responsibility. Nevertheless, for philosophers, retaining the legitimacy of our ordinary attitudes toward human actions, and at the same time regarding them as causally determined, has been so attractive that a majority of them are confirmed compatibilists. Galen Strawson points out that a compatibilist may believe any of at least the following:

(i)   That determinism (D) is true, that D does not imply that we lack the free will required for moral responsibility (F), but that we in fact lack F.

(ii) That D is true, that D does not imply that we lack F, but that it has not been shown whether or not we have F.

(iii) That D is true, and that we have F.

(iv) That D is true, that we have F, and that our having F requires that D be true.

(v)   That D may or may not be true [i.e., we do not know whether D is true], but that in any case we have F.

(vi) That D is not true, but that we have F, and would have F even if D were true.

(vii) That D is not true, that we do not have F, but that F is nonetheless compatible with D.[3]

James calls adherents of positions (iii) and (iv) *soft determinists*. My discussion of compatibilism focuses on those who hold that whether or not D is true we have F, a position that subsumes (iii)–(vi). From now on, I will use the term "compatibilism" to refer to this position.

3.   Galen Strawson, *Freedom and Belief* (Oxford: Oxford University Press, 1986), p. 5.

In the current discussion, we can distinguish two prominent routes to compatibilism. The first type, developed by P.F. Strawson, specifies that contrary to what incompatibilists assume, the truth of determinism is irrelevant to questions of moral responsibility. According to this sort of view, the basis of moral responsibility is found in reactive attitudes such as indignation, moral resentment, guilt, and gratitude. For example, the fact that agents are typically resented for certain kinds of immoral actions is what constitutes their being blameworthy for performing them. Justification for claims of blameworthiness and praiseworthiness ends in the system of human reactive attitudes. Because moral responsibility has this type of basis, the truth or falsity of determinism is immaterial to whether we are justified in holding agents morally responsible. Strawson's position appears to fall under (v) in our table.

The second and most common type of route to compatibilism tries to distinguish causal circumstances of actions that exclude moral responsibility from those that do not. What underlies this approach is the conviction that moral responsibility requires some type of causal integration between the agent's psychology and his action, while it does not demand the absence of causal determination. This route to compatibilism is typically explored by surveying our intuitions about blameworthiness and praiseworthiness in specific cases — cases involving, for example, coercion, addiction, mental illness, hypnotism, and brainwashing. These reactions are used to discover the conditions on causal integration that moral responsibility requires. Varieties of this sort of view have been developed by Aristotle, Augustine, Leibniz, and Hume, and in the twentieth century by R. Hobart, A.J. Ayer, Harry Frankfurt, Gary Watson, and John Fischer, and with respect to praiseworthiness, by Susan Wolf. Proponents of this route maintain views that range from (iii)–(vi).

In the fourth chapter, I contest each of these two compatibilist strategies. I argue that contrary to Strawson's view, determinism can indeed be relevant to the attitudes and judgments that comprise our practice of holding people morally responsible. In addition, I contend that the causal integrationist accounts fail to provide sufficient conditions for moral responsibility, and that as a result, none can plausibly capture conditions under which agents are both determined and morally responsible. To defend this conclusion, I devise effective counterexamples to these conditions, and a general argument that no relevant distinctions can be made between cases in which agents are determined in ways compatibilists think are consistent with moral responsibility and those in which agents are determined in ways that clearly undermine moral responsibility. I maintain that as a result, we are forced to deny that agents are morally responsible if their actions are causally determined, even if these agents meet compatibilist conditions on moral responsibility.

Hard determinists argue that moral responsibility is incompatible with determinism, and because determinism is true, we lack the sort of free will required for moral responsibility. Proponents of this position are relatively uncommon, but Spinoza, Holbach, Priestley, C.D. Broad, B.F. Skinner, Galen Strawson, and Bruce Waller defend this view, or ones similar to it. Critics have expressed many worries about views of this type. They have argued, for example, that hard determinism threatens our self-conception as deliberative agents, that it undermines the reactive attitudes that lie at the core of human interpersonal relationships, that if hard determinism were true, there would be no reason to be moral, and then perhaps even morality itself would be incoherent.

I argue for a position closely related to hard determinism. Yet the term "hard determinism" is not an adequate label for my view, since I do not claim that determinism is true. As I understand it, whether an indeterministic or a deterministic interpretation of quantum mechanics is true is currently an open question. I do contend, however, that not only is determinism incompatible with moral responsibility, but so is the sort of indeterminacy specified by the standard interpretation of quantum mechanics, if that is the only sort of indeterminacy there is. Furthermore, I argue that we have no evidence for indeterminacy of the kind that would be required for agent-causal libertarianism, and that therefore, we have no evidence that we are morally responsible. Supplying an expression to designate this position presents a challenge. Richard Double has coined "no-free-will-either-way theory," but this term suggests the view of G. Strawson that whether or not determinism is true we could not, metaphysically, have the sort of free will required for moral responsibility, and indeed this is how Double defines it.[4] I maintain, by contrast, that there is a coherent indeterminist scenario in which we have this sort of free will, the one in which we are libertarian agent-causes, and that it may well be that agent-causal libertarianism is metaphysically possible. Here is my terminological pro-

---

4. Richard Double, *Metaphilosophy and Free Will* (New York: Oxford University Press, 1996), p. 102.

posal. Traditionally, 'incompatibilism' has been taken to refer to the claim that the sort of free will required for moral responsibility is incompatible with causal determinism. The denotation of this term might be extended to include the view that moral responsibility is incompatible with the sort of indeterminacy specified by the standard interpretation of quantum mechanics, if that is the only sort of indeterminacy there is. Then, since the 'hard' in James's term 'hard determinism' indicates the denial of the sort of free will required for moral responsibility, I will designate my position 'hard incompatibilism.'

Strawson sets out an instructive table of nine possible positions on determinism (D) and the sort of free will required for moral responsibility (F), using t for 'true,' f for 'false,' and ? for 'don't know'[5]:

	1	2	3	4	5	6	7	8	9
D	t	f	t	f	t	f	?	?	?
F	f	t	t	f	?	?	f	t	?

As Strawson points out, incompatibilists can occupy any of these positions except for 3, 5, or 8. Position 1 is the classical hard determinist view, 2 is classical libertarianism. I understand hard incompatibilism as subsuming positions 1, 4, and 7. Within position 7, one can differentiate two sub-positions, a no-free-will-either-way theory and the sort of view for which I argue.

In the last three chapters, I set out my hard incompatibilist position. The fifth chapter features the argument that our best theories about the nature of the physical world do indeed undermine moral responsibility. There I also contend that many of the practical reasons for opposing the hard incompatibilist denial of moral responsibility are not as compelling as they might at first seem. Rejecting the claim that we are morally responsible does not, for example, threaten our self-conception as deliberative agents, and neither does it jeopardize moral principles and values. For many, by far the most worrisome threat posed by the denial of moral responsibility is that it would render unjustified our responses to human evil. Hence, the entire sixth chapter assesses hard incompatibilism's legitimate options for dealing with criminals. I maintain that while severe punishment – involving death or confinement in prisons of a sort common in our society – is ruled out by hard

---

5. Galen Strawson, *Freedom and Belief*, p. 6.

incompatibilism, preventive detention and programs for rehabilitation can be justified.

The seventh chapter examines hard incompatibilism's impact on the meaning of life, and in particular on the attitudes and emotions that have bearing on our most fundamental concerns. Hard incompatibilism, I claim, does not significantly threaten our hopes for meaning in life through success in our projects. While this view does render certain emotional attitudes irrational, those that are legitimate by its standards are sufficient to sustain good interpersonal relationships. Finally, hard incompatibilism holds out promise for challenging a pervasive type of anger that is destructive to our well-being, and thereby encouraging a sort of equanimity that has significant value for human life.

I will now clarify several key conceptual issues. First, in my view, for an agent to be *morally responsible for an action* is for this action to belong to the agent in such a way that she would deserve blame if the action were morally wrong, and she would deserve credit or perhaps praise if it were morally exemplary. The desert at issue here is basic in the sense that the agent, to be morally responsible, would deserve the blame or credit just by virtue of having performed the action, and not, for example, by way of consequentialist considerations. This characterization leaves room for an agent's being morally responsible for an action even if she does not deserve blame, credit, or praise for it − if, for example, the action is morally indifferent. Alternatively then, but less clearly, for an agent to be morally responsible for an action is for it to be imputable to her.

I oppose the idea that to judge a person morally responsible essentially involves having an attitude toward her. Rather, I think that to make a judgment of this sort is most fundamentally to make a factual claim. To defend this position adequately would involve turning back a non-cognitivist position on judgments about moral responsibility, a task I will not undertake. But there are two considerations, analogs of which will be familiar from discussions on moral realism, in favor of my view. First, judging a person morally responsible for an action that is morally indifferent, or for an action that is not morally indifferent but generally expected, like feeding and clothing one's children, need not be accompanied by any discernible attitude. Second, it seems possible to imagine rational but emotionless beings who yet have a deep concern for right and wrong, and who believe that agents are morally responsible. Such beings would believe wrongdoers to be morally responsible without having any emotional attitudes, such as indignation or moral resentment, toward them. It is of course consistent with the view that judgments about moral responsibility are factual that such judgments are typically accompanied by attitudes.

Furthermore, in this book, I take moral responsibility to apply primarily to decisions. I do not broach the topic of responsibility for omissions. I also do not consider the notion of responsibility for consequences of decisions. The view that responsibility for decisions is especially important is driven by the sense that responsibility is fundamentally a matter of control, a kind of control agents would have primarily over their decisions, in conjunction with the fact that decisions are causally prior to consequences of decisions. Intuitions about "moral luck" cases support this view. Suppose two agents, A and B, are psychologically identical and each makes the decision to shoot an innocent person, and then carries out the decision. However, A's bullet does not reach the intended victim because it hits a bird instead, whereas B's bullet kills the victim. A common intuition here is that A and B are equally blameworthy in some especially important respect, an intuition captured by the notion that responsibility for decisions is especially important.

In my conception, being morally responsible is distinct from behaving responsibly – that is, behaving morally – and from taking responsibility for something – making a sincere commitment to a task in one's community, for example, or to care for someone. It is also different from the legitimacy of holding oneself and others morally accountable, where this amounts to the legitimacy of demanding that agents explain how their decisions accord with the moral point of view, and that they consider what their decisions reveal about their moral character and dispositions. Now the issue in the debate about determinism and moral responsibility is not whether determinism threatens the legitimacy of holding oneself and others morally accountable, if, for example, this legitimacy consists just in the fact that it would be effective for moral improvement. For nothing about determinism suggests that such procedures would not be effective for this purpose.[6] Arguing that

6. Hilary Bok claims that "to say that we are responsible for our conduct in this sense is to say that we can appropriately hold ourselves accountable for it: that it can legitimately be laid at our door or reckoned to our charge." She then characterizes holding oneself accountable as follows. "When I take some action to reflect my will, I attribute it to myself, and ask what it reveals about my will and my character, and about the ways they might be improved. To do this is to hold myself accountable for my action" (Hilary Bok, *Freedom and Responsibility* Princeton: Princeton University Press, 1998, p. 152).

determinism is compatible with moral responsibility construed in this way therefore avoids the issue in the traditional debate, and moreover, it is difficult to see why anyone might think this sort of compatibility would be controversial. The debate is not about behaving responsibly, taking responsibility, or the effectiveness of holding oneself and others morally accountable (in these senses), since determinism does not threaten these notions at all.

I think it is important to distinguish whether we are free in the sense required for moral responsibility from whether it is valuable to be free in this sense. Here I am resisting a trend initiated (to my knowledge) by Daniel Dennett.[7] His attempt to recast the debate in terms of the question, "What is free will such that we should want it?" potentially confuses two issues: Do we have the sort of free will required for moral responsibility? and do we want the sort of free will required for moral responsibility? It could be, for instance, that we are free in the sense required for moral responsibility, but since being free in this sense is not especially valuable to us, we would not want it much. It is important to frame the issue so as to make conceptual room for views of this type.

Finally, when the hard incompatibilist disavows freedom of the sort required for moral responsibility, he is not denying that we have freedom of every kind. In fact, hard incompatibilism is consistent with our having most of the sorts of freedom that have appeared on the philosophical landscape. When the hard incompatibilist disavows freedom of the sort required for moral responsibility, he is not also

Subsequently, she argues that responsibility in this sense is not undermined by determinism. This claim is correct, I believe, but it may be misleading for her to call herself a compatibilist because she maintains this view. For responsibility in this sense is not at issue in the traditional debate. Bok's argument for what she calls compatibilism faces a dilemma. If what it means for an agent to be morally responsible is for it to be legitimate to hold him morally accountable because doing so is effective for promoting moral development, then her argument does not join the traditional debate. If, however, she were to agree that moral responsibility at least includes the notion of fundamental desert, then she has not provided an argument against the incompatibilist view that determinism undermines moral responsibility. But although I disagree with Bok on how the debate should be characterized and on where the arguments are owed, I endorse much of her picture of agents as legitimately held morally accountable and free, for example, in the sense that they can select from among epistemically possible alternatives. For positions related to Bok's, see Moritz Schlick, "When Is a Man Responsible?" in *Problems of Ethics*, tr. David Rynin (New York: Prentice-Hall, 1939), pp. 143–56; J.J.C. Smart, "Free Will, Praise, and Blame," *Mind* 70 (1961), pp. 291–306.

7. Daniel Dennett, *Elbow Room* (Cambridge: MIT Press, 1984), especially pp. 153–72.

denying that we have many of the sorts of freedom compatibilists have thought to be sufficient for moral responsibility, such as the ability to choose in accord with one's values, or the capacity to be responsive to the reasons there are for acting. In addition, he is not denying that we might have and strive for freedom from coercion by tyrannical governments, or from authoritarian social situations, or from unhappy conditions in our personal lives. One can be a hard incompatibilist and consistently claim that we can aspire to the freedom from the control of the harmful passions that Spinoza prized. A view of this sort by no means rules out various sorts of freedom connected with religious ideals – St. Paul's Christian freedom, for example, or Buddhism's freedom from desire or from the self.

The aim of this book, then, is to show that the reasons for accepting hard incompatibilism are substantial, and that this view does not have the deep practical problems often associated with it. We must begin by evaluating the opposing positions. This methodological requirement springs from a characteristic that hard incompatibilism does not share with its rival positions. Both libertarians and compatibilists must devise positive accounts, whereas hard incompatibilism is essentially a negative position. It is the view that there is no freedom of the sort required for moral responsibility, and thus, to show that if it is true, one must successfully argue that any account according to which we have this sort of freedom is dubious or mistaken. The positive task of hard incompatibilism is to explain how we might live without this kind of freedom – as hard incompatibilists. But to defend the truth of this position, one need not provide such an account. For hard incompatibilism might be true while at the same time living as if it is would be practically impossible. As we shall see, however, this concern is unfounded.

1

Alternative Possibilities and Causal Histories

The claim that moral responsibility for an action requires that the agent could have done otherwise is surely attractive. Moreover, it seems reasonable to contend that a requirement of this sort is not merely a necessary condition of little consequence, but that it plays a significant role in explaining why an agent is morally responsible. For if an agent is to be blameworthy for an action, it seems crucial that she could have done something to avoid being blameworthy – that she could have done something to get herself off the hook. If she is to be praiseworthy for an action, it seems important that she could have done something less admirable. Libertarians have often grounded their incompatibilism precisely in such intuitions. As a result, they have often defended the following principle of alternative possibilities:

(1) An action is free in the sense required for moral responsibility only if the agent could have done otherwise than she actually did.

or a similar principle about choice:

(2) An action is free in the sense required for moral responsibility only if the agent could have chosen otherwise than she actually did.

I shall argue that despite resourceful attempts to defend conditions of this sort, any such requirement that is relevant to explaining why an agent is morally responsible for an action falls to counterexamples. I maintain instead that the most plausible and fundamentally explanatory incompatibilist principles concern the causal history of an action, and not alternative possibilities.[1] These claims leave open the prospect of alternative-possibilities conditions necessary for moral responsibility but nevertheless irrelevant to explaining why an agent is morally responsible. I believe that there could well be such conditions.

LEEWAY VS. CAUSAL HISTORY INCOMPATIBILISM

Familiarly, arguments of the kind devised by Harry Frankfurt provide an especially formidable challenge to alternative possibility conditions.[2] The standard versions deploy examples with a particular sort of structure. Here is one of Fischer's cases:

Black is a nefarious neurosurgeon. In performing an operation on Jones to remove a brain tumor, Black inserts a mechanism into Jones's brain which enables Black to monitor and control Jones's activities. Jones, meanwhile, knows nothing of this. Black exercises this control through a computer which he has programmed so that, among other things, it monitors Jones's voting behavior. If Jones shows an inclination to decide to vote for Carter, then the computer, through the mechanism in Jones's brain, intervenes to assure that he actually decides to vote for Reagan and does so vote. But if Jones decides on his own to vote for Reagan, the computer does nothing but continue to monitor – without affecting the goings-on in Jones's head. Suppose Jones decides to vote for Reagan on his own, just as he would have if Black had *not* inserted the mechanism into his head.[3]

---

1. I argued for this view in "Determinism *Al Dente* (1985), and later in "Alternative Possibilities and Causal Histories," *Philosophical Perspectives* 14 (2000). For similar positions, see Eleanore Stump, "Intellect, Will, and the Principle of Alternate Possibilities," in *Christian Theism and the Problems of Philosophy*, ed. Michael Beaty (Notre Dame, IN: University of Notre Dame Press, 1990), pp. 254–85, reprinted in *Moral Responsibility*, ed. John Martin Fischer and Mark Ravizza (Ithaca: Cornell University Press, 1993), pp. 237–62; "Libertarian Freedom and the Principle of Alternative Possibilities," in *Faith, Freedom, and Rationality*, ed. Jeff Jordan and Daniel Howard Snyder (Lanham, MD: Rowman and Littlefield, 1996), pp. 73–88; Linda Zagebski, *The Dilemma of Freedom and Foreknowledge* (New York: Oxford University Press, 1991), Chapter 6, Section 2.1; "Does Libertarian Freedom Require Alternate Possibilities?" *Philosophical Perspectives* 14 (2000); Robert Heinaman, "Incompatibilism without the Principle of Alternative Possibilities," *Australasian Journal of Philosophy* 64 (1986), pp. 266–76; Michael Della Rocca, "Frankfurt, Fischer, and Flickers," *Noûs* 32 (1998), pp. 99–105; David Hunt, "Moral Responsibility and Unavoidable Action," *Philosophical Studies* 97 (2000), pp. 195–227.
2. Harry G. Frankfurt, "Alternate Possibilities and Moral Responsibility," *Journal of Philosophy* 1969, pp. 829–839; John Martin Fischer, "Responsibility and Control," in *Moral Responsibility*, Fischer, ed. (Ithaca: Cornell University Press, 1986), pp. 174–190.
3. Fischer, "Responsibility and Control," p. 176.

2

Fischer's intuition is that Jones could be responsible for voting or deciding to vote for Reagan, although he could not have done or chosen otherwise. Jones could not have done or even have chosen otherwise, because the device would have arrested the deliberative process before it resulted in any alternative choice. The conclusion of the argument is that conditions (1) and (2) are mistaken.

Fischer has contended that this type of argument does not refute the claim that moral responsibility requires that the actual causal history of the action not be deterministic. It leaves untouched the view that moral responsibility requires that one's action not actually result from a deterministic causal process that traces back to factors beyond one's control – back to causal factors that one could not have produced, altered, or prevented.[4] I believe that this contention of Fischer's is correct. Notice that this Frankfurt-style case does not specify that Jones's action is causally determined in this way. If it were specified that his choice is deterministically produced by factors beyond his control, by, for example, Martian neuroscientists, then the intuition that he could be morally responsible might well fade away. Furthermore, it seems possible for one's action not to result from a deterministic causal process that traces back to factors beyond one's control while one cannot do or choose otherwise. For, as is clear from the Frankfurt-style case, the factors that make it so that an agent cannot do or choose otherwise need not also determine him to act as he does, since they need not be part of the actual causal history of his action at all.

This reflection suggests a different requirement on the sort of freedom we are seeking to characterize:

(3) An action is free in the sense required for moral responsibility only if it is not produced by a deterministic process that traces back to causal factors beyond the agent's control.

Condition (3) specifies a necessary condition on the sort of freedom required for moral responsibility that I believe any incompatibilist should endorse. One might note that even if it is not a necessary condition on moral responsibility that the agent could have done or chosen otherwise, the incompatibilist can still claim that one is not morally responsible for an action if one could not have done or chosen otherwise due to the choice's resulting from a deterministic causal process that traces back to factors beyond one's control.

4.   Fischer, "Responsibility and Control," pp. 182–85.

3

In his central condition on moral responsibility (UR, for "ultimate responsibility"), Kane expresses one aspect of this intuition very nicely:

(U): For every X and Y (where X and Y represent occurrences of events and/or states), if the agent is personally responsible for X, and if Y is an *arche* (or sufficient ground or cause or explanation) for X, then the agent must also be personally responsible for Y.

(Kane spells out the alternative-possibilities intuition in the (R)-part of (UR).)[5] Conditions such as (3) and (U), I believe, have a critical role in explaining why agents would be morally responsible. If such conditions are not met by an agent's decision, he lacks a certain kind of control over this decision, and it is for this reason that he is not morally responsible. The sort of control at issue is that the agent must in an appropriate sense be the ultimate source or cause of the action. Kane expresses the point in this way:

What (U) thus requires is that if an agent is ultimately responsible for an action, the action cannot have a sufficient reason of any of these kinds *for which the agent is not also responsible*. If the action did have such a sufficient reason for which the agent was not responsible, then the action, or the agent's will to perform it, would have its source in something the agent played no role in producing. Then the *arche* of the action, or of the agent's will to perform it, would not be "in the agent," but in something else.[6]

What lies at the core of the intuition expressed by (3) and (U) is a claim about origination, which might be formulated as follows:

(O) If an agent is morally responsible for her deciding to perform an action, then the production of this decision must be something over which the agent has control, and an agent is not morally responsible for the decision if it is produced by a source over which she has no control.

---

5. Robert Kane, *The Significance of Free Will* (New York: Oxford University Press, 1996), p. 35. (UR) in its entirety is: (UR): An agent is *ultimately responsible* for some (event or state) E's occurring only if (R) the agent is personally responsible for E's occurring in a sense which entails that something the agent voluntarily (or willingly) did or omitted, and for which the agent could have voluntarily done otherwise, either was, or causally contributed to, E's occurrence and made a difference to whether or not E occurred; and (U) for every X and Y (where X and Y represent occurrences of events and/or states) if the agent is personally responsible for X, and if Y is an *arche* (or sufficient ground or cause or explanation) for X, then the agent must also be personally responsible for Y. Thus, if there is a sufficient ground for an agent's decision in events that precede the agent's birth (together with laws of nature), then presuming that an agent cannot be personally responsible for events that precede her birth or for laws of nature, she cannot be personally responsible for the decision.
6. Kane, *The Significance of Free Will*, p. 73.

Ted Honderich also stresses the importance of a notion of origination for our sense of moral responsibility.[7] I think that (O) expresses the most fundamental and plausible incompatibilist intuition about how an agent's moral responsibility is grounded.[8] It explains not only why one might think that determinism and moral responsibility are incompatible, but also why one might believe that an agent cannot be morally responsible for a decision if it occurs without any cause whatsoever. For such a decision is produced by nothing, and hence the production of the decision is not something over which the agent has control. I shall clarify this condition and examine the surrounding issues more thoroughly in Chapter 2.

We might call those who incline toward the view that an alternative possibilities condition has the more important role in explaining why an agent would be morally responsible *leeway incompatibilists*, and those who are predisposed to maintain that an incompatibilist condition on the causal history of the action plays the more significant part *causal history incompatibilists*.[9] Leeway incompatibilists would argue that the actual causal history of a morally responsible action must be

---

7. Ted Honderich, *A Theory of Determinism* (Oxford: Oxford University Press, 1988), e.g., pp. 194–206.

8. Gary Watson, although he is not an incompatibilist, also maintains that the condition on origination is the fundamental incompatibilist claim; "Responsibility and the Limits of Evil," in *Responsibility, Character and the Emotions*, ed. Ferdinand Schoeman (Cambridge: Cambridge University Press, 1987), pp. 256–86, at p. 282.

9. In "Compatibilists Could Have Done Otherwise: Responsibility and Negative Agency" (*The Philosophical Review* 103 (1994), pp. 453–88), Alison McIntyre convincingly argues that an analog of Frankfurt's argument undermines the Principle of Possible Actions for omissions. But she also attempts to undermine any indeterminist requirement for moral responsibility with a Frankfurt-style case (pp. 472–78). A princess rises from her seat at the opera for a photo opportunity, and while it is customary for her to sit down after one minute, she decides to stand for four minutes. But a scientist has placed a force field around her, so that had she decided to sit down after one minute she would have remained standing for an additional three. Yet it is clear she is morally responsible for standing for the four minutes. About this case McIntyre says: ". . . even if her decision to stand for four minutes is not causally determined, it is nevertheless causally determined, once she has stood for a minute, that she will stand for three more minutes. To grant that the Princess can be morally responsible for standing for the last three minutes is *ipso facto* to grant that an agent can be morally responsible for behavior that is causally determined." But this is not a situation in which an agent is responsible for an action that is produced by a deterministic process that traces back to factors beyond her control. McIntyre's case specifies external factors that prevent the Princess from performing the action in question, but these external factors play no role in the actual causal history of the action. In fact, her case is consistent with the action's being freely produced by a libertarian agent-causal power. Hence, condition (3) survives McIntyre's argument, and I maintain that this condition withstands any argument that employs a Frankfurt-style strategy.

indeterministic, but they would be amenable to the claim that this is so only because an indeterministic history is required to secure alternative possibilities. Causal history incompatibilists would lean toward the position that the role the causal history plays in explaining why an agent would be morally responsible is independent of facts about alternative possibilities.

Against causal history incompatibilism, Fischer argues that "there is simply no good reason to suppose that causal determinism in itself (and apart from considerations pertaining to alternative possibilities) vitiates our moral responsibility."[10] Fischer, I believe, is mistaken on this point. To be sure, one incompatibilist intuition that we seem naturally to have is that if we could in no sense do otherwise, then we could never have refrained from the wrongful actions we perform, and thus we cannot legitimately be held blameworthy for them. But another very powerful and common intuition is that if all of our behavior were "in the cards" before we were born – in the sense that things happened before we came to exist that, by way of a deterministic causal process, inevitably result in our behavior – then we cannot legitimately be blamed for our wrongdoing. By this intuition, if causal factors existed before a criminal was born that by way of a deterministic process, inevitably issue in his act of murder, then he cannot legitimately be blamed for his action. If all of our actions had this type of causal history, then it would seem that we lack the kind of control over our actions that moral responsibility requires.

Now I do not believe that in the dialectic of the debate, one should expect Fischer, or any compatibilist, to be moved much by this incompatibilist intuition alone to abandon his position. In my view, the more powerful, and indeed the best, type of challenge to compatibilism develops the claim that causal determination presents in principle no less of a threat to moral responsibility than does covert manipulation. We shall turn to that challenge in Chapter 4. Nonetheless, what this intuition should show at this stage is that there might well be a coherent incompatibilist position that could survive the demise of alternative-possibilities requirements.[11]

FLICKERS AND ROBUSTNESS

Thus in my view it is the intuition expressed by (O) rather than one associated with an alternative-possibility condition that is the most fun-

---

10. Fischer, *The Metaphysics of Free Will* (Oxford: Blackwell, 1994), p. 159.
11. Della Rocca, in "Frankfurt, Fischer, and Flickers," develops a similar theme.

damental and plausible underlying ground for incompatibilism. But this claim has not yet been thoroughly tested. Perhaps some version of an alternative-possibilities condition on moral responsibility can survive any Frankfurt-style argument. Libertarians have contended that according to any argument of this kind, there must be some factor that the neurophysiologist's device is rigged up to detect that could but does not actually occur in the agent, such as an intention to do otherwise.[12] The possible occurrence of this factor — this "flicker of freedom," to use Fischer's term — might then function as the alternative possibility that is required for moral responsibility.[13] Libertarians, in particular, are predisposed to locate the source of moral responsibility in the will, and if moral responsibility requires alternative possibilities, it must require, more precisely, the possibility of willing to do otherwise. But it is not implausible that the formation of an intention to do otherwise should count as willing to do otherwise, and hence the possibility of forming such an intention would assist in explaining moral responsibility for the choice or action at issue.

Fischer, however, argues that one can construct different Frankfurt-style stories in which the intervening device detects some factor prior to the formation of the intention. One might, for example, imagine that Jones will decide to kill Smith only if Jones blushes beforehand. Then Jones's failure to blush (by a certain time) might be the alternative possibility that would trigger the intervention that causes him to kill Smith. Supposing that Jones acts without intervention, we might well have the intuition that he is morally responsible, despite the fact that he could not have done or chosen otherwise, or formed an alternative intention. He could have failed to blush, but as Fischer argues, such a flicker is of no use to the libertarian, since it is not sufficiently *robust*, it is too "flimsy and exiguous" to play a part in grounding moral responsibility.[14]

I agree with Fischer, and here is a first pass at characterizing robustness. The intuition underlying the alternative-possibilities requirement

---

12. Peter van Inwagen, *An Essay on Free Will* (Oxford: Oxford University Press, 1983), pp. 166–80. In my view, the intention to perform an action is produced by the choice to perform the action, and hence succeeds and does not precede it. Thus an intention to perform an action could not serve as a sign for intervention that would preclude a choice to perform it.

13. Fischer provides a lucid discussion and criticism of this strategy in *The Metaphysics of Free Will*, pp. 134–47.

14. Fischer, *The Metaphysics of Free Will*, pp. 131–59; "Recent Work on Moral Responsibility," *Ethics* 110 (1999), pp. 93–139.

is that if, for example, an agent is to be blameworthy for an action, it is crucial that he could have done something to avoid being blameworthy. If having an alternative possibility does in fact play a role in explaining an agent's moral responsibility for an action, it would have to be robust at least in the sense that as a result of securing that alternative possibility, the agent would *thereby* have avoided the responsibility he has for the action he performed – it would be his securing of that alternative possibility per se that would explain why the agent would have avoided the responsibility. Failing to blush in Fischer's scenario does not meet this criterion of robustness. For if Jones had failed to blush, he would not thereby have avoided responsibility for evading killing Smith – it would not be the failure to blush per se that would explain why Jones would not be blameworthy. By typical libertarian intuitions, one robust sort of alternative possibility would involve willing to do otherwise than to perform the action the agent in fact wills to perform.[15]

A LIBERTARIAN OBJECTION TO
FRANKFURT-STYLE ARGUMENTS

It might now seem that any alternative-possibilities condition on moral responsibility can be defeated by a Frankfurt-style argument that employs a non-robust flicker of freedom. But perhaps this line of defense for Frankfurt-style arguments is too quick. An important kind of objection against these sorts of arguments was initially raised by Kane and then systematically developed by David Widerker. (A close relative has been advanced by Carl Ginet, which we will consider shortly.[16]) The general form of the Kane/Widerker objection is this. For any Frankfurt-style case, if causal determinism is assumed, the libertarian will not have, and cannot be expected to have, the intuition that the agent is morally responsible. If, on the other hand, libertarian indeter-

15. See also Mele's characterization of robustness, which I endorse, in "Soft Libertarianism and Frankfurt-Style Scenarios," *Philosophical Topics* 24 (1996), pp. 123–41, at pp. 126–7.
16. Kane, *Free Will and Values* (Albany: SUNY Press, 1985), p. 51 n. 25, and *The Significance of Free Will*, pp. 142–4, 191–2; David Widerker, "Libertarianism and Frankfurt's Attack on the Principle of Alternative Possibilities," *The Philosophical Review* 104 (1995), pp. 247–61; Carl Ginet, "In Defense of the Principle of Alternative Possibilities: Why I Don't Find Frankfurt's Arguments Convincing," *Philosophical Perspectives* 10 (1996), pp. 403–17; see also Keith D. Wyma, "Moral Responsibility and Leeway for Action," *American Philosophical Quarterly* 34 (1997), pp. 57–70. Fischer provides a clear and helpful account of these views in "Recent Work on Moral Responsibility," pp. 111–12.

minism is presupposed, an effective Frankfurt-style scenario cannot be devised, for any such case will fall to a dilemma. In Frankfurt-style cases, the actual situation always features a prior sign by which the intervener can know that the agent will perform the action he does, and that signals the fact that intervention is not necessary. If in the proposed case, the sign causally determines the action, or if it is associated with something that does so, the intervener's predictive ability can be explained. But then the libertarian would not have the intuition that the agent is morally responsible. If the relationship between the sign and the action is not causally deterministic in such ways, then the libertarian can claim that the agent could have done otherwise despite the occurrence of the prior sign. Either way, some principle of alternative possibilities emerges unscathed.

Widerker's particular version of the objection has the following structure.[17] The case at issue is the one we have just encountered, in which Jones wants to kill Smith, but Black is afraid that Jones might become fainthearted, and so he is prepared to intervene if Jones fails to show a sign that he will kill Smith. The sign that he will kill Smith is his blushing at t1. The important features of the scenario are these:

(1) If Jones is blushing at t1, then, provided no one intervenes, he will decide at t2 to kill Smith.
(2) If Jones is not blushing at t1, then, provided no one intervenes, he will not decide at t2 to kill Smith.
(3) If Black sees that Jones shows signs that he will not decide at t2 to kill Smith – that is, he sees that Jones is *not* blushing at t1 – then Black will force Jones to decide at t2 to kill Smith; but if he sees that Jones is blushing at t1, then he will do nothing.

Finally, suppose that Black does not have to show his hand, because

(4) Jones is blushing at t1, and decides at t2 to kill Smith for reasons of his own.[18]

Although the case is meant to show that Jones is morally responsible despite the fact that he could not have done otherwise, Widerker claims that this conclusion is not forced on the libertarian:

17. Cf. Ishtayaque Haji, *Moral Appraisability* (New York: Oxford University Press, 1998), pp. 34–5.
18. Widerker, "Libertarianism and Frankfurt's Attack on the Principle of Alternative Possibilities," pp. 249–50.

Note that the truth of (1) cannot be grounded in the fact that Jones's blushing at t1 is, in the circumstances, causally sufficient for his decision to kill Smith, or in the fact that it is indicative of a state that is causally sufficient for that decision, since such an assumption would . . . [not be] accepted by the libertarian. On the other hand, if (1) is not thus grounded, then the following two options are available to the libertarian to resist the contention that Jones's decision to kill Smith is unavoidable. He may either reject (1), claiming that the most that he would be prepared to allow is

(1a) If Jones is blushing at t1, then Jones will *probably* decide at t2 to kill Smith . . .

But (1a) is compatible with Jones's having the power to decide not to kill Smith, since there remains the possibility of Jones's acting out of character. Or the libertarian may construe (1) as a conditional of freedom in Plantinga's sense . . . that is, as

(1b) If Jones is blushing at t1, then Jones will *freely* decide at t2 to kill Smith, [in a sense that allows that the agent could have decided otherwise][19]

in which case the libertarian may again claim that in the actual situation when Jones is blushing at t1, it is within his power to refrain from deciding to kill Smith at t2.[20]

Widerker's is a very important objection, and it serves as a test for the effectiveness of any Frankfurt-style argument. One point of clarification: If the libertarian that Widerker supposes Frankfurt must convince is simply presupposing a principle of alternative possibilities, then one could not expect that a Frankfurt-style argument would dislodge his view. But Widerker, I think, does not intend that his libertarian simply presuppose this principle, but rather only the claim that moral responsibility is incompatible with an action's having a deterministic causal history. I will proceed with this understanding of Widerker's objection.

PROBLEMS FOR RECENT ATTEMPTS TO ANSWER WIDERKER

Several critics have tried to construct Frankfurt-style arguments that escape this objection. The cases used in these arguments divide into two categories:

19. This bracketed phrase does not occur in Widerker's text, but it clearly expresses his meaning.
20. Widerker, "Libertarianism and Frankfurt's Attack on the Principle of Alternative Possibilities," p. 250.

(a) Those in which the relationship between the prior sign and the action is causally deterministic, and the indeterminism that makes for the agent's libertarian freedom is present in the causal history of the action before the prior sign,

and

(b) those in which the prior sign is eliminated altogether.

Eleonore Stump and Ishtiyaque Haji have constructed examples in category (a),[21] while David Hunt and Alfred Mele, together with David Robb, have devised scenarios in category (b).[22]

In my view, the cases that have been devised in each of these categories face significant problems. First, (a)-type situations are difficult to construct so that they are effective against Widerker's objection. Stump's and Haji's examples have serious drawbacks. In Stump's case, Grey, the neurosurgeon, wants to ensure that Jones will vote for Reagan. Grey finds that every time Jones decides to vote for Republicans, the decision regularly correlates with the completion of a sequence of neural firings in Jones's brain that always includes, near the beginning, the firing of neurons a, b, and c. Jones's deciding to vote for Democratic candidates is correlated with the completion of a neural sequence that always includes, near the beginning, the firing of neurons x, y, and z. Whenever Grey's neuroscope detects the firing of x, y, and z, it disrupts that sequence, with the result that the sequence is not brought to completion. Instead, the device activates a coercive mechanism that makes Jones vote Republican. Crucially, Stump specifies that the firing of x, y, and z does not constitute a decision, and in her view the occurrence of this sequence would not count as a robust alternative possibility. If, on the other hand, the neuroscope detects the firing of a, b, and c, it allows the sequence to proceed to completion and the decision to vote Republican to occur.[23] Stump specifies that the decision is indeed a causal outcome of the neural sequence.[24] What makes the agent libertarian is that the neural sequence is not the outcome of a causal chain that originates in a cause outside him. Rather, it is the outcome of a causal chain that originates, at least to a significant extent, in an act of

21. Stump, "Libertarian Freedom and the Principle of Alternative Possibilities"; Haji, *Moral Appraisability*, p. 36.
22. Alfred Mele and David Robb, "Rescuing Frankfurt-Style Cases," *The Philosophical Review* 107 (1998), pp. 97–112; David Hunt, "Moral Responsibility and Unavoidable Action."
23. Stump, "Libertarian Freedom and the Principle of Alternative Possibilities," pp. 77–8.
24. Ibid., p. 79.

the agent which is not the outcome of a causal chain that originates in a cause outside the agent. Here, Stump suggests the Aquinas-inspired view that the neural sequence is the outcome of a causal chain that originates in the agent's intellect and will.[25]

But as Stewart Goetz points out, to assess this case, one needs to know more about the psychological features of the act performed by the agent to cause the neural process. If this originating act is causally determined, then Stump's agent would appear not to be free in the libertarian sense. If it is not causally determined, then he might well have robust alternative possibilities for action. If the originating act is an intention to make a decision, for example, and if the indeterminism of that act allows for the agent to have avoided intending to make the decision, then the case might well include a robust alternative possibility after all.[26] Note that in Stump's setup, the agent's performance of that act – which constitutes the agent's crucial libertarian causal role – precedes the possible intervention.[27]

More generally, the challenge for Stump is to characterize the agent's causal role so that (i) her action is not causally determined (by factors beyond her control), and (ii) her action does not involve robust alternative possibilities. A case of the sort that Stump devises is subject to the following dilemma: If the indeterminism (whether or not it is a characteristic of the sort of agent's act she has in mind) that occurs prior to the neural sequence is significant enough to make the action a libertarian freely willed action, then it has not been ruled out that the indeterministic juncture features a robust alternative possibility. If Stump were to reject the claim that there is a robust alternative possibility at this point, then it would remain open to a libertarian (like Widerker) to deny that the agent has genuine libertarian free will. Perhaps it is possible to embellish Stump's example to answer this objection. However, it is not clear to me that there could be a plausible Frankfurt-style case in which the action is not causally determined by factors beyond the agent's control (in a way that would satisfy the libertarian) and she lacks robust alternative possibilities if the intervention would occur after the crucial indeterministic juncture.

25. Stump, "Libertarian Freedom and the Principle of Alternative Possibilities," pp. 80–5.
26. Stewart Goetz, "Stumping for Widerker," *Faith and Philosophy* 16 (1999), pp. 83–9. In this article, he develops this and other criticisms in further detail.
27. Stump replies to Goetz's objection in "Dust, Determinism and Frankfurt: A Reply to Goetz," in *Faith and Philosophy* 16 (1999), pp. 413–22, but in my view she does not lay to rest the worry I just described.

In Haji's example, the sort of libertarian agency attributed to the agent consists in its being undetermined which of various considerations will enter the mind of the agent in deliberation. So, at the outset of Jones's deliberation, it is causally open whether he will kill Smith, because it is causally undetermined whether various considerations will enter his mind at the onset of his musings. The infallible predictor, Black,

> intervenes if and only if he believes that Jones will not make the decisive best judgment that favors the decision to kill Smith which he, Black, wants Jones to make. Specifically, should Jones make the judgment that he ought not to kill Smith, *then* (and only then) will Black intervene and cause Jones to alter the judgment.[28]

There is no need for Black to intervene "as Jones decides appropriately on his own," and one will have the intuition that Jones could be morally responsible for his decision. One problem for Haji's case is that it was open to Jones to have made the decisive best judgment that he ought not to kill Smith, and this alternative possibility seems robust. For it appears plausible that if Jones had made the decisive best judgment that he ought not to kill Smith, he would thereby have avoided the responsibility he has for the action he actually performed – it would be his securing of this alternative possibility per se that would explain why he would have avoided this responsibility. Another difficulty for Haji's example is that many libertarians would not let the sort of indeterminacy he specifies be significant for moral responsibility because it fails to provide the agent with enhanced control. A case in which the relevant considerations indeterministically enter the mind of the agent, whereupon his judgment and decision are determined, would seem to exhibit no more control by him than a situation in which such considerations deterministically enter the mind of the agent, whereupon the agent's judgment and decision are causally determined.[29]

28. Haji, *Moral Appraisability*, p. 36. Haji attributes the inspiration for this sort of libertarianism to Mele, in *Autonomous Agents* (New York: Oxford University Press, 1995), p. 216. This kind of libertarianism is also suggested by Daniel Dennett, in "Giving Libertarians What They Say They Want," in his *Brainstorms* (Montgomery, VT: Bradford Books, 1978), at p. 295.
29. See, for example, Randolph Clarke, "Agent Causation and Event Causation in the Production of Free Action," *Free Will*, ed. Derk Pereboom (Indianapolis: Hackett, 1997), pp. 273–300, at p. 286 (the original and longer version of this article appears in *Philosophical Topics* 24, 1996, pp. 19–48).

Cases in category (b) exemplify a different strategy for opposing alternative-possibility conditions. In these cases, there are no prior signs to guide intervention, not even non-robust flickers of freedom. One ingenious scenario in this category is presented by Mele and Robb.[30] The example features Bob, who inhabits a world in which determinism is false:

At t1, Black initiates a certain deterministic process P in Bob's brain with the intention of thereby causing Bob to decide at t2 (an hour later, say) to steal Ann's car. The process, which is screened off from Bob's consciousness, will deterministically culminate in Bob's deciding at t2 to steal Ann's car unless he decides on his own to steal it or is incapable at t2 of making a decision (because, e.g., he is dead at t2). . . . The process is in no way sensitive to any "sign" of what Bob will decide. As it happens, at t2 Bob decides on his own to steal the car, on the basis of his own indeterministic deliberation about whether to steal it, and his decision has no deterministic cause. But if he had not just then decided on his own to steal it, P would have deterministically issued, at t2, in his deciding to steal it. Rest assured that P in no way influences the indeterministic decision-making process that actually issues in Bob's decision.

Mele and Robb claim that Bob is plausibly morally responsible for his decision. I think that their argument may in fact be successful, but that their development of the case raises one problem that could undermine it. Mele and Robb discuss several potential problems for their scenario, one of which is whether we can make sense of what would happen at t2 if P and Bob's indeterministic deliberative process were to diverge at t2. Here is how they handle the difficulty:

The issue may be pictured, fancifully, as follows.[31] Two different "decision nodes" in Bob's brain are directly relevant. The "lighting up" of node N1 represents his deciding to steal the car, and the "lighting up" of node N2 represents his deciding *not* to steal the car. Under normal circumstances and in the absence of preemption, a process's "hitting" a decision node in Bob "lights up" that node. If it were to be the case both that P hits N1 at t2 and that x does not hit N1 at t2, then P would light up N1. If both processes were to hit N1

---

30. Mele and Robb, "Rescuing Frankfurt-Style Cases."
31. (Mele and Robb's note.) The picture obviously is neuro-fictional, but it is still useful nonetheless.

at t2, Bob's indeterministic deliberative process, x, would light up N1 and P would not. The present question is this. What would happen if, at t2, P were to hit N1 and x were to hit N2? That is, what would happen if the two processes were to "diverge" in this way? And *why*?

We extend Bob's story as follows. Although if both processes were to hit N1 at t2, Bob's indeterministic deliberative process, x, would preempt P and light up N1, it is also the case that if, at t2, P were to hit N1 and x were to hit N2, P would prevail. In the latter case, P would light up N1 and the indeterministic process would not light up N2. Of course, readers would like a story about why it is that although x would preempt P in the former situation, P would prevail over x in the latter. Here is one story. By t2, P has "neutralized" N2 (but without affecting what goes on in x). That is why, if x were to hit N2 at t2, N2 would not light up.[32] More fully, by t2 P has neutralized all of the nodes in Bob for decisions that are contrary to a decision at t2 to steal Ann's car (e.g., a decision at t2 not to steal anyone's car and a decision at t2 never to steal anything).[33] In convenient shorthand, by t2 P has neutralized N2 and all its "cognate decision nodes." Bear in mind that all we need is a conceptually possible scenario, and this certainly looks like one.[34]

The aspect of this story that might raise the libertarian's eyebrows is P's neutralization of N2 and all its cognate decision nodes. For he might be tempted to claim that P's neutralizing procedure is equivalent to P's causal determination of Bob's decision to steal the car. On the other hand, Mele and Robb do specify that P's neutralizing activity does not affect what goes on in Bob's indeterministic decision-making process, and so it would seem that P would not causally determine the decision. How can we shed light on this difficulty?

Let us examine an approach in category (b) that more vigorously exploits the neutralization idea. A strategy of this type has become known as "blockage," and has been developed by David Hunt.[35] Here

---

32. (Mele and Robb's note.) What would happen if Bob's indeterministic deliberative process were to hit N2 at some time tn prior to t2? In one version of the story, N2 would light up at tn — Bob would decide at tn not to steal the car — but then at t2, when P hits N1, Bob would change his mind and decide to steal it. In another version — the one we prefer, because of its relative simplicity — P neutralizes N2 as soon as Black initiates P.

33. (Mele and Robb's note.) David Hunt independently makes a similar suggestion in his article, "Moral Responsibility and Unavoidable Action" in *Philosophical Studies* 97 (2000). See note 1.

34. Mele and Robb, "Rescuing Frankfurt-Style Cases," pp. 104–5.

35. Fischer, contribution to a symposium on Kane's *The Significance of Free Will*, *Philosophy and Phenomenological Research* 60 (2000), pp. 141–8; Hunt, "Moral Responsibility and Unavoidable Action."

is a way of presenting this sort of approach that I think is especially powerful. Consider two situations.

Situation A. Ms. Scarlet deliberately chooses to kill Colonel Mustard at t1, and there are no factors beyond her control that deterministically produce her choice. When she chooses to kill the Colonel, she could have chosen not to kill him. There are no causal factors that would prevent her from not making the choice to kill Colonel Mustard.

In these circumstances, Ms. Scarlet could be morally responsible for her choice. But then, against an alternative-possibilities principle, one might employ a counterfactual version of this situation:

Situation B. Ms. Scarlet's choice to kill Colonel Mustard has precisely the same actual causal history as in A. But before she even started to think about killing Colonel Mustard, a neurophysiologist had blocked all the neural pathways not used in Situation A, so that no neural pathway other than the one employed in that situation could be used. Let us suppose that it is causally determined that she remain a living agent, and if she remains a living agent, some neural pathway has to be used. Thus every alternative for Ms. Scarlet is blocked except the one that realizes her choice to kill the Colonel. But the blockage does not affect the actual causal history of Ms. Scarlet's choice, because the blocked pathways would have remained dormant.

One might, at least initially, have the intuition that Ms Scarlet could be morally responsible for her choice in B as well. Yet for an incompatibilist, this intuition might well be undermined on more careful reflection about whether in B Ms Scarlet retains libertarian freedom. One important question about such blockage cases is one Fischer asks: Could neural events bump up against, so to speak, the blockage?[36] If so, there still may be alternative possibilities for the agent. But if not, it might seem, as Kane suggests, that the neural events are causally determined partly by virtue of the blockage.[37]

---

36. Fischer, "Recent Work on Moral Responsibility," p. 119.
37. Kane suggests this response in his reply to Fischer in the symposium on *The Significance of Free Will* in *Philosophy and Phenomenological Research* 60 (2000), p. 162: In [a case in which every other alternative is blocked except the agent's making A at t], of course, there *are* no alternative possibilities left to the agent; every one is blocked except the agent's choosing A at t. But now we seem to have determinism pure and simple. By implanting the mechanism in this fashion, a controller would have predetermined exactly what the agent would do (and when); and, as a consequence, the controller, not the agent, would be ultimately responsible for the outcome. Blockage by a controller that rules out all relevant alternative possibilities is simply predestination; and on my view at least, predestination runs afoul of ultimate responsibility.

In response, one might point out that in the standard Frankfurt-style cases, the relevant action is inevitable, but the intuition that the agent is morally responsible for it depends on the fact that it does not have an actual causal history by means of which it is made inevitable. What makes the action inevitable is rather some fact about the situation that is not a feature of its actual causal history, and hence the action's being inevitable need not make it the case that it is causally determined. But then how is the blockage case different from the standard Frankfurt-style cases? After all, the blockage does not seem to affect the actual causal history of the action.

Nevertheless, perhaps Kane's response can be defended. Two-situation cases of the above sort might be misleading just because it is natural to assume that the actual causal history of an event is essentially the same in each, given that the only difference between them is a restriction that would seem to have no actual effect on the event. But consider a simple two-situation case modelled on a reflection of Hunt's.[38] Imagine a universe correctly described by Epicurean physics: At the most fundamental level all that exists is atoms and the frictionless void, and there is a determinate downward direction in which all atoms naturally fall – except if they undergo uncaused swerves.

Situation C. A spherical atom is falling downward through space, with a certain velocity and acceleration. Its actual causal history is indeterministic because at any time the atom can be subject to an uncaused swerve. Suppose that the atom can swerve in any direction other than upwards. In actual fact, from t1 to t2 it does not swerve.

A counterfactual situation diverges from C only by virtue of a device that eliminates alternative possibilities and all differences thereby entailed:

Situation D. The case is identical to C, except that the atom is falling downward through a straight and vertically oriented tube whose interior surface is made of frictionless material, and whose interior is precisely wide enough to accommodate the atom. The atom would not have swerved during this time interval, and the trajectory, velocity, and acceleration of the atom from t1 to t2 are precisely what they are in C.

---

38. From Hunt's personal correspondence with Fischer, cited in Fischer's "Recent Work on Moral Responsibility," pp. 119–20.

One might initially have the intuition that the causal history of the atom from t1 to t2 in these two situations is in essence the same. However, this intuition could be challenged by the fact that the restrictions present in D but not in C may change this causal history from one that is essentially indeterministic to one that is essentially deterministic. For since the tube prevents any alternative motion, it would seem that it precludes any indeterminism in the atom's causal history from t1 to t2. And if the tube precludes indeterminism in this causal history, it would appear to make the causal history deterministic. Whether this line of argument is plausible is difficult to ascertain, but it is not obviously implausible.

This problem could make it hard to assess moral responsibility in blockage cases. Sympathy for Frankfurt-style arguments is generated by the sense that moral responsibility is very much a function of the features of the actual causal history of an action, to which restrictions that exist but would seem to play no actual causal role are irrelevant. However, in a scenario in which such restrictions, despite initial appearances, could be relevant to the nature of the actual causal history of an action after all, one's intuitions about whether the agent is morally responsible might become unstable. My own view is not that actual causal histories in blockage cases are clearly deterministic, but only that these considerations show that they may be. This type of problem should make one less confident when evaluating these difficult kinds of Frankfurt-style cases. Since Mele and Robb's development of their case involves something very much like a blockage scenario, one might as a result also be less confident about the ultimate success of their argument.

A NEW FRANKFURT-STYLE SCENARIO

I propose a case of a different sort, one that doesn't fit either category (a) or (b):

Tax Evasion, Part 1. Joe is considering whether to claim a tax deduction for the substantial local registration fee that he paid when he bought a house. He knows that claiming the deduction is illegal, that he probably won't be caught, and that if he is, he can convincingly plead ignorance. Suppose he has a very powerful but not always overriding desire to advance his self-interest no matter what the cost to others, and no matter whether advancing his self-interest involves illegal activity. Furthermore, he is a libertarian free agent. Crucially, his psychology is such that the only way that in this situation he could fail to choose to evade taxes is for moral reasons. (As I use the phrase here, "failing to choose to evade taxes" will encompass both not choosing to evade taxes and choosing not to evade taxes.) His psychology is not, for example, such that he could fail to choose to evade taxes for no reason or simply on a whim. In fact, it is causally necessary for his failing to choose to evade taxes in this situation that a moral reason occur to him with a certain force. A moral reason can occur to him with that force either involuntarily or as a result of his voluntary activity (e.g., by his willing to consider it, or by his seeking out a vivid presentation of such a reason). However, a moral reason occurring to him with such force is not causally sufficient for his failing to choose to evade taxes. If a moral reason were to occur to him with that force, Joe could, with the his libertarian free will, either choose to act on it or refrain from doing so (without the intervener's device in place). But to ensure that he chooses to evade taxes, a neuroscientist now implants a device which, were it to sense a moral reason occurring with the specified force, would electronically stimulate his brain so that he would choose to evade taxes. In actual fact, no moral reason occurs to him with such force, and he chooses to evade taxes while the device remains idle.

In this situation, Joe could be morally responsible for choosing to evade taxes despite the fact that he could not have chosen otherwise.[39] The prior sign does not causally determine his decision. There are indeed alternative possibilities which involve a moral reason occurring to him with a certain force. In one type of possibility, Joe makes this happen voluntarily. But such a possibility is insufficiently robust to ground his moral responsibility for tax evasion. Again, the deeper intuition underlying the alternative-possibilities requirement is that if, for example, an agent is to be blameworthy for an action, it is crucial that he could have done something to avoid this blameworthiness. If alternative possibilities were to play a role in explaining an agent's moral responsibility for an action (in a way independent of an intuition about its actual causal history), it would be because as a result of securing an alternative possibility instead, he would thereby have avoided the responsibility he has for the action he performed. However, if Joe had made a reason for an alternative action occur to him with a certain force, he would not thereby have avoided responsibility for evading taxes. For his making the reason for an alternative action occur to him is compatible with his

---

39. I pursue this strategy in "Alternative Possibilities and Causal Histories." Independently, David Hunt, in "Moral Responsibility and Avoidable Action," pp. 214–16, also considers making the prior sign a necessary condition of the alternative decision, but he is skeptical about this approach. See note 1.

never deciding to perform the alternative action, or even ever being inclined to perform that action, and choosing to evade taxes instead.

It is important to the example that the trigger for intervention be that a moral reason occur to Joe with a certain force, and not simply that a moral reason occur to him. For one might plausibly argue that it is a necessary condition on blameworthiness that the agent understands that his action is morally wrong, which in Joe's case would seem to require some awareness of moral reasons.[40] At the same time, Joe's blameworthiness would not require that moral reasons occur to him with any particularly strong force.

This example fits neither description (a) or (b). Rather, it is a case that has the following features:

(i) The agent clearly has free will according to most libertarian views.
(ii) What would trigger the intervention is a "flicker" that is insufficiently robust to explain the agent's moral responsibility for the decision in question.
(iii) It does not ground the truth of the analog of Widerker's

    (1) If Jones is blushing at t1, then, provided no one intervenes, Jones will decide at t2 to kill Smith,

which is

    (1′) If a moral reason does not occur to Joe with a certain force, then, provided no one intervenes, he will decide to evade taxes,

in causal determinism, while at the same time not endorsing the analog of Widerker's

    (1a) If Jones is blushing at t1, then Jones will [only] *probably* decide at t2 to kill Smith,

and

    (1b) If Jones is blushing at t1, then Jones will *freely* decide at t2 to kill Smith, [in a sense that allows that the agent could have decided otherwise],

which are

    (1a′) If a moral reason does not occur to Joe with a certain force, then he will (only) probably decide to evade taxes,

40. Thanks to Michael McKenna for suggesting that I make this point explicit.

20

and

> (1b′) If a moral reason does not occur to Joe with a certain force, then he will freely decide to evade taxes (in a sense that allows that the agent could have decided otherwise).

For the absence of what would trigger the intervention at some particular time (the role of this absence is played by Jones's blushing at t1 in Widerker's case, and by the non-occurrence of a moral reason with the requisite force at some particular time in Tax Evasion), or a state indicated by this absence, will not, together with all the other actual facts about the situation, causally determine the decision. Joe's decision is not causally determined by the non-occurrence at any particular time of a moral reason with sufficient force. For at any point in the causal history of the action prior to the choice, a moral reason could have occurred to him with sufficient force, even as a result of his own (undetermined) voluntary activity. But (contra 1a) the decision will occur (and not just probably occur) in the absence of what would trigger the intervention, even though it is not causally determined, because what would trigger the intervention is causally necessary (but not causally sufficient – thus not causally determining) for the decision's not occurring. Hence, (contra 1b) there is a libertarian sense in which the agent can freely decide to perform the action, but without its being the case that he could have decided otherwise.

Seeing how this example responds to Kane's version of the objection highlights the value of having the cue for intervention be causally necessary but not sufficient for the action, while ensuring that up to the time of the decision itself, the agent is not causally determined to make it. Kane argues, first of all, that supposing a Frankfurt-style case is to convince the libertarian, then if the agent in the example decides on his own, this decision must be causally undetermined. Now if the intervention does occur, the agent is not morally responsible. But if the neuroscientist "does not intervene to predetermine the outcome and the indeterminacy remains in place until the choice is made – so that the outcome is [a "self-forming willing"] – then the agent . . . is ultimately responsible for it. However, then it is also the case that the agent *could have done otherwise*."[41] However, let the cue for intervention be the

41. Kane, *The Significance of Free Will*, p. 142.

relevant sort of causally necessary condition, such as, in our example, the occurrence to the agent of a moral reason with a certain force. Then, if the neuroscientist does not intervene, even though the indeterminacy remains in place until the choice is made, it is not the case, contrary to Kane's supposition, that the agent could have decided or could have done otherwise. For in order to decide otherwise, a moral reason would have had to occur with the requisite force, and then the device would have been activated.

One might reply that in order for Joe to be responsible for his action, his moral psychology must have been set up by crucial choices of his for which there were robust alternative possibilities.[42] But to see that this sort of answer is mistaken, consider:

Tax Evasion, Part 2. Joe was raised in a context in which people are typically self-interested in the sort of way he is now. His parents, for example, had this sort of psychological profile. But he was also raised to reflect critically on his values as soon as he was able. Like most of us, he initially accepted his family's values, and he held them very strongly. Joe then learned about competing positions, but upon serious reflection, he rejected them. Suppose that for him to abandon his initial moral view it was causally necessary that a reason for accepting a competing position occur to him with a certain force, and this could occur either involuntarily or as a result of his voluntary activity. Were such a reason to occur to him with that force, he could still choose to retain or reject his values (in the absence of the neuroscientist's device). But the neuroscientist, knowing all of this about his psychology, sets up his device before Joe begins critical reflection on his moral views, so that if a reason to accept a competing view were to occur to him with the specified force, it would electronically stimulate his brain to retain his initial moral position. But in actual fact, the device remains inert, for although he considers reasons to accept competing views, these reasons never occur to him with force sufficient to trigger the device.

Thus, although Joe's moral psychology was not set up by crucial choices of his for which there were robust alternative possibilities, he could still be morally responsible for evading taxes. Consequently, this type of objection can be answered. Even presupposing libertarianism, we have not yet encountered a principle of alternative possibilities that plausibly has a significant role in explaining moral responsibility.

42. Kane suggests a reply of this sort to a similar case, in personal correspondence.

Another type of attack on Frankfurt-style strategies has been advanced by Michael Otsuka, Keith Wyma, and Michael McKenna.[43] Otsuka contends that a necessary condition on blameworthiness is that the agent, as a result of voluntary endeavor, could have behaved in such a manner for which he would have been entirely blameless. Wyma, in a similar vein, claims that a person is morally responsible for something she has done, A, only if she has failed to do something she could have done, B, such that doing B would have rendered her not morally responsible for A. McKenna argues that in all of the successful Frankfurt-style cases, the agent has the power either to be the author of his action or not, and that it is precisely this sort of alternative possibility that is significant for moral responsibility. (McKenna's condition differs from the others in the respect that it employs the notion of a power, a point that I will ignore for now but address later.)

These authors assume that their conditions could not be falsified by Frankfurt-style cases because the successful versions involve the possibility that the agent could have voluntarily done, or been the author of, something that would have triggered the intervention, whereupon she would not have been morally responsible for the act in question. Fischer argues that these conditions could be undermined by cases in which the intervention would be triggered by an involuntary flicker, so that the agent does not have a voluntary alternative possibility.[44] However, in setting up an involuntary-flicker case, one must be careful to avoid the problem that Widerker raises, and to do this one must ensure that Joe remains a libertarian free agent. We might try to devise a scenario that meets these specifications by changing Joe's psychology in Tax Evasion, Part 1, so that in his situation, a vivid presentation by an external source would now be required for a moral reason to occur to him with the requisite force. Because of the strength of his self-interest and the level of his commitment to morality, since the benefit to himself at stake is significant, and the

---

43. Michael Otsuka, "Incompatibilism and the Avoidability of Blame," *Ethics* 108 (1998), pp. 685–701; Keith D. Wyma, "Moral Responsibility and Leeway for Action," Michael McKenna, "Alternative Possibilities and the Failure of the Counterexample Strategy," *Journal of Social Philosophy* 28 (1997), pp. 71–85. Fischer provides a helpful account of these positions in "Recent Work on Moral Responsibility," pp. 117–19.
44. Fischer, "Recent Work on Moral Responsibility," p. 120.

damage to others that would result is not especially great, Joe could not make a moral reason occur to him with such force voluntarily, and he could not voluntarily seek the sort of external presentation of moral reasons that would make them occur to him with this force. The relevant facts about the history of his psychology are given by Tax Evasion, Part 2, except that now he could not make a moral reason occur to him with sufficient force because of the strength of his self-interest and the weakness of his moral commitment, and the extent to which these features of his psychology have become ingrained. This last specification is psychologically plausible – there is much that typical agents could not bring themselves to do because of their commitments.

Again (without the intervener's device in place), if a moral reason were to occur to him with the specified force, Joe could, with the power of his libertarian free will, either decide to act on it or act against it. The neuroscientist's device is set up so that it would intervene if a moral reason occurred to him with this force, but he decides to evade taxes without the device intervening. If Joe could be morally responsible for deciding to evade taxes in this case, then it would directly undermine Otsuka's condition, since Joe could not, as a result of his voluntary endeavor, have behaved in such a manner for which he would not have been entirely blameless. It would show McKenna's to be mistaken, for Joe lacks the power not to be the author of the tax evasion, and similarly for Wyma's, since it is not the case that he failed to do something he could have done, such that doing it would have rendered him not morally responsible for evading taxes.

But the leeway incompatibilist might argue that if Joe were morally responsible despite his not meeting these conditions, it would be because his not meeting them is explained by his moral psychology, which, in turn, results from certain crucial choices of his that do fulfill conditions of the general sort we are now examining. Joe's inability to make a moral reason occur to him with sufficient force is explained by the fact that he chose to retain the self-interested moral conception that he was raised to hold. Although he could not have chosen otherwise than to retain this conception, he failed to do something he could have voluntarily done – have a reason for accepting a competing moral position occur to him with a certain force – such that doing so would have rendered him not morally responsible for making this choice (because then the device would have been activated). This claim suggests the following alternative possibilities principle:

An agent is morally responsible for something she has done, A, only if she has failed to do something she could have done, B, such that doing B would have rendered her not morally responsible for A, or if she could not have done something that would have rendered her not morally responsible for A, this fact is explained by choices this agent made in the past, $C_{1...n}$, which are such that at the time she made them she could have done something, $D_{1...n}$, such that doing $D_{1...n}$ would have rendered her not morally responsible for $C_{1...n}$.

It is not obvious to me that this principle has a counter-example, and that therefore it could be an alternative-possibilities condition necessary for moral responsibility. We might revise Part 2 of Tax Evasion so that for Joe to have abandoned his initial moral view, it was causally necessary that a reason for accepting a competing position occur to him with sufficient force, but that such a reason could occur to him only involuntarily, and never as a result of his voluntary activity. But then we would want to know why his psychology has this feature, and the sort of explanation that suggests itself is that he had been so thoroughly indoctrinated by his upbringing that his ability to evaluate his moral view rationally has been impaired by factors beyond his control. But there would be a strong pull to claiming that Joe is not morally responsible in this situation. There may be another way to construct a counter-example to this principle, but it is not obvious to me how one might do so.

I favor a different kind of objection to the sort of condition that McKenna, Wyma, and Otsuka advocate. First of all, it may be that a condition is necessary for some phenomenon A but sometimes holds by virtue of features that do not illuminate A, features that are irrelevant to explaining the nature of A. I believe that even if it turns out that conditions of the sort at issue are necessary for moral responsibility, they can hold by virtue of features of a situation that are explanatorily irrelevant to what would make an agent morally responsible, and that as a result the condition at issue fails to illuminate the nature of the phenomenon. As we will now see, what is missing from this sort of condition is an epistemic element.

Consider Wyma's view, according to which an agent is morally responsible for something she has done, A, only if she has failed to do something she could have done, B, such that doing B would have rendered her morally non-responsible for A. Suppose that Joe could have voluntarily taken a sip from his coffee cup prior to his deciding to take the illegal deduction, not understanding that this action would preclude his evading taxes, because unbeknownst to him, taking the sip would have triggered a bomb that would have killed him. In this situation, he could have behaved voluntarily in such a manner that would have precluded the action for which he was in fact blameworthy, as a result of which he would not have been morally responsible for this action. But whether he could have voluntarily taken the sip from the coffee cup, not understanding that it would render him blameless in this way, is intuitively irrelevant to explaining whether he is morally responsible for tax evasion. We might say that despite the fact that Joe could have voluntarily taken a sip from his coffee cup, and doing so would have rendered him not morally responsible for evading taxes, this alternative possibility is nevertheless insufficiently robust to have an important role in grounding moral responsibility. Because this sort of alternative possibility would render Wyma's proviso satisfied, conditions of this sort, despite being necessary for moral responsibility, would appear not to have a significant role in explaining its nature.

As a result, we need to embellish the notion of a robust alternative possibility to incorporate this epistemic dimension. Accordingly, an alternative-possibilities condition more plausibly relevant to explaining an agent's moral responsibility for an action must capture the notion that she could have willed otherwise in the following more robust sense: she could have willed something that she understood would, per se, get her off the hook. Here is the final notion of robustness I favor:

Robustness. For an alternative possibility to be relevant to explaining why an agent is morally responsible for an action, it must satisfy the following characterization: she could have willed something different from what she actually willed such that she understood that by willing it she would thereby be precluded from moral responsibility for the action.

However, in Tax Evasion, Joe does not have an alternative possibility available to him that is robust in this sense. True, he could have willed that a moral reason not to evade taxes occur to him with a particular force. But if he had made a reason for an alternative action occur to him with that force, he, as far as he could know, would not thereby have avoided responsibility for evading taxes. For, given his understanding, his making this sort of reason for an alternative action occur to him is compatible with his never deciding to perform the alternative action, or even ever being inclined to perform that action. In addition, Joe does not understand that willing the occurrence of this moral reason would actually preclude him from responsibility for doing A.

Indeed, if he were voluntarily to make this sort of moral reason occur to him, the intervention would take place, and he would not then have been responsible for A. Still, he does not know that the intervention would then take place and that as a consequence of this intervention he would perform A but not be responsible for it.

Despite all of this, Joe is morally responsible for his action. Consequently, if Wyma's condition were refined in such a way as to preclude its being satisfied by alternative possibilities irrelevant to explaining why the agent is morally responsible, then it could be shown to be false. The same type of point can be made about Otsuka's and McKenna's provisos. Conditions of this sort seem to purchase technical indefeasibility at the cost of explanatory relevance to moral responsibility.

There is a feature of McKenna's condition we have not yet addressed. He believes that what is crucially necessary for moral responsibility is a power for alternatives of a certain sort – for him, a power to be the author of one's action or not. He is not alone in maintaining a position of this general type. For example, both John Duns Scotus and William of Ockham argue that moral responsibility requires a power not to choose to perform the action.[45] A crucial fact about this sort of condition is that it could be satisfied even if the agent cannot currently activate this power, for the notion of retaining a power while the agent currently cannot activate it is coherent. For even when Maurice Greene is asleep, it would seem true that he retains the power to run 100 meters in less than 10 seconds, despite the fact that his being asleep is currently an impediment to his activating this power. So, similarly, in the standard Frankfurt-style cases, one might argue that no matter what arcane flicker the intervening device is set up to sense, the agent retains the power not to choose to perform the action or not to be the author of her action, despite the fact that she cannot activate the power because of the device. The Scotus/Ockham proposal is that none of these Frankfurt-style arguments undermine the following condition:

(4) An action is free in the sense required for moral responsibility only if the agent has the power not to choose to perform the action.

Indeed, as Maurice Greene's situation shows, there are cases in which it is natural to agree that an agent has a power even though it cannot

---

45. Marilyn Adams, "Duns Scotus on the Will as Rational Power," *Via Scoti: Methodologica ad Mentem Joannis Duns Scoti*, ed. Leonardo Sileo (Rome: PAA Edizioni Antonianum, 1995), pp. 839–854; and "The Structure of Ockham's Moral Theory," *Franciscan Studies* XXIV (1986), 1–35.

currently be exercised. However, it would be implausible to maintain that no matter what the nature of the external impediment, the agent still retains the power. Suppose, for example, that a patient has a tumor that puts pressure on his brain so that he can no longer do cutting-edge mathematics. If the tumor were not putting pressure on the brain, he could do the mathematics. But imagine that it is causally impossible to remove the tumor, or for its existence to cease in any other way, without the patient's dying. Then, it would seem, he lacks the power to do cutting-edge mathematics. Analogously, suppose that in Tax Evasion, the neurophysiologist has implanted his device in Joe's brain, which is triggered by the occurrence of the moral reason, but she has also made it causally impossible to remove or disable the device without killing him. As a result, he permanently cannot choose not to evade taxes. Under these circumstances, Joe would appear to lack the power not to evade taxes. But, still, he could be morally responsible. Therefore even condition (4) would seem mistaken.[46]

GINET'S CHALLENGE

Ginet's response to Frankfurt-style arguments resembles but is yet interestingly different from Widerker's and Kane's. I believe that Tax Evasion, with a little embellishment, answers the challenge Ginet devises for those who defend these arguments, either by providing a direct counter-example to his alternative-possibilities condition, or in any case by leaving only alternative possibilities that are explanatorily irrelevant in the way we just explored. Ginet begins his discussion with the following case – let's call it **Intervener**.

Black sets up a mechanism that monitors Jones's actions and that would cause Jones's doing B by t3 if Jones has not already done B by some deadline t2. We must suppose that had this mechanism been triggered at t2, it would have causally necessitated Jones's doing B by t3 in such a way as to render Jones unable to avoid doing B by t3, and that there was no time at which Jones knew or should have known about this mechanism. The mechanism is not triggered because Jones does B at t1, before t2.

Ginet contends that Jones may be responsible for doing B at the precise time at which he did it (t1), but not for doing B by t3, "because,

46. McKenna, "Alternative Possibilities and the Failure of the Counterexample Strategy." Haji criticizes McKenna's view in *Moral Appraisability*, pp. 30–34.

owing to the presence of Black's mechanism, Jones could not have avoided it [doing B by t3], but he may be responsible for the obtaining of the temporally more specific state of affairs, which he could have avoided."[47] He then issues this challenge to defenders of Frankfurt-style arguments:

This finding as to what Jones is and is not responsible for depends on there being a difference between the time at which Jones actually does B and the time at which Jones would do B if he were caused to do it by Black's mechanism. A defender of Frankfurt's argument might think that my finding could be blocked by revising the example so that this difference is eliminated, so that the precise time at which Jones actually does B and the precise time at which Black's mechanism would cause Jones to do B are the same.[48]

Ginet thinks that there is no case that could answer his challenge,

[1] For in order to ensure that the two times are the same Black's mechanism would have to be set up so that it would be triggered by the absence of some condition whose actual presence is causally sufficient to ensure that Jones does B at t1.

[2] That is, it would have to be posited, first, that there occurred at a time t0 prior to Jones's doing B at t1 a condition C that was causally sufficient for his doing B at t1 and, second, that Black's mechanism was rigged so that, had C failed to occur at t0, the mechanism would have causally necessitated Jones's doing B at t1.

[3] Condition C at t0 must be such that, its obtaining makes it the case that it is not open to Jones after t0 to avoid doing B at t1, that is, from t0 Jones could not avoid doing B at t1. Otherwise, if there were no such condition C whose presence at t0 forces Jones's doing B at t1 and whose absence at t0 would cause Black's mechanism to force Jones's doing B at t1, there would be nothing in the example that entails that Jones could not avoid doing B at t1.[49]

In Ginet's view, whether Jones could be responsible for anything in this case depends on whether he could have prevented the occurrence of C at t0, whether he knew or could have known how he could do this,

47. Ginet, "In Defense of the Principle of Alternative Possibilities," p. 406.
48. Ibid., p. 407.
49. Ibid., pp. 407–8.

and whether he knew or should have known that it would mean that from t0 he would be unable to avoid doing B at t1. If these conditions are not met, then Jones's doing B at t1 will be unavoidable for him even independently of Black's mechanism, and claiming that he is morally responsible would therefore beg the question against the opponent. If these conditions are fulfilled, then Jones would not be responsible for doing B at t1, but rather for "his allowing or contributing the occurrence of a prior condition that he knows will make his doing B at t1 unavoidable."[50]

First, one's intuition about this case might well diverge from Ginet's, for one might think that Jones could indeed be morally responsible for doing B by t3, since he does B by t3 on his own without any intervention. I, for one, have this intuition, and if it is plausible, then Ginet's objection will have been nipped in the bud. Moreover, Ginet's defense of his intuition that Jones is not responsible for doing B by t3 – "owing to the presence of Black's mechanism, Jones could not have avoided it [doing B by t3]" – would seem to beg the question against Frankfurt.

Second, even if Ginet is right that Jones would not be morally responsible for doing B by t3, perhaps a version of Tax Evasion can meet Ginet's challenge, without being problematic in the way that claims [1]-[3] suggest. As a first pass (let's call this case Tax Evasion/Ginet), let us suppose that the intervener can know that at the time (t1) when Joe gets to the crucial point in filling out his tax form – the space most appropriate for entering registration fees as deductions – he will decide to enter the local registration fee (= action B), unless a moral reason occurs to him with sufficient force, and he can make that moral reason occur to him voluntarily. The condition causally relevant to his decision is his moral psychology, which obtains during some appropriate time prior to t1. The mechanism is set up so that if a moral reason occurs to him with the specified force during his deliberation, it causes him to do B at t1. But in fact, the moral reason does not occur to him, and he does B at t1 on his own.

Notice that in this case, there is no condition C that obtains at some time t0 prior to t1 that is (without the mechanism) causally sufficient for Joe's doing B at t1. As a candidate, one might propose: no moral reason occurring with sufficient force at t0. But this condition is not causally sufficient for Joe to do B at t1 (without the mechanism in

50. Ginet, "In Defense of the Principle of Alternative Possibilities," p. 409.

place), since after t0 it is causally possible that he voluntarily make a moral reason occur to him with the requisite force, whereupon he could avoid B at t1. Thus, in this example, Ginet's [1] and [2] are not satisfied. Someone might contend that these facts about the case would undermine its success, for by analogy with [3], if there is no condition C whose presence at t0 forces Joe's doing B at t1 and whose absence at t0 would cause the mechanism to force him to do B at t1, there would be nothing in the example that entails that he could not avoid doing B at t1. This claim is mistaken. We can set up Joe's moral psychology so that it does not force him to do B at t1, supposing instead that there is a necessary condition for his avoiding B at t1, which he could voluntarily produce at any time, and is such that the mechanism is set up to detect and react to it.

In correspondence, Ginet argues that my example does not entail Joe's not avoiding doing B at t1 rather than a bit later. For it would take some non-zero interval − call it x − for the mechanism to detect the occurrence of the reason and then cause Joe's doing B. If M were to occur between t1−x and t1, Joe would be caused to do B at a time later than t1.

In response, the alternative possibilities left open are insufficiently robust to explain why Joe is morally responsible for doing B at t1. The possibilities at issue fit this description: Joe makes the moral reason occur to him between t1−x and t1, and the intervention occurs that causes Joe to do B at some time slightly later than t1. As I have argued, for an alternative possibility to be relevant to explaining an agent's moral responsibility for an action, it must satisfy the following characterization: she could have willed something different from what she actually willed such that she understood that by willing it she would thereby be precluded from moral responsibility for the action. However, if Joe had made a moral reason occur to him with the specified force, he, as far as he could understand, would not thereby have avoided responsibility for evading taxes. In addition, he could not have understood that willing the occurrence of the moral reason after t1−x and before t1 would preclude his doing B at t1, and a fortiori that it would preclude his responsibility for doing B at t1, or for doing B at all. For he has no inkling of the fact that so willing would cause the intervention that would preclude his doing B at t1, or that so willing would cause the intervention that would preclude his responsibility for doing B at t1, or for doing B at all. Thus, despite the unavailability of a robust alternative possibility, Joe is morally responsible for doing B at t1.

Consequently, the alternative possibilities that this scenario leaves open are not relevant to explaining why Joe is morally responsible for doing B at t1 in the actual situation. So even if the alternative-possibilities condition that Ginet has in mind is necessary for moral responsibility, it is nevertheless not pertinent to explaining why agents are morally responsible for their actions.

Furthermore, with a little more amplification, I suspect Tax Evasion/Ginet may yet provide a successful counter-example to Ginet's challenge. First, the case might be revised so that Joe is not responsible for doing B at an instant, but rather during some very short temporal interval. To get this result, one might specify that Joe does not in any sense intend his decision to occur at any instant in particular, but rather he only times it to occur during some very short temporal interval. He is not even aware that there is an instant, as opposed to some very short temporal interval, at which he might time his decision, or at which his decision eventually occurs. To add to the plausibility of this specification, note that there must be a limit to the human capacity to time decisions – there must be a limit to the control a human being has over exactly when a decision of hers will take place. Consequently, there will be some small interval of time – perhaps some very small fraction of a second, call it n – such that no human being can control at which point in that interval she makes a decision. It may be that despite this limitation, an agent could still be responsible for making a decision at an instant if she intends to make it at that instant (supposing that this is psychologically possible). But in the absence of such an intention, it seems reasonable to conclude that the agent is not responsible for making a decision at a particular instant as opposed to being responsible for making it during some interval with a minimum length n. Let us suppose that Joe times his decision to occur during some interval i of length just slightly greater than n.

Moreover, it is possible to make machines that work very quickly. In particular, it is possible to make an intervention machine such that the time it takes to detect the occurrence of a moral reason and then cause a decision is much shorter than n. Now, in Ginet's objection, x is the time it takes for the mechanism to detect the occurrence of the reason and then cause Joe's doing B. If M were to occur between t1−x and t1, Joe would be caused to do B at a time later than t1. However, given that Joe is responsible for doing B not at some instant, but rather during the interval i slightly longer than n surrounding the instant t1, and x is sufficiently shorter than n, it will be impossible for the mechanism to cause Joe to do B outside of i. That is, if we make the plausible assumption that as a matter of psychological fact, Joe cannot make the moral reason occur to him during the interval i in which he is timing his decision to occur – he can't do these two things "at once." Hence, in the sense in which Joe is responsible for making a decision at a specific time, Joe could not have done otherwise than to do B at a specific time, and yet he is morally responsible for his decision. Thus it seems that Ginet's challenge has been met.

AN OBJECTION TO CAUSAL-HISTORY INCOMPATIBILISM

I have argued that the proposed alternative-possibilities conditions that are plausibly relevant to explaining why an agent is morally responsible for an action all fall to counter-example. However, I began by suggesting that the incompatibilist intuition about actual causal histories (represented by condition (3)) is more fundamental than any incompatibilist intuition about alternative possibilities (expressed by conditions such as (1) and (2)). The causal-history condition has not been threatened by any Frankfurt-style argument, and it is sufficient to keep the case for incompatibilism very much alive even if no alternative-possibilities condition on moral responsibility is true. In the next few chapters, I will develop and revise this condition, and provide further reasons to think that it is true.

I close this chapter by examining an important objection to the sort of incompatibilism that I favor. One of van Inwagen's strategies for establishing incompatibilism is independent of considerations regarding alternative possibilities, and instead attempts to establish this position by way of a "direct argument."

If determinism is true, then there is some state of the world in the distant past P that is connected by the laws of nature to any action A that one performs in the present. But since no one is responsible for the state of the world P in the distant past, and no one is responsible for the laws of nature that lead from P to A, it follows that no one is responsible for any action A that is performed in the present.[51]

51. Van Inwagen, *An Essay on Free Will*, pp. 182–8; the summary is from Mark Ravizza, "Semi-Compatibilism and the Transfer of Non-Responsibility," *Philosophical Studies* 75 (1994), pp. 61–93, at p. 63.

This argument expresses the incompatibilist intuition that I have regarding determinism. But Ravizza (later, together with Fischer)[52] objects to a version of this argument, which he summarizes as follows:

If (i) there are conditions for which no one is, or ever has been, even partly responsible, and (ii) these conditions are sufficient to ensure a given event, and (iii) these conditions *play a role in the actual sequence that brings about this event*, then it follows that no one is responsible for the event in question.

Fischer and Ravizza claim that there are counter-examples that undermine these contentions. Suppose that Betty freely explodes some dynamite with the intention of starting an avalanche at T1, which crushes the enemy base at T3. But there is also a glacier in the area that is gradually melting, shifting, and eroding. At the very same time that Betty's dynamite explodes to start the avalanche, the erosion of the glacier starts the avalanche. Suppose, in addition, that the glacier would have started the avalanche even if Betty had not exploded the dynamite. Here we have a situation in which (i), (ii), and (iii) above are satisfied, and yet the agent is morally responsible for the consequence in question, and therefore the direct argument has been undermined.

Notice, however, that the condition that in my view specifies the preferred incompatibilist intuition about determinism,

(3) An action is free in the sense required for moral responsibility only if it is not produced by a deterministic process that traces back to causal factors beyond the agent's control,

would not rule out Betty's moral responsibility for her action in this situation. For Fischer's and Ravizza's case does not specify that Betty's action is produced by a deterministic process that traces back to causal factors beyond her control. Fischer and Ravizza's case of simultaneous overdetermination may show that sometimes factors beyond an agent's control make consequences of her action inevitable, and that she still might be responsible for those consequences. Nothing in my position, so far, rules out this possibility. For, as Betty's case itself demonstrates, factors beyond an agent's control might render the consequences of an action inevitable while not causally determining the action or decision

52. Ravizza, "Semi-Compatibilism and the Transfer of Non-Responsibility," p. 75; Fischer and Ravizza, *Responsibility and Control: A Theory of Moral Responsibility*, pp. 151–69, especially pp. 159–63.

itself, allowing her to be responsible for the action (and thereby perhaps even for those consequences).

However, one may construct a related challenge that might seem more threatening to my position. Suppose that Plum, the neurophysiologist, has implanted a device in Betty's brain so that at the very instant that she, by her libertarian free will, makes the decision to set off the dynamite, it also causes this decision, and that this device would have caused the decision in the absence of Betty's making it. Perhaps it is intuitive that she could still be morally responsible for her decision in this situation. But in this case, there are causal factors beyond Betty's control that produce her decision, so my condition (3) would seem to be undermined.

However, I think that this conclusion can be resisted. Suppose that Betty could indeed be morally responsible in this situation. Then, rather than reject the incompatibilist intuition about actual causal histories, I would argue that a more precise version of (3) is

(3′) An action is free in the sense required for moral responsibility only if there is at least one causal history that produces the action that is not a deterministic causal history that traces back to factors beyond the agent's control.[53]

Nevertheless, it is not obvious that I would be forced to make this move. One problem for this case of overdetermination is that an attempt to spell it out might reveal details that would undermine the intuition that the agent is morally responsible (at least for incompatibilists). This is a lesson to be learned from the Mele–Robb scenario, which is very similar in structure. In developing that case, Mele and Robb invoked what seems to be blockage, and blockage may in the last analysis amount to causal determinism. Similarly, spelling out this overdetermination case might also reveal blockage and causal determination. A related problem is that the intuition that Betty is morally responsible might be unstable.[54] For these reasons, I will set the complications raised by this sort of case aside, and retain (3) as

53. Thanks to Michael McKenna and Carl Ginet for suggesting this formulation.
54. Ginet, for example, suggests (in personal correspondence) that Betty may not be responsible for her action, though she may be responsible for its being the case that it would have happened even if Plum's device had not been there. But perhaps Ginet's intuition is explainable by the fact that his intuitions generally tend to track the Principle of Alternative Possibilities.

the expression of the fundamental incompatibilist intuition about determinism.

A FINAL WORD

A resolute causal-history incompatibilism would diminish the importance of two debates between incompatibilists and compatibilists that have been difficult to resolve (Kane makes an analogous point[55]). The first debate concerns whether "she could have done otherwise" should be analyzed conditionally — for example, as "if she had chosen otherwise she would have done otherwise." Compatibilists have contended for the conditional analysis, incompatibilists have argued against it, and it has been suggested that the controversy ends in stalemate. However, if whether an agent could have done otherwise is not crucial to moral responsibility, then the status of this controversy loses significance. The second debate is about the status of the "consequence" argument. Van Inwagen contends that if physicalist determinism is true, there is a clear sense in which no agent could have done otherwise than what he in fact did.[56] By van Inwagen's characterization, physicalist determinism is true just in case a proposition that expresses the entire state of the universe at some instant in time, in conjunction with the physical laws, entails any proposition that expresses the state of the universe at any other instant.[57] So, if physicalist determinism is true, given the entire state of the universe at some instant in time, every subsequent state of the universe is thereby rendered inevitable. Suppose Ms. Peacock murdered Mr. Green last Tuesday. Given physicalist determinism, Ms. Peacock's crime is inevitable given the state of the universe 100 years before she was born and the state of the natural laws. So if Ms. Peacock were able to do otherwise last Tuesday, then she must at that time have been able to cause the state of the universe 100 years before she was born to have been different from what it in fact was, or to change the

---

55. Kane, *The Significance of Free Will*, pp. 58–9.
56. Van Inwagen, "The Incompatibility of Free Will and Determinism," in *Free Will*, Gary Watson, ed. (Oxford: Oxford University Press, 1982), pp. 96–110; *An Essay on Free Will*, pp. 55–78. Perhaps the earliest version of this argument is Carl Ginet's in his "Might We Have No Choice," in *Freedom and Determinism*, ed. Keith Lehrer (New York: Random House, 1966), pp. 87–104; for a comprehensive discussion of these issues see John Martin Fischer, *The Metaphysics of Free Will*, pp. 1–130, and for a catalog of sources for the argument see Fischer's pp. 218–9, note 10.
57. Van Inwagen, "The Incompatibility of Free Will and Determinism," p. 47.

natural laws. Since she was able to do neither, last Tuesday she could not have done otherwise than to murder Mr. Green. Compatibilists have challenged this sort of argument in various ways, and it has been suggested that this debate too ends in a stalemate. But, again, if whether an agent could have done otherwise is not crucial to moral responsibility, how this debate is resolved becomes less momentous.[58]

As I have indicated, leeway incompatibilists would tend to advocate an incompatibilist condition on the actual causal history of an action only because it makes the existence of alternative possibilities a prerequisite for moral responsibility, for it is a condition about alternative possibilities that is more significant for explaining why agents would be morally responsible. One might place incompatibilists on a continuum ranging from those who hold that moral responsibility requires that an agent could have done otherwise, to the most radical causal incompatibilists, who maintain that even in a blockage case, an agent can be morally responsible so long as the actual causal history of the action has the right features. My own view is that moral responsibility requires that the action's actual causal history have certain indeterministic features, but that it might well be that alternative possibilities – not necessarily of the robust sort – are entailed by the actual causal history's having these features. Nevertheless, the aspect of the action that has the important role in explaining why agents would be morally responsible is the nature of the actual causal history, and not the alternative possibilities.

---

58. For discussions of these "dialectical stalemates" see Fischer, *The Metaphysics of Free Will*, pp. 83–5, Kane, *The Significance of Free Will*, pp. 44–58, and Bok, *Freedom and Responsibility*, pp. 98–103.

2

Coherence Objections to Libertarianism

INTRODUCTION

Critics of libertarianism have contended that indeterministically free action cannot be reconciled with certain provisions in action theory that libertarians themselves would want to endorse. Specifically, they have argued that a libertarian theory of action cannot allow for agents to be morally responsible for freely willed action, for freely willed action to meet plausible general requirements on explanation, and for freely willed action to be rational. These kinds of criticisms are sometimes categorized as *coherence objections* to libertarianism. According to another sort of complaint against libertarianism, the free will it espouses does not harmonize with the empirical evidence. Our choices produce physical events in the brain and in the rest of the body, and these events would seem to be governed by physical laws. The libertarian position must make it credible that our choices could be free in the sense it advocates given the evidence we have about these physical laws, and according to the objection, this cannot be done. This challenge gives rise to a family of *empirical objections* to libertarianism, the subject of the next chapter.

The concern of this chapter is the coherence of libertarianism, predominantly the first of the three mentioned coherence objections – whether a plausible libertarian theory of free will can allow for moral responsibility. It might be named the Humean challenge, since its classical presentation is found in Hume's *Treatise of Human Nature*; it is sometimes called the *Mind* objection, for the journal in which various versions of it were presented and discussed in the mid-twentieth century.[1] My aim will be to develop a version of this argument adapted to my causal history incompatibilist concerns. I shall touch on the coherence objections regarding explanation and rationality of action. In my view, very fine work has been done by philosophers such as Ginet, Kane, Clarke, and O'Connor to show that libertarianism can withstand them – work to which I have little to add.[2] I will, however, consider two objections in this general category to agent-causal libertarianism specifically.

The version of the Humean challenge I will develop has the following structure: Libertarians agree that a decision's being causally determined by factors beyond the agent's control would preclude moral responsibility. However, if causal determinism rules out moral responsibility, then it is no remedy simply to provide slack in the causal net by making the causal history of actions indeterministic.[3] Such a move would yield one incompatibilist requirement for moral responsibility – leeway for decision and action – but it would not supply another – sufficiently enhanced control. In particular, it would not provide the capacity to be the origin of one's decisions and actions that according to incompatibilists is unavailable to compatibilists. This formulation of the objection departs from Hume's original version, since he denies that determinism undermines moral responsibility. Instead, it develops this general sort of challenge from the point of view

1. David Hume, *Treatise of Human Nature* (Oxford: Oxford University Press, 1978), pp. 399–412, esp. pp. 411–2; cf. R. Hobart, "Free Will as Involving Determinism and Inconceivable without it," *Mind* 43 (1934), pp. 1–27; P.H. Nowell-Smith, "Free Will and Moral Responsibility," *Mind* 57, pp. 45–65; Alfred J. Ayer, "Freedom and Necessity," in Alfred J. Ayer, *Philosophical Essays* (London: Macmillan, 1954), reprinted in *Free Will*, ed. Gary Watson (Oxford: Oxford University Press, 1982), pp. 15–23.

2. Carl Ginet, "Reasons Explanation of Action: An Incompatibilist Account," in *Agents, Causes, and Events*, Timothy O'Connor, ed. (Oxford: Oxford University Press, 1995), pp. 69–94; O'Connor, "Agent Causation," O'Connor, ed. (Oxford: Oxford University Press, 1995), pp. 170–200; Kane, *The Significance of Free Will*, pp. 174–9; Randolph Clarke, "A Principle of Rational Explanation," *The Southern Journal of Philosophy* 30 (1992), pp. 1–12; "Contrastive Rational Explanation of Free Choice," *Philosophical Quarterly* 46 (1996), pp. 185–201, and "On the Possibility of Rational Free Action," *Philosophical Studies* 88 (1997), pp. 37–57. Significant challenges to a libertarian theory of rational action are posed by Galen Strawson in *Freedom and Belief* (Oxford: Oxford University Press, 1986), pp. 25–60, esp. 52–6, and "The Impossibility of Moral Responsibility," *Philosophical Studies* 75, pp. 5–24; Richard Double, *The Non-Reality of Free Will*, and "The Principle of Rational Explanation Defended," *Southern Journal of Philosophy* 31 (1993), pp. 431–9.

3. Hume, *A Treatise of Human Nature*, II, iii, 2 (p. 411); A.J. Ayer, "Freedom and Necessity," in *Free Will*, ed. Gary Watson, p. 18; Ted Honderich, *A Theory of Determinism*, pp. 184ff, 332–4.

of an incompatibilist who favors origination as a requirement for moral responsibility.

In the discussion of this objection, we must keep in mind the defining features of the two versions of libertarianism distinguished in the Introduction. According to agent-causal theory, freedom of the sort required for moral responsibility is accounted for by the existence of agents who possess a causal power to make choices without being determined to do so.[4] In this view, it is crucial that the kind of causation involved in an agent's making a free choice is not reducible to causation among states of the agent or events involving the agent, but is rather irreducibly an instance of a substance causing a choice not by way of states or events. The agent, fundamentally as a substance, possesses the causal power to make choices without being determined to do so. Chisholm, Taylor, Clarke, and O'Connor advance views in this category. In event-causal libertarianism, by contrast, actions are caused solely by way of states or events. Some type of indeterminacy in the production of appropriate states or events is considered a decisive requirement for moral responsibility.[5] Ginet and Kane develop views of this sort. I shall argue that the event-causal libertarianisms are under-

4. Theories of agent causation have been advanced by Thomas Reid, *The Works of Thomas Reid, D.D.*, 8th edition, Sir William Hamilton, ed. (Edinburgh, 1895), reprinted with an introduction by H.M. Bracken (Hildesheim: Georg Olms Verlag, 1967); cf. William Rowe, *Thomas Reid on Freedom and Morality* (Ithaca: Cornell University Press, 1991); Roderick Chisholm, "Human Freedom and the Self," in ed. Gary Watson, *Free Will*, pp. 24–35 and *Person and Object* (La Salle: Open Court, 1976), pp. 53–88; Richard Taylor, *Action and Purpose* (Englewood Cliffs: Prentice-Hall, 1966), pp. 99–152, and *Metaphysics*, 4th ed. (Englewood Cliffs: Prentice-Hall, 1992), pp. 33–50; John Thorp, *Free Will* (London: Routledge & Kegan Paul, 1980); Randolph Clarke, "Toward a Credible Agent-Causal Account of Free Will," *Noûs* 27 (1993), pp. 191–203, reprinted in *Agents, Causes, and Events*, Timothy O'Connor, ed. (Oxford: Oxford University Press, 1995), pp. 201–15, and "Agent Causation and Event Causation in the Production of Free Action," *Philosophical Topics* 24 (1996), pp. 19–48; and Timothy O'Connor, "Agent Causation," pp. 173–200.

5. Philosophers who have been sympathetic to event-causal libertarianism include Lucretius, *De Rerum Natura*, translated by W.H.D. Rouse, Loeb Classical Library (Cambridge: Harvard University Press, 1982), 2.216–293: ". . . but what keeps the mind itself from having necessity within it in all actions . . . is the minute swerving of the first beginnings at no fixed place and at no fixed time" (2.289–293); Carl Ginet, "Reasons Explanation of Action: An Incompatibilist Account." Robert Kane, "Two Kinds of Incompatibilism," in *Agents, Causes, and Events*, ed. Timothy O'Connor (Oxford: Oxford University Press, 1995), pp. 115–50, and *The Significance of Free Will*; Robert Nozick, *Philosophical Explanations* (Cambridge: Harvard University Press, 1981), pp. 291–397; David Wiggins, "Towards a Reasonable Libertarianism," in T. Honderich, ed., *Essays on Freedom of Action* (London: Routledge and Kegan Paul, 1973).

mined by my version of the Humean objection, but that it is not obvious that agent-causal libertarianism also falls to it.[6]

Let us begin by considering how this objection fares against versions of event-causal libertarianism. Ginet provides a clear account of one such position:

Every action, according to me, either is or begins with a causally simple mental action, that is, a mental event that does not consist of one mental event causing others. A simple mental event is an action if and only if it has a certain intrinsic phenomenological quality, which I've dubbed the "actish" quality and tried to describe by using agent-causation talk radically qualified by "as if": the simple mental event of my volition to exert force with a part of my body phenomenally seems to me to be intrinsically an event that does not just happen to me, that does not occur unbidden, but it is, rather, as if I make it occur, as if I determine that it will happen just when and as it does . . . A simple mental event's having this intrinsic actish phenomenological quality is sufficient for its being an *action*. But its having the quality entails nothing either way as to whether it satisfies the incompatibilist requirement for *free* action (which is that it not be causally necessitated by antecedent events) . . . I make my own free, simple mental acts occur, not by causing them, but simply by being their subject, by their being my acts. They are *ipso facto* determined or controlled by me, provided they are free, that is, not determined by something else, not causally necessitated by antecedent states and events.[7]

In Kane's variety of event-causal libertarianism, the paradigm case of an action for which an agent is responsible is one of moral or prudential struggle, in which there are reasons for and against performing the action in question. In his conception, the sequence that produces the action begins with the agent's character and motives, and proceeds through the agent's making an effort of will to act, which results in the choice for a particular action. The effort of will is a struggle to choose in one way in a situation in which there are countervailing

6. O'Connor holds a similar view, cf. "Indeterminacy and Free Agency: Three Recent Views," *Philosophy and Phenomenological Research* 53 (1993), pp. 499–526.
7. Ginet, "Freedom, Responsibility, and Agency," *The Journal of Ethics* 1 (1997), pp. 85–98, at p. 89.

pressures. When an agent is morally responsible, this effort of will is explained by the agent's character and motives. In the case of a freely willed choice, this effort of will is *indeterminate*, and as a result the choice produced by the effort is *undetermined*. Kane explains this last specification by drawing an analogy between an effort of will and a quantum event:

> Imagine an isolated particle, such as an electron, moving toward a thin atomic barrier. Whether or not the particle will penetrate the barrier is undetermined. There is a probability that it will penetrate, but not a certainty, because its position and momentum are not both determinate as it moves towards the barrier. Imagine that the choice (to overcome temptation) is like the penetration event. The choice one way or the other is *undetermined* because the process preceding it and potentially terminating in it (i.e. the effort of will to overcome temptation) is *indeterminate*.[8]

The effort of will is indeterminate in the sense that its causal potential does not become determinate until the choice occurs. Before this pivotal interaction, there are various ways in which this causal potential can be resolved, and thus when it is resolved, the resulting choice will be undetermined. In response to objections, Kane cautions against construing his view in such a way that the indeterminacy occurs after the effort is made: "One must think of the effort and the indeterminism as fused; the effort *is* indeterminate and the indeterminism is a property of the effort, not something that occurs before or after the effort."[9] In his view, if an agent is morally responsible for a choice, either it must be free in this sense or there must be some such free choice that is (or perhaps has a decisive role in) its sufficient ground, cause, or explanation.[10] Furthermore, Kane strengthens his account by endeavoring to show how the particle analogy for free choice might actually work in the functioning of the brain's neural networks.[11]

Any Humean challenge to views like these must be presented with care, for as several commentators have pointed out, an agent can indeed be responsible for an event that is indeterministic in a very basic

8. Kane, *The Significance of Free Will*, p. 128; cf. "Two Kinds of Incompatibilism," p. 129.
9. Kane, "Responsibility, Luck, and Chance: Reflections on Free Will and Indeterminism," *Journal of Philosophy* 96 (May 1999), pp. 217–40, at p. 232.
10. Kane, *The Significance of Free Will*, p. 35.
11. Kane, *The Significance of Free Will*, pp. 128–30.

sense.[12] To use one of Kane's examples, it may not be determined that the radioactive material the employee places in the executive's desk will give him cancer, but this fact does not undermine the claim that the employee can be morally responsible for his developing cancer if he in fact does.[13] Kane is surely right about this. However, as Galen Strawson suggests, if the indeterminism is located elsewhere in the causal history of the action, responsibility is more clearly threatened.[14] Suppose the indeterminism is located not in the consequences of the decision, as in the above case, but rather in the decision to act itself. For example, if the agent's deciding to place the radioactive material in the desk is an indeterministic event, then one might have more reason to doubt that the agent is morally responsible than in the type of case Kane cites (as he recently acknowledges[15]).

Let us develop this suggestion more carefully. Event-causal libertarianisms might allow agents to be responsible for decisions characterized by two distinct types of causal histories. In the first sort, (a), events of type

(E) **an agent's being in circumstances C** (where C includes the agent's character, motives, and external circumstances)

cause events of type

(F) **the agent's deciding to do A**

but E's do not deterministically cause F's.

In the second sort, (b), events of type (F) occur without being caused at all.

Events with either sort of causal history will be indeterministic events. On a first approximation of the Humean objection, agents will not be morally responsible for decisions with either sort of causal history because they are not sufficiently within the agent's control. But

12.   J.L. Austin, "Ifs and Cans," in Bernard Berofsky, ed. *Free Will and Determinism* (New York: Harper and Row, 1966), pp. 295–321; Philippa Foot, "Free Will as Involving Determinism," *The Philosophical Review* 66 (1957), reprinted in her *Virtues and Vices* (Berkeley and Los Angeles: University of California Press, 1978), pp. 62–73; G.E.M. Anscombe, *Causality and Determinism* (Cambridge: Cambridge University Press, 1971); Kane, *The Significance of Free Will*, pp. 54–6.
13.   Kane, *The Significance of Free Will*, p. 55, cf. "Responsibility, Luck, and Chance," pp. 226–7.
14.   Strawson, *Freedom and Belief*, p. 8.
15.   Kane, "Responsibility, Luck, and Chance," p. 230ff.

Kane has advanced two lines of defense against this claim. First, he argues that decisions can be indeterministic and yet possess a number of characteristics we associate with agent control and with responsibility. If decisions are undetermined, then agents could still make them voluntarily, intentionally, knowingly, on purpose, and as a result of their efforts. They may yet have reasons for making these decisions, they might choose for these reasons, rather than by mistake, accident, or chance, and they may want to choose for these reasons more than any others. Agents might nevertheless not be coerced or compelled in choosing, and they may not be controlled by other agents or circumstances.[16] Indeterminism is therefore consistent with an impressive sort of control in action, and, Kane believes, enough control for moral responsibility.

In my view, Kane is indeed right to the extent that he shows that indeterminism allows for significant control in action. But compatibilists, familiarly, also appeal to the same sorts of claims as Kane does to defend against the objection that determinism does not allow for control sufficient for responsibility. Since incompatibilists wish to deny that compatibilists can secure this sort of control, one might question whether Kane's defense can, in the final analysis, accommodate what incompatibilists are most fundamentally after.

Kane's second strategy for defending event-causal libertarianism appeals to the phenomenology of choice and action. (Note that in Ginet's view, phenomenology also plays a critical role.) Kane argues that if the phenomenology of indeterministic action were such that the initiation of an action were experienced as an uncaused, involuntary event, not resulting from one's effort of will, then this would provide good reason to believe that no genuine choice is involved, and that the agent is not morally responsible. But if the initiation of the action were indeterministic and experienced as voluntary and as resulting from one's own effort of will, then the agent's moral responsibility is not challenged. Kane describes a case of a businesswoman who is on the way to an important meeting when she observes an assault in an alley. An inner struggle ensues between her moral conscience, which urges her to stop and call for help, and her career ambitions, which tell her she cannot miss the meeting. She resolves the struggle by making the decision to help the victim. Kane imagines in this case that the effort of will is inde-

---

16. Kane, *The Significance of Free Will*, p. 179, "Responsibility, Luck, and Chance," pp. 237–9.

terminate, and as a result the decision is undetermined. He then remarks:

Now indeterminism may in some instances undermine choice . . . We imagined that Jane had reached a point in her deliberation at which she favored vacationing in Hawaii when, owing to a quantum jump in her brain, she found herself intending to vacation in Colorado. The case was odd because she did not have the sense of voluntarily doing anything . . . she would be reluctant – and we would be reluctant – to say she *chose* anything in such a case . . . So indeterminism can sometimes undermine choice. But there is no legitimate reason to generalize from cases like Jane's and say it must always do so. Consider the businesswoman by contrast. Her experience, unlike Jane's, is of consciously and voluntarily choosing to follow her moral conscience and to return to help the victim, thereby resolving a preceding uncertainty in her mind. Also, in the businesswoman's case, unlike Jane's, the indeterminate process discovered by the neuroscientists immediately preceding the choice was experienced by her as her own effort of will, not merely as a random occurrence in her brain that happened to influence the outcome. Given these circumstances, it would be hasty, to say the least, to lump the two cases together and draw conclusions about the businesswoman's case from Jane's . . . Why would the businesswoman conclude that she did not really choose in such circumstances (rather than that her choice was undetermined) just because, *under very different circumstances,* Jane did not really choose?[17]

In Kane's view, the phenomenology of action is decisive, or at least counts very heavily, for determining whether an agent is morally responsible for an indeterministic decision.

However, this sort of phenomenological consideration is also available to the compatibilist as a response to the objection that when an agent is causally determined, he does not choose in a way for which he is responsible, and this fact should give the incompatibilist pause. A compatibilist might argue that if one experienced one's causally determined decision as resulting from an outside determining force, one would thereby have reason to believe that one was not making a responsible choice. If, by contrast, a causally determined decision were experienced as voluntary and resulting from one's own effort of will, there would be a strong reason to believe that one was making a choice for which one was responsible. An incompatibilist would reject this

---

17. Kane, *The Significance of Free Will*, pp. 182–3.

45

compatibilist defense on the ground that the metaphysical facts about the causal history of the action – that the decision is causally determined – is ultimately decisive for the agent's responsibility. But it would seem implausible to claim that the phenomenology should carry more weight when the threat to moral responsibility is indeterministic rather than deterministic.

Because they are available to compatibilists, these last two responses give rise to a more refined version of our objection. I will grant, for purposes of argument, that event-causal libertarianism allows for as much responsibility-relevant control as compatibilism does.[18] However, following a suggestion of Clarke's, I shall argue that if decisions were indeterministic events of the sort specified by this theory, then agents would have no more control over their actions than they would if determinism were true, and such control is insufficient for responsibility.[19]

We might amplify this objection by turning to Kane's UR (for "ultimate responsibility"), which delineates his crucial conditions for moral responsibility. UR has two components. The first (in essence – Kane's formulations are more precise[20]) is that to be ultimately responsible for an event, the agent must have voluntarily been able to do otherwise. The second is that to be ultimately responsible for an event, the agent must be responsible for any sufficient ground or cause or explanation of the event. Now if actions are undetermined events of the sort Kane specifies, then the first component of UR might be satisfied, and agents could have the requisite leeway for alternative actions. Moreover, the second component will be satisfied, since there will be no sufficient conditions of actions for which agents are not morally responsible. However (as we saw in the last chapter), for Kane the second component is a consequence of a more fundamental requirement about

---

18. Clarke develops the claim that indeterminism can allow for as much control as determinism in "Indeterminism and Control," *American Philosophical Quarterly* (1995), pp. 125–38, and in "Modest Libertarianism," *Philosophical Perspectives* 14 (2000).

19. Clarke voices a challenge of this form to indeterminist theories generally, "On the Possibility of Rational Free Action," p. 45.

20. (UR) An agent is *ultimately responsible* for some (event or state) E's occurring only if (R) the agent is personally responsible for E's occurring in a sense which entails that something the agent voluntarily (or willingly) did or omitted, and for which the agent could have voluntarily done otherwise, either was, or causally contributed to, E's occurrence and made a difference to whether or not E occurred; and (U) for every X and Y (where X and Y represent occurrences of events and/or states) if the agent is personally responsible for X, and if Y is an *arche* (or sufficient ground or cause or explanation) for X, then the agent must also be personally responsible for Y. Kane, *The Significance of Free Will*, p. 35.

the origination of action: "If the action did have such a sufficient reason for which the agent was not responsible, then the action, or the agent's will to perform it, would have its source in something that the agent played no role in producing . . . ultimately responsible agents must not only be the sources of their actions, but also of the *will* to perform the actions."[21] In my view, this quotation expresses the deepest and most plausible incompatibilist intuition, and it also undermines Kane's position.

As we have seen, the core incompatibilist claim about origination can be expressed, somewhat roughly, as follows:

(O) If an agent is morally responsible for her deciding to perform an action, then the production of this decision must be something over which the agent has control, and an agent is not morally responsible for the decision if it is produced by a source over which she has no control.

On the basis of this principle, an agent cannot be responsible for decisions determined to occur by factors beyond his control. But the principle also entails that an agent cannot be responsible for decisions that are indeterministic in the sense that they are not produced by anything at all, for then their production is not something over which the agent has control. This last consideration undermines event-causal libertarianisms according to which an agent can be responsible for decisions of type (b), in which events of type (F) – the agent's deciding to do A – occur without being caused at all. We shall have to see whether it also undermine's a view like Kane's.

Between these two extremes – one deterministic and the other maximally indeterministic – lie a range of events for which factors beyond the agent's control contribute to their production but do not determine them, while there is nothing that supplements the causal contribution of these factors to produce the events. By analogy, according to the standard interpretation of quantum mechanics, preceding events causally influence which quantum event will occur from among a range of possibilities by determining the probabilities governing this range, but these preceding events do not causally determine which of the possible quantum events will occur. Similarly, one can imagine that preceding events causally influence which decision an agent will make without causally determining any particular decision.

21. Kane, *The Significance of Free Will*, p. 73.

But from the incompatibilist point of view, an agent cannot be responsible for decisions if they are events of this sort either. If there are factors beyond the agent's control that contribute to a decision's production without determining it, while there is nothing that supplements the contribution of these factors to produce the decision, then its production exhibits only a combination of the first two types of responsibility-undermining factors. We have already seen that by incompatibilist intuitions, an agent is not responsible for decisions determined by factors beyond his control. However, if these factors, rather than determining a single decision, simply leave open more than one possibility, and the agent plays no further role in determining which possibility is realized, then we have no more reason to hold him responsible than we do in the deterministic case.

We might call those events for which factors beyond the agent's control determine their occurrence *alien-deterministic events* and those that are not produced by anything at all *truly random events*. The range of events between these two extremes − for which factors beyond the agent's control contribute to their production but do not determine them, while there is nothing that supplements the contribution of these factors to produce the events − we might designate *partially random events*. By incompatibilist standards, an agent cannot be morally responsible for a decision if it is an event that lies anywhere on this continuum, because the agent does not have a suitable role in its production. The agent will then not be the source of the decision in a sense sufficient for moral responsibility.

On Ginet's and Kane's conceptions, are free choices indeed partially random events (or perhaps even totally random events on Ginet's account) for which agents cannot be morally responsible? At this point, one might suggest that there is an additional resource available to bolster Ginet's and Kane's account of morally responsible decision. For convenience, let us focus on Kane's view (I suspect that Ginet's position will not differ significantly from Kane's on this issue). One might argue that in Kane's conception, the character and motives that explain an effort of will need not be factors beyond the agent's control, since they could be produced partly as a result of the agent's free choices. Consequently, it need not be that the effort, and thus the choice, is produced solely by factors beyond the agent's control and no further contribution of the agent. But this move is unconvincing. To simplify, suppose that it is character alone, and not motives in addition, that explains the effort of will. Imagine first that the character that explains the effort is not a product of the agent's free choices, but rather that there are factors beyond his control that determine this character, or nothing produces it, or factors beyond his control contribute to the production of the character without determining it and nothing supplements their contribution to produce it. Then, by incompatibilist standards, the agent cannot be responsible for his character. But in addition, neither can he be responsible for the effort that is explained by the character, whether this explanation is deterministic or indeterministic. If the explanation is deterministic, then there will be factors beyond the agent's control that determine the effort, and the agent will thereby lack moral responsibility for the effort. If the explanation is indeterministic, given that the agent's free choice plays no role in producing the character, and nothing besides the character explains the effort, there will be factors beyond the agent's control that make a causal contribution to the production of this effort without determining it, while nothing supplements the contribution of these factors to produce the effort. Here, again, the agent cannot be morally responsible for the effort.

However, prospects for moral responsibility for the effort of will are not improved if the agent's character is partly a result of his free choices. For consider the first free choice an agent ever makes. By the above argument, he cannot be responsible for it. But then he cannot be responsible for the second choice either, whether or not the first choice was character-forming. If the first choice was not character-forming, then the character that explains the effort of will for the second choice is not produced by his free choice, and then by the above argument, he cannot be morally responsible for it. Suppose, alternatively, that the first choice was character-forming. Because the agent cannot be responsible for the first choice, he also cannot be responsible for the resulting character formation. But then, by the above argument, he cannot be responsible for the second choice either. Since this type of reasoning can be repeated for all subsequent choices, Kane's agent can never be morally responsible for effort of will.

Given that such an agent can never be morally responsible for his efforts of will, neither can he be responsible for his choices. For in Kane's picture, there is nothing that supplements the contribution of the effort of will to produce the choice. Indeed, all free choices will ultimately be partially random events, for in the final analysis there will be factors beyond the agent's control, such as his initial character, that partly produce the choice, while there will be nothing that supplements their contribution in the production of the choice, and by the most attractive incompatibilist standard, agents cannot be responsible for such partially random events.

These considerations undermine event-causal libertarianisms in which agents are responsible for actions of sort (a), in which events of type

(E) **an agent's being in circumstances C** (where C includes the agent's character, motives, and external circumstances)

cause events of type

(F) **the agent's deciding to do A**

but E's do not deterministically cause F's,

when the events of type (F) are partially random in the sense defined. Given both Kane's and Ginet's accounts, decisions will at best be partially random events of this sort (perhaps sometimes totally random events on Ginet's account). While these event-causal libertarianisms facilitate leeway for action, they do not supply the enhanced control – that agents be the sources of their actions – that libertarianism very plausibly requires. One might suggest that if decisions were underlain by complex, perhaps chaotic arrangements of such events, the enhanced control would emerge.[22] However, as long as the decisions themselves are at best partially random events, agents will not have the enhanced control required for moral responsibility, no matter how complex the underlying structure of the decisions is.

RANDOMIZING MANIPULATORS

Let us now consider a response Kane gives to an interesting objection of Mele's – the "luck" objection – to see whether it can answer the objection just developed. (Bruce Waller, Richard Double, and Mark Bernstein have also advanced objections of this general sort.[23]) Accord-

---

22. Kane, *The Significance of Free Will*, pp. 128–30.
23. Alfred Mele, "Review of Kane's *Significance of Free Will*," *Journal of Philosophy* 95 (1998), pp. 581–4, and in "Ultimate Responsibility and Dumb Luck," *Social Philosophy and Policy* 16 (1999), pp. 274–93. The core idea behind Mele's view can be dramatized by van Inwagen's "rollback" objection, that God might have allowed the world to revert back to all of the initial conditions of the decision of one of these agents, and in about half the cases the agent decides one way and in the other half the other way (*An Essay on*

ing to the luck objection, if two agents (say in two possible worlds) have all the same powers, capacities, states of mind, moral character (and the like) prior to choice, and feature exactly the same efforts of will, and yet make different decisions, then the difference is just a matter of luck, and it is difficult to see how these agents could possess the control required for moral responsibility. In reply, Kane first cites the case of "husband" who angrily slams his fist down on a glass table top, intending to break it. Due to indeterminism in his efferent neural pathways, the momentum of his arm is indeterminate, and as a result it is undetermined if the table will break right up to the moment when it is struck.[24] Now consider husband*, who has the same capacities, motives, character, and efforts prior to choice as husband does, but his blow does not break the table. It does not follow from this possibility that husband is not morally responsible for breaking the table top. Kane defends the claim that husband could be responsible by pointing out that he succeeded in something he was trying to do, despite the presence of indeterminism.

Kane then has us consider to a case in which a decision (as opposed to a consequence of a decision) is undetermined because the effort of will is indeterminate. Imagine businesswoman* who has the same capacities, motives, character, and efforts prior to choice as the businesswoman in the case described earlier, except that she decides to try to make the meeting on time and not to help the victim. Kane contends that here too both businesswoman and her counterpart succeed in something they were trying to do, and thus each of them can be morally responsible for her decision:

But if they both succeeded in what they were trying to do (because they were both simultaneously trying to do both things), and then having succeeded, they both *endorsed* the outcomes of their respective efforts (that is, their choices) as what they were trying to do, instead of disowning or disassociating from those choices, how can we *not* hold them responsible? It just does not follow that, because they made exactly the same efforts, they chose by chance.[25]

In my view, Kane provides an impressive answer to the argument that Mele advances. At the very least, he puts the ball back in Mele's court.

Free Will, pp. 126–50); cf. Bruce Waller, "Free Will Gone Out of Control," *Behaviorism* 16 (1988), pp. 149–67; Richard Double, *The Non-Reality of Free Will*, pp. 192–211; and Mark Bernstein, "Kanean Libertarianism," *Southwest Philosophy Review* 11 (1995), pp. 151–57.

24. Kane, "Responsibility, Luck, and Chance," p. 227.
25. Ibid., p. 235.

However, does this answer help to show that Kane's theory allows for agents to be the sources of their actions in the way required? Notice that the considerations he adduces to secure responsibility in his example are again also available to the compatibilist. As a result, I think that his reply does not advance the case that this sort of indeterminism can supply the enhanced control that according to Kane himself moral responsibility demands.

Kane claims that in his account agents have *plural voluntary control* over a set of options, which means "being able to bring about *whichever* of the options you will or most want, *when* you will to do so, for the reasons you will to do so, without being coerced or compelled in doing so."[26] Nevertheless, one might be skeptical about the sense in which the businesswoman has the control required to bring about any of her two options for choice. In my view, it is not a sense that makes her a source of her decision in the way that moral responsibility requires. To strengthen the case for this claim, imagine businesswoman★★, whose capacities, character, motives, and efforts are qualitatively identical to those of businesswoman. Businesswoman★★ also makes the choice to help the victim. But intimately involved in this choice is not the usual determining manipulator featured in arguments against compatibilism, but a randomizing manipulator who spins a dial that will land on one of two positions.[27] Imagine that the spinning of the dial is a metaphysically indeterministic event, and that it is not merely indeterministic relative to the spinner's knowledge and power.[28] In addition, suppose

---

26. Kane, "Responsibility, Luck, and Chance," pp. 237–8.
27. Randomizers of various sorts are used in arguments against event-causal libertarianism by van Inwagen in *An Essay on Free Will*, pp. 132–4, and by Mele in "Ultimate Responsibility and Dumb Luck," p. 277.
28. Clarke ("On the Possibility of Rational Free Action," p. 43) mentions that although it is commonly thought that processes such as coin tosses are epistemically and not physically indeterministic, there are numerous reasons to doubt this view. Here he quotes David Lewis: [F]or instance, the making and breaking of chemical bonds is chancy, so is the coherence of solids that stick together by means of chemical bonding, so is the elasticity of collisions between things that might bond briefly before they rebound . . . There is chance enough in the processes by which the coin leaves the fingers; in the processes whereby it bounces off air molecules and sends them recoiling off, perhaps to knock other molecules into its path; in the process whereby the coin does or doesn't stretch a bit as it spins, thereby affecting its moment of inertia; and in the processes whereby it settles down after first touching the table. In ever so many minute ways, what happens to the coin is a matter of chance. Postscript B to "A Subjectivist's Guide to Objective Chance," in David Lewis, *Philosophical Papers*, Volume II (New York: Oxford University Press, 1986).

that the dial's landing on a position just *is* the crucial indeterministic component of the neurophysiological realization of the choice to perform the action, and that it is not simply an indeterministic event that deterministically causes one choice rather than the other. Also, suppose the dial's landing on a position does not supplement the agent's normal neurophysiological processes, but rather replaces the crucial indeterministic component in these processes.[29] Businesswoman★★'s effort, from the psychological point of view, is exactly qualitatively identical to businesswoman's. The position the dial lands on therefore makes the salient difference as to which decision the agent makes. If the dial lands on one position, her efforts of will result in one choice, and if it lands on the other, they produce the alternative choice. Imagine that her efforts of will are indeterminate in the sense that their causal potential does not become determinate until the choice occurs. Before the choice occurs, there are various ways in which this causal potential can be resolved. (If one is tempted to reply that the two agents will not be neurophysiologically the same and thus will not be psychologically the same, and thus will not feature the same efforts, assume instead that the various indeterministic components of the *microphysical* realization of businesswoman★★'s effort are suitably supplied by the randomizing manipulator.) Suppose, in addition, that businesswoman★★, just like businesswoman, has reasons for making the choice, she chooses for these reasons, she wants to choose for these reasons more than any others, and she is not be coerced or compelled in choosing. It is yet implausible that indeterminacy of the sort exhibited by businesswoman★★'s decision provides for moral responsibility, and this is intuitively because she lacks the control over her decision that moral responsibility demands. More fundamentally, she is not the source of her decision in the sense that moral responsibility requires. It is incumbent on a defender of Kane's view to provide a principled difference between businesswoman★★ and businesswoman that would explain why an agent could be responsible for the decision that fits Kane's theory but not for the one produced by the manipulator. This I believe cannot be done.

One might argue that two disanalogies could undermine this sort of argument. First, given how we have described the example, the randomizing factor might not be in the agent's head, and second, given this description, the agent might not experience her decisions as

29. Thanks to Robert Bishop for prodding me to state some of these specifics.

resulting from her own effort of will. But it is easy to set up the example so as to preclude these worries. We could specify that the randomizing device could be inserted into the agent's brain, with the proviso that the spinning be performed by an external manipulator. Furthermore, we could stipulate that the agent experiences the decision as voluntary and as resulting from her own effort of will. However, making these changes could hardly make the difference as to whether our agent is morally responsible, and thus we have reason to believe that event-causal libertarianism can be undermined. As a result, an analog to a prominent argument against compatibilism (I develop the argument involving traditional determining manipulators in Chapter 4) can be used to show that the control Kane's agents have fares no better than the compatibilist sort in achieving moral responsibility.

As a result of this discussion, we can see that the incompatibilist causal condition on moral responsibility (3) that I introduced in the last chapter,

(3) An action is free in the sense required for moral responsibility only if it is not produced by a deterministic process that traces back to causal factors beyond the agent's control,

can be extended so as to exempt agents from moral responsibility for certain kinds of indeterministic events:

(5) An action is free in the sense required for moral responsibility only if the decision to perform it is not an alien-deterministic event, nor a truly random event, nor a partially random event.

Condition (5) provides the key to assessing whether particular libertarian theories are undermined by the Humean objection. Let us call it the Causal History Principle. In my view, what explains its truth follows:

(O) If an agent is morally responsible for her deciding to perform an action, then the production of this decision must be something over which the agent has control, and an agent is not morally responsible for the decision if it is produced by a source over which she has no control.

For an agent to be morally responsible for a decision, she must be its source in this especially strong sense.

I have argued that event-causal libertarianism lacks any significant advantage over compatibilism in securing moral responsibility because it does no better in providing the enhanced control that would be required. For, in the last analysis, what libertarian views of this sort add to determinism is *just* indeterminism in the causal history of actions, and while this modification may provide leeway for decision and action, it does not bestow on the agent the capacity to be the source of decision and action in the sense that moral responsibility demands. On the other hand, agent causation can be viewed as simply positing, as a primitive, agents who have the ultimate control that cannot be secured by event-causal libertarianism – agents who can be the sources of action in a way that from the incompatibilist point of view, confers moral responsibility. More exactly, this theory posits, as a primitive feature of agents, the causal power to choose without being determined by events beyond the agent's control, and without the choice being a truly random or partially random event. This causal power cannot in turn be analyzed into event-causal relations of any sort. In the best version of this position, free choices are identical to activations of this agent-causal power.[30]

30.   This view is defended by Keith De Rose, "Review of William Rowe's *Thomas Reid on Freedom and Morality*," *Philosophy and Phenomenological Research* 53 (1993), pp. 945–9. In William Rowe's interpretation of Thomas Reid's view, an agent's exertion of an agent-causal power is required to produce a free choice. William Rowe, "Two Concepts of Freedom," in *Agents, Causes, and Events*, ed. Timothy O'Connor, (New York: Oxford University Press, 1995), pp. 151–71; cf. William Rowe, *Thomas Reid on Freedom and Morality*. The agent-causal power cannot be viewed as reducible to causal relations among events, but rather must be regarded as a metaphysically fundamental capacity, possessed by agents, to cause actions without being causally determined to cause them. But for Rowe, Reid's requirement gives rise to a worry about a massive proliferation of causal steps. For a choice to perform an action to be free, it would seem that the exertion of the agent-causal power that produces the choice must itself be freely chosen. But then, by Reid's requirement, the agent would have to cause a further exertion of an agent-causal power in order to cause the exertion of the agent-causal power that produces the choice to perform the action. Thus, "In order to produce any act of will whatever, the agent must cause an infinite number of exertions" (*Thomas Reid on Freedom and Morality*, p. 148). To avoid a regress, Rowe suggests that the agent's free choice is not caused by any exertion of a causal power, but is rather a basic act, and "a basic act of an agent is one that she causes but not by any exertion of power or any other act"("Two Concepts of Freedom," p. 162). At this point, De Rose argues the libertarian should identify the agent's causing of a choice with an activation of an agent-causal power, an activation that is not caused by any further exertion or act on the part of the agent. On this proposal, free choices can be explained as activations of agent-causal powers,

Nevertheless, one might maintain that the agent-causal view has no advantage over event-causal libertarianism in providing for moral responsibility because for the most basic sort of action, the notion of causation itself is irrelevant to moral responsibility. For example, Ginet's position is that an agent's causing simple mental acts would have no such advantage over his simply performing such acts, where "performing" can be analyzed non-causally – just in terms of the agent's being the subject of the act.[31] The answer that the advocate of agent causation should provide is that event-causal libertarianism does not provide agents with any more control than compatibilism does, and hence a way must be found to enhance an agent's control to the appropriate degree. The relevant sort of control involves two factors. The first is the absence of external determination, which both event-causal libertarianism and agent causation provide. But the second is the capacity of the agent to be the source of his decisions and actions, and this is the factor that event-causal libertarianism is missing. To be the source of one's decisions and actions is plausibly to be their cause. Hence, it is a credible hypothesis that being the agent-cause of one's decisions and actions is required for the control that moral responsibility demands.

The agent-causal theorist claims that by contrast with event-causal libertarian choices, agent-caused choices do not fall on the continuum we have devised. Agent-caused choices are not alien-deterministic events because the agent is not causally determined to cause them. They are not truly random events, since they are caused not by nothing, but at least partly by the agent. If these agent-caused choices were partially random events, their causal history would be exhausted by the causal contribution of factors beyond the agent's control. But in the agent-causal theory, the agent plays a fundamental causal role in the causation of the choice, and factors beyond his control do not causally determine him to make it.

However, even agent-causal theory conceived in this way must confront an objection similar to the one that undermines event-causal libertarianism. According to this objection, the agent-causal theorist must admit that there are events of type

(G) **the agent's causing the choice for A**

---

while a regress is avoided. As De Rose points out, Rowe himself suggests such a solution in one place, cf. *Thomas Reid on Freedom and Morality*, p. 150.

31. Ginet, "Freedom, Responsibility, and Agency," p. 89.

The agent, however, could not cause events of type G, for it is absurd to claim that the agent causes himself to cause a choice. But since the agent could not cause events of type G, he cannot be responsible for them. In fact, events of this sort would seem to be partially or truly random. Because the agent cannot be responsible for such events, he cannot be responsible for the choices embedded in them. If an agent cannot be morally responsible for his causing of his choices, he cannot be responsible for his choices either.

Ginet presents a version of this objection against O'Connor's agent-causal libertarianism. In O'Connor's view, in a case of agent causation, *the agent's causing an event e* is not itself an event for which there are sufficient causal conditions.[32] Hence, Ginet sees him as vulnerable to the objection that this more complex event will be an undetermined event over which, according to agent-causal theorists, agents cannot have sufficient control for moral responsibility. Ginet remarks:

I don't see why it would be absurd to suppose that we are entitled to say that in causing *e* the agent exercised control over *e* only if we are also entitled to say that the agent exercised control over [his] causing *e*.[33]

(Ginet, as we have seen, does believe that agents can be morally responsible for undetermined events, and this is the perspective from which he is making the objection to O'Connor.) Chisholm's reply to this sort of objection is that when an agent causes a choice by virtue of his agent-causal power, he does indeed cause an event of type G, for which he can therefore be morally responsible.[34] I believe that he is close to right about this. In the conception of agent causation I would favor, when an agent-cause acts freely, what he does most fundamentally is to cause a choice for an action. He could be morally responsible for this choice because he causes it by virtue of his agent-causal power. At this point, one should note that it is a logical consequence of the agent's causing a choice for an action that an event of type G occurs. It follows logically from the fact that Mary causes a choice to save her child that the event *Mary's causing the choice to save her child* occurs. Therefore, by causing a choice, it is at the very least true that the agent also brings

32. O'Connor, "Agent Causation," pp. 185–7.
33. Ginet, "Freedom, Responsibility, and Agency," p. 91.
34. Chisholm raises and attempts to answer this objection in "Reflections on Human Agency," *Idealistic Studies* 1 (1971), pp. 33–46, at pp. 40–3. See also O'Connor's discussion of this issue, pp. 184–7.

about an event of type G, albeit as a logical consequence of his causing the choice, which is explanatorily prior to the event of type G. In Chisholm's favor, perhaps it could be said that an agent causes any contingent event whose occurrence is a logical consequence of his causing a choice. Then, by causing a choice, the agent will also cause an event of type G. I will not go so far as to endorse this claim. However, whether or not agents cause the logical consequences of their acts, it is plausible that agents, as agent-causes, could be morally responsible not only for the choices they immediately cause, but also for the events whose occurrence is a logical consequence of their causing of these choices – whether or not they merely bring about such events or actually cause them. Even though it is not true that if an agent is morally responsible for an action, he will be morally responsible for any logical consequence of it, he could indeed be responsible for some of them. Agents, as agent-causes, could then be morally responsible for events of type G. Consequently, the agent-cause of a choice to perform an action could be morally responsible both for the choice to perform the action and for the event of his causing the choice to perform the action, and our objection has been answered.

Someone might point out that as a result of an instance of agent-causation, the agent would not simply bring about the event of *his causing the choice*, but also the event of *his bringing about of his causing the choice*, and also of *his bringing about of his bringing about of his causing the choice*, ad infinitum, and this critic might contend that this consequence is absurd. In reply, Chisholm embraces the conclusion that an agent-cause indeed causes an infinite number of events to occur whenever he causes a choice.[35] I believe that he is also close to right about this. Whenever such an agent causes a choice, he brings about an infinite number of events as a logical consequence of the fundamental interaction, his causing of a choice. If it could be said that an agent causes any contingent event whose occurrence is a logical consequence of his causing a choice, then the agent, by causing a choice, would also cause an infinite number of events to occur. But, again, I will not go so far as to endorse this stronger claim. The appearance of oddity here can be dispelled by noticing that a similar phenomenon occurs in any instance of ordinary event causation. Whenever event A causes event B, A does not merely cause B, but A also brings it about that *A's causing B* occurs, and hence A also brings it about that *A's bringing about A's causing B*

35. Chisholm, "Reflections on Human Agency," *Idealistic Studies* 1 (1971), pp. 40–3.

occurs, ad infinitum. Here also it is clear that the event A causing the event B is fundamental, and the fact that A brings it about that *A's causing B* occurs is just a trivial logical consequence of the more fundamental and explanatorily prior interaction. Thus, agent causation and ordinary event causation are exactly similar in this respect, and we can dismiss this sort of phenomenon as harmless. Accordingly, agent-causal theory, so far, might well allow for moral responsibility, and the type of objection that undermines the event-causal libertarianisms can be resisted by this version of libertarianism.

OBJECTIONS TO THE AGENT-CAUSAL THEORY'S NOTION OF CAUSATION

Whether agent-causal libertarianism can secure the kind of control required for moral responsibility depends crucially on whether the sort of causation proposed by the theory could exist. However, critics have expressed their doubts about the coherence of this notion of causation. For example, it is sometimes claimed that the main problem for agent-causal theory is that an agent, fundamentally as a substance, simply cannot be the first term of a causal relation. It is not problematic, on this conception, to regard agents as causes, so long as it turns out that any causation by agents is reducible to causation among events. After all, as C.D. Broad points out, anyone can agree that substances such as trees and cars are causes, given that a statement such as

"The car caused the splashing of the water that ruined her dress"

reduces to a statement like

"The car's passing through the water caused the splashing of the water that ruined her dress."[36]

But according to agent-causal theory, agent-causal relations do not reduce to causal relations among events, and as a result, the notion of agent-causation is incoherent.

The notion of agent causation might be incoherent if an account of causation of the Humean sort were correct. If causation in fact reduces, as Humeans have proposed, to regularity among events or to

36. C.D. Broad, "Determinism, Indeterminism, and Libertarianism," in his *Ethics and the History of Philosophy* (London: Routledge and Kegan Paul, 1952), pp. 195–217, reprinted in *Determinism, Free Will, and Moral Responsibility*, Gerald Dworkin, ed. (Englewood Cliffs: Prentice-Hall, 1970), pp. 149–71, p. 169.

counter-factual dependence among events, then a type of causal claim that cannot be reduced in this way would be ruled out by virtue of what causation is. Many philosophers indeed defend Humean analyses of causation. However, the main problem with an objection of this sort is that such analyses are not obviously true. According to the competing view, causation is an irreducible relation, and thus the causal relation is metaphysically basic. As a first response, agent-causal theorists can claim that causal relations are indeed irreducible. Clarke, for example, suggests this strategy, and as he points out, there are good reasons independent of agent-causal theory to favor an anti-reductionist "realist" position on causation.[37] In his view, the relation of causation is a basic constituent of the universe, and the fundamental notion of causation is that of producing, bringing about, or making happen.

Nevertheless, one might still contend that causal claims have no content unless they can be given some reductive account. A view of this sort may be behind the famous objection to agent-causation that Chisholm presents in the form of the rhetorical question: What is the difference between saying, of an event A, that A just happened and saying that someone caused A to happen?[38] Yet one cannot simply presume that unless causal relations are reducible, propositions expressing causal relations are empty of content. Clarke's response to Chisholm's question, and the one that I think the advocate of agent-causation is well-advised to provide, is that when an agent causes A to happen, the irreducible relation of causation obtains between the agent and event A, while when A just happens, this relation fails to obtain. To this Clarke adds that the very irreducible causal relation that according to the realist can be a relation between events can also be a relation between an agent, fundamentally, and an event.[39]

Bok argues that this last move "is unhelpful in the absence of an explanation of what it means for causal relations to hold between agents and their actions, if (as libertarians insist) the claim that such a relation exists is not equivalent or reducible to the claim that some state of the agent, or some event in whose description she figures, causes her actions."[40] She provides this analogy:

37. Clarke, "From Agent Causation and Event Causation in the Production of Free Action," in *Free Will*, Derk Pereboom, ed., pp. 277–82.
38. Chisholm, "Human Freedom and the Self," p. 30.
39. Clarke, "Agent Causation and Event Causation in the Production of Free Action," p. 280.
40. Bok, *Freedom and Responsibility*, p. 44.

We understand what it means to be someone's sister. But it does not follow that we understand what it would mean to be the sister of an event. It would not help to be told that our relation to such an event would be the exact same relation that we now stand in to our siblings. What we need, rather, is an explanation of how we could stand in that relation to an event: how, for instance, our mothers might in some nonmetaphorical sense have given birth to one. Likewise, we cannot assume that it makes sense to say that agents can stand in the same causal relation to events that other events do, absent some explanation of how an agent can produce an event in some way that is not reducible to event causation.[41]

Bok is right to argue that Clarke's claim that the agent-causal relation is the same as the event-causal relation does not, all by itself, provide us with a thorough understanding of the agent-causal relation. Still, in my view Clarke's claim does provide logical space for the existence of the agent-causal relation. It gives us a (very short) story about the nature of the agent-causal relation that involves no logical incoherence. To see this, one might note two disanalogies between the sister-event relation and the agent-event causal relation. First, it is virtually as analytic as a truth can be that the sister relation holds only between a female of a species and another member of that same species, and this is a fact that is well understood. This fact rules out a sister-event relation. But although it is well understood that the causal relation holds between events, and that all of our well-established cases of causal relations are between events, it is not virtually an analytic truth that the causal relation holds only between events. Second, there are no cases that make it intuitive that a sister relation holds between a sister and an event, and indeed the claim that this relation can hold between a sister and an event is thoroughly unintuitive. By contrast, it is not similarly unintuitive that choices can be caused by agents, fundamentally, not by events. In fact, from the introspective point of view it may be difficult to find an event, or a set of events, that could have been the cause of my choice for chocolate over strawberry ice cream, (supposing, say, that I don't prefer one over the other), but it is yet plausible to claim that I caused this choice (by making it). These considerations afford credibility to the idea that I, fundamentally as an agent, cause this choice.

A further aspect of Bok's argument is that agent-causal libertarianism requires an explanation of how an agent, fundamentally, can produce an event. Mele delivers a similar challenge:

41. Bok, *Freedom and Responsibility*, pp. 44–5.

61

In the absence of an account of how agent causation "works," one might as well just say that there is such a thing as agents' *control* – a mysterious thing that cannot be characterized in any detail, and is not manifested in, as van Inwagen puts it, "'normal' causation, a relation that takes *events* or *states of affairs* or some such, and not *persons* as its terms."[42]

According to this sort of objection, positing an agent-causal power is empty because no satisfying account can be provided for the mechanism by which this power operates. In reply, either the agent-causal power is constituted of more basic causal powers, or it is basic in the sense that it is not constituted of more basic causal powers. If the former is true, then there could be a constitutional account of the mechanism by which the power operates, which would give the agent-causal hypothesis content. By analogy, the causal powers of a computer are constituted of more basic causal powers, and a computer engineer might be able to provide the requisite constitutional account. Some agent-causal theorists suppose that the agent-causal power emerges from more basic neurophysiological powers, and indeed that these neurophysiological causal powers are powers for events to cause events. So far, of course, no account along these lines has been provided, but then, in general, neurophysiological accounts of powers of agency are incomplete at best. One cannot reasonably reject agent-causal theory on the ground that it has not yet provided a constitutional explanation of agent-causal powers when science has not developed to a point where the sort of account in question could be given.

On the other hand, it might be that the agent-causal power is basic in the sense that it has no constitution. Then there may well be no mechanism by means of which the agent-causal power operates. However, for the agent-causal theorist to claim that there is no such mechanism does not obviously make the theory empty either. By analogy, it is not empty to suggest that the causal powers of an electron are basic in this sense. If these powers are basic, then there would be no mechanism by means of which the electron transmits causal power. More generally, for fundamental event-causal relations, there would be no mechanisms by means of which causal power is transmitted, and thus no explanation as to how the causation works. But it would not be right to hold the agent-causal theory to a standard that event-causal theory cannot meet. I suspect that the best way to pursue

---

42. Mele, *Autonomous Agents*, p. 199.

the emptiness charge against an agent-causal view of this sort would be to argue that such a causal power could not be physically realized, and then no satisfactory account of how it interacts with the brain and body could be produced. Perhaps this sort of project might be successful, but whether it would is also not obvious.

A DISPARITY BETWEEN CAUSATION AND EXPLANATION?

A further objection to agent causation, first stated by Broad[43] and then developed by Ginet, focuses on a disparity between the agent-causal theory's account of the causation and the contrastive explanation of the *timing* of an action. Ginet also raises a similar issue for causation and contrastive explanation of the *sort* of action at issue:

On the agent-causation theory, the immediate cause of the occurrence of a particular sort of simple mental event at a particular time is the agent herself, *per se* and not in virtue of any event of which she is the subject. But the agent *per se* cannot *explain* why the event happened precisely when it did rather than at some slightly different time. Only some difference between the agent at one time and the agent at the other times, some temporally located property, could do that. Nor, it might be added, can the agent *per se* explain why that particular sort of event rather than some other sort happened just then. What sense can it make, then, to say that the agent as such is the *cause* of the occurrence of that particular sort of event rather than some other sort, and is the cause of its occurring at that particular time rather than at some other time?[44]

The agent-causal theory asserts that agents cause events to happen at particular times. Ginet challenges this claim by arguing that the theory provides no explanation as to why such an event occurred at some particular time rather than at some other time (for example, at some nearby time), and it does not make sense to say that an agent caused an event to occur at some particular time rather than at some other time without there being an explanation for the event's occurring at this time rather than at some other time. The reason the theory cannot explain why an event that an agent caused occurred at some particular time rather than at some other is that only temporally located properties could serve this function, and an agent is not a temporally located property.

In response, Clarke argues that the agent-causal theorist might claim that part of the cause of an action may be an event, for example, the

43. Broad, "Determinism, Indeterminism, and Libertarianism," p. 169.
44. Ginet, "Freedom, Responsibility, and Agency," pp. 93–4.

agent's acquisition of certain reasons, and that such an event may help explain an action's occurring at a certain time.[45] O'Connor maintains that "a full explanation of why an agent-caused event occurred, will include, among other things, an account of the reasons upon which the agent acted," and that as a result, the agent-causal theory has resources to explain the timing of such an event.[46] To the reasons and the agent's acquisition of reasons as explanatory resources one might add the agent's weighing of the reasons and the motivational force that results from the agent's weighing of the reasons. But Ginet argues that there are nevertheless cases in which the agent-causal theory would want to say that the agent causes an event at one particular time rather than at some other time, but yet where no explanation for why the event occurred at that time rather than some other time is available:

. . . my reason for picking up the phone does not explain why I picked it up precisely when I did rather than a few seconds earlier or later, and I need not have had any reason for choosing that precise time rather than a slightly different earlier or later one. It is possible that there was nothing at all explains why the one thing was the case rather than any alternative . . . But in that case, it seems natural to infer, there was nothing that *caused* the one rather than any alternative.[47]

Similarly, for the "sort of event" problem, "my reason for picking up the telephone was that I wanted to make a call. But that reason does not explain why I used my left *rather than* my right hand to pick it up, and indeed I need not have had any reason for using one hand rather than the other."[48] I might have good reasons for choosing strawberry ice cream and equally good reasons for choosing chocolate, I might weigh these reasons equally, and the resulting motivational force may be the same for each option. But yet I might choose chocolate, and the agent-causal theory would want to claim that the chocolate-choosing event was agent-caused. Yet for each of these two cases, Ginet would argue that nothing explains the occurrence of the event rather than the alternative, and thus it would be natural to infer that nothing caused the occurrence rather than the alternative.

---

45. Clarke, "Agent Causation and Event Causation in the Production of Free Action," pp. 298–9.
46. O'Connor, "Agent Causation," p. 184.
47. Ginet, "Freedom, Responsibility, and Agency," pp. 94–5.
48. Ginet, "Freedom, Responsibility, and Agency," p. 94.

However, an understanding of the resources of agent-causal theory will indicate that the asymmetry that Ginet suggests is not clearly a feature of the view. The theory can specify that the agent, by virtue of his agent-causal power, can cause a choice of a particular sort and at a particular time. There is no incoherence in this claim. The agent-causal power that equips the agent to cause the ice-cream choice thus enables the agent to cause this particular choice rather than the strawberry ice-cream choice, and to cause this choice at t1 rather than at some other time. Moreover, one might also then claim that it is also the agent that causally explains the occurrence of the chocolate rather than the strawberry ice-cream choice, and that the agent explains the occurrence of this choice at t1 rather than at some other time. For after all, doesn't citing the causes of something count as causally explaining it? Now, if one is accustomed to causal explanations adducing only events (as perhaps we all are), it will seem strange that a causal explanation would advert not to events but only to an agent, or an agent by virtue of a causal power. But this sort of explanation, I think, is no stranger than the hypothesis that agents, fundamentally, are causes. One might propose that because such explanations are not featured in mature sciences, they are thereby ruled out. However, this verdict assumes that these sciences allow us to understand the notion of explanation well enough to rule out agent-causal explanation. In my view, the strangeness of agent-causal explanations should perhaps make one wary of them, but it does not support an argument that agent-causal libertarianism is incoherent.[49]

GALEN STRAWSON'S ARGUMENT AGAINST THE COHERENCE OF LIBERTARIANISM

The specific type of agent-causal libertarianism whose coherence I defend is relevantly similar to what Galen Strawson calls the

49. An issue for agent-causal libertarianism raised by Thomas Nagel (*The View From Nowhere* (Oxford, Oxford University Press, 1986), p. 116) and Kane ("Two Kinds of Incompatibilism," pp. 121–4), among others, is whether agent-causal libertarianism is deficient in it that postulates events for which there are no contrastive explanations. Clarke (in "Contrastive Rational Explanation of Free Choice") argues that it would seem that contrastive explanations of particular types are often available for libertarian free actions. For example, if an agent has stronger reasons to perform one action rather than another, then this fact can explain why he performed the action and not the alternative, even if the reasons do not determine him to act as he does. But for certain kinds of contrasts, such as why the agent in the example given caused the chocolate ice cream rather than

"Leibnizian" libertarian picture of agent causation. According to this picture, the agent's reasons (made up of beliefs and desires) constitute only one part of the causation of a free decision, since they may incline but do not all by themselves cause the agent to choose. The agent's causation of a choice constitutes the remaining part. But, Strawson contends, rational actions must have a full causal explanation in terms of the agent's reasons alone. More precisely, rational actions must have an explanation in terms of reasons the agent has that indicates all of what there was about the agent, mentally speaking, that causally brought it about that she performed the action she did.[50] Otherwise, only the "reasons" part of the action's cause would be rational, and the remaining mental aspects would not be. "Upon what," he asks, "are the decisions about actions now supposed to be based, other than upon its reasons?"[51] The decisions cannot be based on further principles of choice or on further reasons, because the same questions can be asked about those. Either those reasons all by themselves cause the decision, in which case the agent-cause has no causal role and the decision is not free, or the agent-cause plays a part that is not rational. Consequently, these agent-caused actions must either be unfree or "rationally speaking random," and thus irrational.

the strawberry ice cream choice, there is no contrastive explanation. However, it is certainly not obvious that the libertarian should give up his view on account of this deficiency. According to the standard interpretation of quantum mechanics, there are many events for which there is no explanation as to why they occur rather than an alternative in the possibility space. Suppose that given the initial conditions, each of two possible subsequent events, E_1 and E_2, has the same probability of occurring. Each of these events is then such that if it occurs, there will be no explanation as to why it occurs rather than the other. Or suppose that in this situation, there is some other event, E_3, with a higher probability of occurring than E_1, but E_1 occurs and E_3 does not. There will be no explanation as to why E_1 occurs rather than E_3. Granted, the standard interpretation of quantum mechanics has not been conclusively established. But since it is such a weighty contender, one cannot have any confidence that conditions with which it is incompatible are true. More importantly, the demand that there always be a contrastive explanation for the occurrence of an event rather than some alternative would rule out the standard interpretation of quantum mechanics prior to any consideration of the evidence for this theory. Surely this is reason to doubt that it is a condition on anything that happens. For a presentation of the opposing view, see Richard Double, *The Non-Reality of Free Will*, and "The Principle of Rational Explanation Defended."

50. Galen Strawson, *Freedom and Belief*, pp. 52–6, cf. "The Impossibility of Moral Responsibility," *Philosophical Studies* 75 (1994), pp. 5–24. Clarke interprets Strawson this way in "On the Possibility of Rational Free Action," and there he indicates that Strawson endorses this interpretation (p. 48, cf. note 24).

51. Strawson, *Freedom and Belief*, p. 53.

Now I think Strawson would be correct in his criticism if, according to the Leibnizian picture, the agent's role in the causation of the decision and the role of her reasons were wholly independent of each other. One might imagine Kane's businesswoman as an agent-cause, struggling whether to act on the moral reasons or on the self-interested ones. If the causal efficacy of these reasons were wholly independent of the agent-cause, and the agent-cause's breaking a stalemate between the sets of reasons were wholly independent of the reasons, then indeed, by my intuitions, the businesswoman would be no more responsible for her decision than she would if the stalemate were broken by a randomizing manipulator. But suppose that the agent-cause's role is not independent of the reasons in this way, but rather that an aspect of her agent-causal power is the capacity to consider and weigh reasons, and thereby to guide her causing of choices. Imagine that the businesswoman exercises this capacity and makes the decision to help the assault victim because in her estimation the reasons to do so outweigh the reasons against, and that is all there is to the mental part of the decision's cause (at least, that is all there is that is relevant to this discussion). Nevertheless, given her agent-causal power she still could have decided against helping the victim even after her consideration and weighing of the reasons. Then how plausible is Strawson's contention that the decision is not rational because the agent-cause's part of the causal story is not itself caused by reasons?

In my view, Strawson's argument sets an implausibly high standard for the rationality of action – that in order to be rational, the entire mental part of the causation of an action must consist in the agent's reasons. For there is nothing in ordinary criteria for rationality of action that precludes the businesswoman under this last description from being rational. Nothing in these ordinary criteria would justify our saying to her: "Although you did decide on the basis of the reasons you considered best, your decision was irrational because the mental part of the cause wasn't wholly determined by these reasons." A more intuitively plausible position on the role reasons must play in fully rational action is that (i) reasons must have a part in the causation of the action, and (ii) these reasons must be the ones the agent considers best (or some such condition), and (iii) the agent must choose as she does because of those reasons, and this is how the reasons have a role in the causation of the action. I believe that ordinary standards for judging actions to be rational require no more than this, and that unless Strawson can make a case that more stringent conditions are appropriate, we have no reason to endorse his argument.[52] The way I would see these conditions playing out in a theory of agent causation for rational action is that the agent would cause a decision on the basis of the reasons she considers best, and that these reasons would have a causal role only by this route. In the production of a rational decision for which the agent is morally responsible, the agent-cause would be a mental causal factor distinct from the reasons, and even a mental factor in the causal explanation distinct from the reasons. Yet the causal role of the reasons and that of the agent-cause would be interdependent in the way specified. Hence, in my view, contrary to what Strawson claims, there is a coherent and plausible model for agent-causal libertarianism according to which agents can make free rational decisions.

THE PROSPECTS FOR AGENT-CAUSAL LIBERTARIANISM

A case can now be made for the claim no objections canvassed so far show that agent-causal libertarianism is incoherent, at least in the sense that it involves no detected logical inconsistency. But this does not mean that it is in the clear. The request for more explanation of what agent causation is like can be regarded as part of an assessment of whether we have any reason to believe that agent causation exists, even if it is coherent. Accordingly, there are other ways in which one might attempt to undermine the hypothesis of agent causation. In my view, the most promising strategy would aim to show that although irreducible causal relations could, in principle, obtain between libertarian agent-causes and events, in actual fact there are empirical considerations that tell against this position.

52. Although I agree with many of Clarke's criticisms of Strawson, here my approach differs from his. Clarke is willing to allow that "for full rationality, it will suffice if there is an explanation in terms of reasons the agent had (and possibly also, I would allow, character traits of the agent) that indicates all of what there was about the agent, mentally speaking, that causally brought it about that she performed the action she did." He then contends that on his version of agent-causal libertarianism, such explanations will be available. For even though the agent herself is an irreducible component in the causation of the action, "the agent herself is not 'something about the agent, mentally speaking'; she is not a feature of herself. All of the mental features of the agent that causally bring about her action are her reasons (and possibly her character traits)" ("On the Possibility of Rational Free Action," p. 49). He then claims that "the explanation that cites the agent's reasons is in no way false or incomplete as a rational explanation, even if it does not tell the entire story about what causally produced the action . . ." (p. 50). The problem with Clarke's specifications is that they could all be satisfied and the action still not be rational, for example, if the agent's role were completely independent of reasons.

3

Empirical Objections to Agent-Causal Libertarianism

INTRODUCTION

The most significant empirical objections to agent-causal libertarianism challenge its capacity to accommodate our best natural scientific theories. Different aspects of this type of libertarianism give rise to two such objections. First, given our scientific understanding of the world, how could there exist anything as fabulous as an agent-causal power? It would appear that our natural scientific theories could not yield an account of a power of this sort. Second, given our scientific understanding, how could there be agent-caused decisions that are freely willed in the sense required for moral responsibility? Such decisions, it would seem, would not be constrained by the laws of nature, and therefore could not exist in the natural world.

Let us begin with the first of these two issues. Some libertarians maintain that there could be no natural scientific account of agent-causal powers. But they do not conclude from this that such powers do not exist, only that they could not be wholly physically realized. For others, a more congenial approach is to avoid non–physicalism by exploiting the resources of nonreductive materialism. According to nonreductive materialism generally construed, causal powers in the purview of sciences such as biology and psychology arise solely as a result of the organization of their material constituents, while they do not reduce to microphysical causal powers. Nonreductive materialism provides an attractive strategy for saving phenomena such as consciousness and belief from the scientific eliminativist's axe, and the libertarian might therefore be encouraged to preserve agent-causal free will by the same approach. A view of this sort is suggested by O'Connor:

... given that there is nothing inconsistent about the emergence of an "ordinary" causal property, having the potential for exercising an irreducible causal influence on the environments in which it is instantiated, it is hard to see just why there could not be a sort of emergent property whose novelty consists in its capacity to enable its possessor directly to effect changes at will.[1]

Thus, the libertarian might affirm that agent-causal powers, although not reducible to microphysical causal powers, can arise as a result of the complex organization of matter.

Views about the nature of agent-causes can be separated into several distinct options. The *materialist* approach can usefully be divided into two categories along the following lines. According to the *ordinary nonreductive materialist* strategy, the agent-causal power is a higher-level power that results from a wholly microphysical constitution by virtue of the organization of its constituents, but the microphysical level remains wholly governed by the physical laws. By the *strong emergentist* scheme, it is also the true that the agent-causal power is a higher-level power that results from a wholly microphysical constitution by virtue of the organization of its constituents. However, because of the nature of the agent-causal power, the microphysical level − in particular, the microphysical constitution of the agent-causal power − is no longer wholly governed by the (ordinary) laws of physics. Finally, according to the *non-physicalist* position, the agent-causal power is partially or wholly non-physically constituted. Familiarly, there are many considerations in the philosophy of mind that bear on the plausibility of non-physicalism, none of which I will discuss here. I will assume that non-physicalism is a coherent possibility. The argument I will develop against the plausibility of agent-causal libertarianism does not depend on any considerations opposing non-physicalism per se.

PROBLEMS FOR THE ORDINARY
NONREDUCTIVIST STRATEGY

In my view, the ordinary non-reductive materialist approach cannot provide libertarians with what they want most − free decisions for which, from the incompatibilist point of view, we can be morally responsible. Suppose that ordinary nonreductive materialism is true, and

---

1. O'Connor, "Agent Causation," p. 179; see also his "Emergent Properties," *American Philosophical Quarterly* 31 (1994), pp. 91–104.

that therefore all microphysical constitutions of higher-level causal powers, including such constitutions of agent-causal powers, are wholly governed by the physical laws. Could there then be agent-caused decisions that are freely willed in the sense required for moral responsibility (hereafter *agent-caused free decisions*)? Consider first the case in which the physical laws are deterministic. If everything is wholly constituted of microphysical entities, and these entities are governed by deterministic laws, then the complete state of the microphysical universe five million years ago, together with these deterministic laws, renders inevitable every subsequent complete microphysical state of the universe. If every subsequent complete microphysical state of the universe is rendered inevitable in this way, and everything is wholly microphysically constituted, then every subsequent state of the universe, whether or not it reduces to the microphysical, is rendered inevitable in this way. Thus, even if nonreductive materialism is true, as long as the microphysical level is governed by deterministic laws, all of our decisions will be rendered inevitable by virtue of previous states of the universe, just as their microphysical realizations are. All of our decisions will then be alien-deterministic events – events for which factors beyond the agent's control determine their occurrence – and none of them could be agent-caused free decisions.

The prospects for the ordinary nonreductive materialist strategy are not improved if the microphysical universe is not a deterministic system, but is instead governed by fundamentally statistical quantum mechanical laws.[2] If everything is wholly constituted of microphysical entities governed by such laws of quantum mechanics, then all of our decisions will be wholly constituted of events on the continuum we discussed earlier. That is, all of our decisions will be constituted of events that are alien-deterministic, or truly random (those not produced by anything at all), or partially random (those for which factors beyond the agent's control contribute to their production but do not determine them, while there is nothing that supplements the contribution of these factors to produce the events). To simplify, the causal history of all of the constituents of any of our decisions will be exhausted by

2. Note, however, that according to David Bohm's interpretation of quantum mechanics, which is a serious contender, the theory is deterministic. For a detailed account of the implications quantum mechanics has for libertarianism, see Barry Loewer, "Freedom from Physics: Quantum Mechanics and Free Will," *Philosophical Topics* 24 (1996), pp. 91–112. Loewer canvasses three interpretations of quantum mechanics, and he argues that in the last analysis, the theory provides scant support for libertarian free will.

the contribution made by factors beyond the agent's control, and nothing else. But if this is so, then the causal history of the decision itself will also be exhausted by the contribution made by factors beyond the agent's control, and nothing else. This picture also admits of no agent-caused free decisions.

Consequently, given ordinary nonreductive materialism, whether the laws of physics are deterministic or fundamentally statistical, events with microphysical constitutions governed by these laws are not sufficiently within our control. If everything is wholly constituted of micro-physical entities governed by either sort of law, no room is left for agent-caused free decisions.

John Dupré argues that determinism at the micro-level does not have any implications for determinism at higher levels of explanation. In his view, the best case from scientific research for determinism would be evidence for causal completeness at the micro-level.[3] But he does not think that a good case of this sort can be made.

Evidence for causal completeness would require that increasingly complex systems of physical particles could be shown to be amenable to causal explanation in terms of the laws said to govern individual particles, evidence, that is to say, for general reductionism.

However, in Dupré's view not only are there general difficulties that confront the project of reductionism, but in addition:

No one has claimed to be able to explain the behavior even of very small collections of particles in terms of the behavior of individual particles; the reduction even of relatively simple parts of chemistry to physics is now looked on with considerable skepticism; and even physics itself is acknowledged to consist of laws the relations between which are obscure . . .[4]

But assuming ordinary nonreductive materialism, there is a mistake in Dupré's contention that the untenability of reductionism shows that determinism at the micro-level has no implications for determinism at higher levels. For determinism could hold at a higher level simply because determinism holds for its entire micro-level constitution, even

---

3. John Dupré, "The Solution to the Problem of the Freedom of the Will," *Philosophical Perspectives* 10 (Oxford: Blackwell Publishers, 1996), pp. 385–402, at p. 390, cf. Dupré, *The Disorder of Things* (Cambridge: Harvard University Press, 1993).

4. Dupré, "The Solution to the Problem of the Freedom of the Will," p. 390. Stump endorses Dupré's line of argument in "Libertarian Freedom and the Principle of Alternative Possibilities," pp. 83–6.

if there are no explanations for types of higher-level phenomena in terms of micro-level phenomena, and even if no higher-level explanation reduces to a micro-level counterpart. For the arguments just advanced are not dependent on the explainability of any types of higher-level phenomena in micro-level terms, nor on the reducibility of any higher-level explanation to a micro-level counterpart. Given ordinary nonreductive materialism, if everything is wholly constituted of microphysical entities governed by deterministic laws, then the complete state of the physical universe at any time, together with these deterministic laws, renders inevitable every subsequent complete microphysical state of the universe. Again, if every subsequent complete microphysical state of the universe is rendered inevitable in this way, and everything is wholly microphysically constituted, then clearly every subsequent state of the universe is rendered inevitable in this way.

More generally, assuming ordinary nonreductive materialism, even if higher-level explanations do not reduce to microphysical counterparts, the laws governing the microphysical constituents will constrain the nature of the entities they make up. Suppose that the explanation as to how telephone systems work has no microphysical reduction. It would be absurd to argue on these grounds that telephone systems are not constrained by the laws governing their microphysical constituents. For instance, the velocity limits for a telephone system's constituent particles will nevertheless limit the speed at which calls can be transmitted. The arguments just advanced focus our attention on a constraint of this type for the powers of agents. Assuming ordinary nonreductive materialism, this constraint would rule out agent-caused free decisions if everything were constituted of entities governed by deterministic laws, and would preclude this sort of freedom even if everything were constituted of entities governed by statistical laws.

STRONG EMERGENTISM AND MICROPHYSICAL CONSTRAINTS

It might be, however, that Dupré is supposing that given the evidence we have against reductionism, strong emergentism is very much a live possibility. On the strong emergentist strategy, the agent-causal power is a higher-level power that emerges from a wholly microphysical constitution by virtue of the organization of the constituents, and because of the nature of this causal power, this microphysical constitution is no longer wholly constrained by the laws of microphysics. The strong emergentist claims that it is possible for a complex organization of material constituents to give rise to causal powers that can yield deviations in these constituents from what the microphysical laws would predict. This strategy avoids the problem we have just raised for ordinary nonreductive materialism, because if the microphysical constitution of the agent-causal power is not governed by the microphysical laws, then we can no longer argue in the way we did that agent-caused free decisions would be impossible.

A serious difficulty for this strategy is that we have no evidence for the existence of this sort of emergence in chemistry, biology, or psychology.[5] A promising materialist strategy would invoke, it would seem, a reasonably well-grounded form of nonreductive materialism to make a case for agent-caused free decisions. However, strong emergence is not confirmed by any of the higher-level sciences. Even if the libertarian were nevertheless to hold out for the possibility of emergence of this sort, the lack of any evidence in the higher-level sciences for its actual occurrence makes it a precarious foundation on which to base a theory of action and moral responsibility.

As a further antidote to an easy acquiescence in this sort of position, it is useful to examine Jaegwon Kim's argument against any distinction between higher- and lower-level causal powers, the argument from explanatory exclusion.[6] I believe that there is a good nonreductivist reply to this argument, but that taking the issue Kim raises seriously will indicate how credible it is that higher-level causal powers are firmly constrained by the laws (ordinarily) governing their microphysical constitutions.

What might the relationship be, Kim asks, between explanation of an event – say, the raising of one's hand – by the higher-level causal powers and its explanation by corresponding microphysical causal powers? The most commonly accepted sort of nonreductivist materialism affirms that whenever there is a higher-level account that causally explains something that happens, there is also a microphysical causal explanation for the microphysical constitution of that event or state. So, for example, suppose there is a genetic causal explanation for a baby's having brown eyes, which tracks a genetic causal power that produces

---

5.   See Brian McLaughlin. "The Rise and Fall of British Emergentism," in *Emergence or Reduction? Essays on The Prospects of Nonreductive Physicalism*, eds. A. Beckerman, H. Flohr, and J. Kim (New York: Walter de Gruyter, 1992).
6.   Jaegwon Kim, "The Myth of Nonreductive Materialism," in his *Supervenience and Mind* (New York: Cambridge University Press, 1993), pp. 265–84.

the brown eyes. At the same time, the constitution of the present token of this genetic causal power is a complex of microphysical causal powers that produces the microphysical constitution of the baby's having brown eyes. But given that both sorts of explanation are causal, what is the relationship between the causation to which the explanation at the genetic level appeals and the causation to which the microphysical explanation appeals? How can *both* be true? It is implausible that each explanation adverts to causal powers that are sufficient for the event to occur, and that hence the event is overdetermined. It is also implausible that each of these causal powers is a partial cause of the event and that each by itself is insufficient for the event to occur.

According to the solution that Kim develops, real causal powers exist at the microphysical level, and micro-physical explanations track genuine causal relationships. Only if the higher-level explanations actually reduce to microphysical explanations does it turn out that the higher-level explanations also track genuine causal powers. This move solves the problem of explanatory exclusion, because if one explanation reduces to another, then they do not compete. In Kim's view, higher-level explanations that do not reduce to microphysical explanations fail to track causal powers, and have some lesser status. Perhaps such explanations express regularities without at the same time tracking genuine causal relationships. This account, which Kim believes is the only possible solution to the problem he raises, undermines any powerful nonreductive view. For if there are no genuinely causal explanations that do not reduce to microphysical explanations, there are no irreducible causal explanations.

On Kim's position, any token higher-level causal power at a time will be identical to a token microphysical causal power at that time. He codifies this claim with respect to mental properties as:

[The Causal Inheritance Principle] If mental property M is realized in a system at t in virtue of physical realization base P, the causal powers of *this instance of M* are identical with the causal powers of P.

He believes that denying this principle would amount to accepting "causal powers that magically emerge at a higher level and of which there is no accounting in terms of lower-level causal powers and nomic connections."[7] The Causal Inheritance Principle implies that there are

7. Kim, "Multiple Realizability and the Metaphysics of Reduction," in his *Supervenience and Mind*, pp. 309–35, at p. 326.

no token causal powers distinct from token microphysical causal powers, a claim that would undercut any robust sort of non-reductivism, for there remains no substantial sense in which there exist causal powers which are not microphysical. Needless to say, strong emergentism is not a possibility given Kim's reductive metaphysics.

It is important to see that even the sort of nonreductive materialism that Fodor endorses, since it is a token-identity theory, plausibly satisfies the Causal Inheritance Principle, and as a result seems to preclude strong emergentism.[8] In Fodor's view, any particular instance of a mental state will be identical to some particular instance of a microphysical state, and it would be natural to infer that the causal powers of any particular instance of a mental state will then be identical with the causal powers of some particular instance of a microphysical state. Fodor's materialism remains nonreductive because types of mental states and mental causal powers are, in his view, not identical with types of physical states and causal powers. Nevertheless, his token-identity theory constrains the nature of the higher-level causal powers very narrowly. What plausibility strong emergentism has derives from the supposition that non-microphysical causal powers might radically transform the ways in which microphysical entities can behave. But if every token causal power is identical to a microphysical causal power, then there are no token non-microphysical causal powers that can play this role. It would seem far-fetched to claim that although there are no token-level non-microphysical causal powers that can have this function, there are nevertheless type-level causal powers of this sort that can have it. Strong emergentism consequently seems ruled out.

Still, on the nonreductive view I wish to defend, Fodor's token identity thesis is false, and the prospects for strong emergentism remain live. We might explore this possibility by asking whether the Causal Inheritance Principle is true, and if it is false, whether Kim is right to suppose that magical emergentism follows. I think that the answer to both of these questions is "no." First, a respectable case can be made for the claim that token entities are typically not identical to their constitutions or realization bases. *The ship of Theseus* is not identical to its current

8. Jerry Fodor, "Special Sciences," *Synthese* 28 (1974), pp. 97–115, reprinted in *Readings in the Philosophy of Psychology*, ed. Ned Block (Cambridge: Harvard University Press, 1980), pp. 120–33. The soundness of the most prominent argument against type-type reductionism about mental states, the argument from the multiple realizability of mental state types, is compatible with both Fodor's token-identity thesis and its denial.

token microphysical realization base because it might remain the same token ship while the token microphysical (or even macrophysical) constitution changes. Or, for a modal as opposed to a temporal argument, the ship might have been the same token ship even if the token microphysical constitution had been different. But this reflection would also seem to support the claim that the token causal powers of the ship are not now identical to the token microphysical causal powers of its constitution. The same sort of argument can be run for causal powers of token genetic or mental entities.[9]

Moreover, on this picture, as higher-level tokens are wholly constituted by microphysical entities, so the causal powers of these higher-level tokens are wholly constituted by the microphysical causal powers of the stuff they are made of. (Hilary Kornblith and I have argued for the following general view about the constitution of token causal powers: The causal powers of a token of kind F are constituted by the causal powers of a token of kind G just in case the token of kind F has the causal powers it does in virtue of its being constituted by a token of kind G.[10]) This picture is not committed to magical emergentism any more than is token physicalism, since it does not admit causal powers that are not wholly constituted of microphysical causal powers. It endorses a weaker but nevertheless plausible version of the causal inheritance principle:

[The Weaker Causal Inheritance Principle] If mental property M is realized in a system at t in virtue of physical realization base P, the causal powers of *this instance of M* are wholly constituted by the causal powers of P.

In addition, since higher-level tokens are fully constituted of microphysical constituents, there will be at least some degree to which causal powers of higher-level tokens can be explained in terms of the causal powers of their micro-physical constituents.[11]

Just as Kim claims that no competition between explanations arises in the case of reduction, so we can now argue that no competition

9. Derk Pereboom and Hilary Kornblith, "The Metaphysics of Irreducibility," *Philosophical Studies* 63 (1991): pp. 125–46, at pp. 131–2.
10. Pereboom and Kornblith, "The Metaphysics of Irreducibility," p. 131.
11. A full constitutional explanation of the token higher-level powers might be limited by the degree to which they are essentially relational. For example, if a perceptual state is individuated partly by its object, then one would not expect this fact about its individuation to be explained by its constitution.

arises in this view either. A clear intuition underlying the explanatory exclusion argument would seem to be that if A is the sufficient (proximal) cause of B, then there cannot be anything spatio-temporally diverse from A that also has a role in (proximally) causing B. But if a token of a higher-level causal power is wholly constituted by a complex of microphysical causal powers, it is not the case that there are two spatio-temporally diverse (groups of) causal powers at work. Rather, these causal powers coincide spatio-temporally (and in this possible world), and they coincide in this way because one is now (actually) wholly made up of the other. Moreover, if the higher-level causal power's being constituted of some specific microphysical causal power in every possible world (as would be the case if they were identical) eliminates competition, why wouldn't the fact that this higher-level power is constituted of this specific microphysical causal power merely in the actual world also eliminate competition? The requirement that this constitution relation hold at every possible world would seem to be irrelevant to the explanatory exclusion issue. Consequently, because it is possible to have wholly spatio-temporally coinciding causal powers that are not identical, it is possible that there be two causal explanations for one event that do not exclude each other and at the same time do not reduce to a single explanation.

On this conception, then, higher-level causal powers are wholly constituted of microphysical causal powers but are in no sense identical to them. Nevertheless, such a picture still suggests that higher-level causal powers would be significantly constrained by their microphysical counterparts. Indeed, to the degree that there is a constitutional explanation of a higher-level causal power in terms of its microphysical constituents, one might well expect that whatever laws govern the microphysical constituents would also constrain the higher-level powers. For the laws that normally govern the microphysical constituents plausibly determine the role they can have in any explanation. If, as on the strong emergentist proposal, the arrangement of the constituents can give rise to causal powers due to which these constituents are no longer governed by these laws, then it is not clear what sort of possibility for constitutional explanation remains. Therefore, strongly emergent causal powers might well have no microphysical constitutional explanation at all, and in that sense their emergence will be magical. This consideration provides a reason for being wary of strong emergentism. Nevertheless, strong emergentism is not conclusively ruled out by this consideration, and thus in what follows, let us still allow for the possibility that there are arrangements of micro-physical constituents that yield higher-level causal powers, with the result that the microphysical level is no longer fully constrained by the laws of physics.

STRONG EMERGENTISM, NON-PHYSICALISM, AND THE PROSPECTS FOR RECONCILIATION WITH PHYSICS

At this stage, then, two proposals for the nature of agent-causal powers remain, strong emergentism and non-physicalism. Against each of these views, we might raise the second sort of empirical challenge we discussed earlier: Given our scientific understanding of the world, how could there be agent-caused decisions that are freely willed in the sense required for moral responsibility? It would seem that on either of these views, if agent-causes are to be capable of such free decisions, they would require the power to produce deviations from the physical laws – deviations from what these laws would predict and from what we would expect given these laws. But such agent-causes would be embed-ded in a world that, by the evidence that supports our current theo-ries in physics, is nevertheless wholly governed by the laws of physics. According to this second type of empirical objection, then, the claim that there are agent-causes is not credible, given this evidence. I shall argue that in the final analysis, this objection has considerable force.

There are two possible kinds of strategies for responding to this objection. The first, *reconciliation*, affirms that agent-causes do not in fact produce deviations from what the physical laws would predict. The second, *overriding*, argues that when libertarian agent-causes make free choices, they actually do produce such deviations. I shall argue that neither of these strategies is credible.

The reconciliation strategy was first developed by Kant for a deter-minist conception of the physical laws. To be morally responsible, he thinks, agents must have *transcendental freedom*, the power to cause an action without being causally determined to cause it.[12] But he also agrees with Hume that everything that we experience – not only the physical, but the psychological as well (i.e., all of nature) – is governed

---

12. Kant, *Critique of Pure Reason* (Cambridge: Cambridge University Press, 1997), A533/B561. Kant characterizes transcendental freedom as "the power of beginning a state from oneself" and as "the idea of a spontaneity that can begin to act from itself, without another cause having to be placed ahead of it so as in turn to determine it to action in accordance with a law of causal connection" (A533/B561, my translation).

by deterministic causal laws. In Kant's view, if we are free, we would have to be free in a way that is inaccessible to experience. His way of stating the view is that we would have to be free as noumena – entities in a realm of which we cannot have experience.

But if we are transcendentally free, how can it be that the empirical aspects of our actions are governed by deterministic laws? Kant thinks that we cannot explain how this is *really* possible – for example, we cannot explain how it is causally possible. We can, however, show that the belief that we are transcendentally free involves no logical contradiction, and this is all that is required at the theoretical (or epistemic) level, in his view, for one to legitimately have this belief given its practical benefits.[13] In particular, we can show theoretically that the claim that we have transcendental freedom does not logically contradict the thesis that nature is a deterministic system.

Kant's view entails that it is logically possible that agents make transcendentally free choices all of which are for just those potential actions whose physical components are causally determined.[14] Kant is right about this, supposing he means that there is no logical contradiction involved in the supposition that every transcendentally free choice ever made dovetails precisely with the way the physical components of actions are causally determined to be. But is this proposal for reconciling transcendental freedom with physical causal determinism credible? There would certainly be nothing incredible about the proposal that a transcendentally free agent should make a free choice on some particular occasion for a possible action whose physical component was causally determined. However, Kant needs a much more substantial proposal, and this one fares differently. It is that all transcendentally free choices should be for just those possible actions whose physical components are causally determined to occur, and that none of these choices be for the alternatives. Aside from highly dubious idealistic attempts to explain how this might be, the wild coincidences implied by this proposal make it incredible.[15] Another way of seeing

---

13. Kant, *Critique of Pure Reason*, A558/B586.
14. Ibid., A538/B566–A558/B586.
15. Perhaps Kant has in mind the hypothesis that all free choices are made timelessly, but as a result of the human mental processing that generates the phenomenal world, all empirical results of these choices are made to come out as deterministic. This suggestion is largely speculative, but see the *Critique of Pure Reason*, A551–2/B579–80. Kant claims that because of our cognitive limitations, we cannot genuinely explain why empirical results of intelligible choices have the character they do: "But why the intel-

this is that if we were agents making transcendentally free choices, one would expect, in the long run, that these choices be evident in our bodies as patterns of divergence from the deterministic physical laws. Kant's proposal that there are no such divergences, although it involves no logical contradiction, would run so sharply counter to what we would expect to occur as to render the proposal incredible.

According to the standard interpretation of quantum mechanics, however, the laws governing matter are statistical and not deterministic. To try to solve this problem of wild coincidences, the libertarian might invoke the indeterminacy in nature indicated by these laws. In the indeterministic context, the reconciliationist claims that despite the existence of libertarian agent-causes who produce effects in the physical world external to the agent, one should nevertheless expect the long-run frequencies of physical events to be just as physical theory would predict. In assessing this indeterminist proposal, one might note that in ordinary cases, quantum indeterminacy only allows for extremely small probabilities of counterfactual choices and actions. To see why this is so, suppose, by analogy, that the soda can on the table remains where it is for the next minute. Given quantum indeterminacy, there is some probability that instead it had moved spontaneously one inch to the left sometime during this minute. However, for this event to have occurred, each of many quantum indeterminacies would have had to be resolved in a specific alternative range of ways, and the probability of this occurring is extremely small. The prospects for counterfactual human actions would seem to be similarly bad. Even if quantum indeterminacy results in the indeterminacy of certain neural events — like the firing of individual neurons, so that at certain times both the probability that the neural event will occur and that it will not are significant — the likelihood of entire physical components of counterfactual actions occurring would still seem to be insignificant.[16] For making a decision involves a physical event of a much larger scale than the firing of a neuron. When we make a decision, a very large number of individual quantum and neural events are involved. Therefore, for a counterfactual decision to have occurred, each of many quantum

ligible character gives us exactly these appearances and this empirical character under the circumstances before us, to answer this surpasses every faculty of our reason, indeed it surpasses the authority of our reason even to ask it . . ." (A557/B585).

16. For an extensive discussion of the relationship between freedom and quantum theory, see Honderich, pp. 304–336 (cf. note 11). See also Daniel Dennett, *Elbow Room: Varieties of Free Will Worth Wanting*, pp. 135–6.

indeterminacies would have had to be resolved in a specific alternative range of ways, and the probability of this occurring is extremely small.

Consequently, it would seem that quantum indeterminacy could not undergird a significant probability for counterfactual events of this magnitude, and that therefore the antecedent probability of the occurrence of the physical component of any counterfactual action is very small. Moreover, the proposal that all or even almost all agent-caused free choices should be for just those possible actions the occurrence of whose physical components has an extremely high antecedent physical probability, and not for any of the alternatives, would appear to fare no better than Kant's. For it too involves coincidences so wild as to render the proposal incredible.

To this challenge the libertarian might reply that the problem of wild coincidences arises only if it turns out that, at the neurophysiological level, counter-factual events do not have significant antecedent probability. But things might be otherwise. There are examples, such as the moving of the needle on a Geiger counter, of microphysical indeterminacies being magnified to significantly indeterminate events at a macrolevel. As Thorp, van Inwagen, and Kane suggest, perhaps similar magnifications occur in the brain.[17] Clarke inspires the suggestion that an agent-causal libertarian might take advantage of macro-level natural indeterminacy by positing agent-causes who, in a particular choice situation in which each of several possible actions have physical components with a significant antecedent probability, have the power to make the difference as to which occurs.[18] In this way, agent causation can be reconciled with the physical laws.

However, this picture does not provide the agent-causal libertarian with a way out of the wild coincidences problem. Suppose that physical components of counterfactual actions do have a significant antecedent probability of occurring. Then, consider the series of possible actions each of which has a physical component whose antecedent probability of occurring is approximately 0.32.[19] Let us first focus just on the class of the physical components to which the antecedent prob-

17. John Thorp, *Free Will* (London: Routledge and Kegan Paul, 1980), pp. 67–71; van Inwagen, *An Essay on Free Will*, pp. 191–201; Kane, *The Significance of Free Will*, pp. 128–30.
18. Randolph Clarke, "Toward a Credible Agent-Causal Account of Free Will," p. 193.
19. Note that this is a class of possible actions. I make this specification because it may be that there is no actual class of this sort that is large enough for the argument to go through.

ability of 0.32 attaches. It would not violate the statistical laws in the sense of being logically incompatible with them if for a large number of instances, the physical components in this class were not actually realized close to 32 percent of the time, but rather, say, 50 percent or even 100 percent of the time. Rather, the force of the statistical law is that for a large number of instances, it would be correct to expect physical components in this class to be realized close to 32 percent of the time. For according to the statistical law, it is overwhelmingly likely that for a large number of instances, these components be actually realized close to 32 percent of the time.

Now consider whether free choices of the sort advocated by the agent-causal libertarian are compatible with what the statistical law leads us to expect about this class. If agent-caused free action were compatible with what according to the statistical law is overwhelmingly likely, then for a large enough number of instances, these possible actions would have to be freely chosen close to 32 percent of the time. Thus, the libertarian proposal to be considered is that in the long run, the possible actions whose physical components have an antecedent probability of 0.32 will almost certainly be freely chosen close to 32 percent of the time. But if the occurrence (or non-occurrence) of these physical components is to be settled by the choices of agent-causes, then their actually being chosen close to 32 percent of the time would constitute a coincidence no less wild than the coincidence of possible actions whose physical components have an antecedent probability of about 0.99 being chosen, in the long run, close to 99 percent of the time. The problem of wild coincidences is therefore independent of the physical components of actions having any particular degree of antecedent probability. Indeed, the problem for the indeterminist version of reconciliationism is essentially the same as that faced by the Kantian proposal just discussed.[20]

Again, there is another way to see this point. In the view under consideration, the standard interpretation of quantum mechanics is true, the brain magnifies significant quantum indeterminacies to the macrolevel, and there are agent-causes who make free choices. We would then expect that in the long run, these choices would be reflected in our bodies as divergences from the statistical laws. The proposal that agent-caused free choices do not diverge from what the statistical laws predict for our bodies, although it involves no logical contradiction, would run

20. Thanks to David Christensen for help in formulating this argument.

so sharply counter to what we would expect as to make the proposal incredible. Both Clarke and Ginet argue that no evidence could tell us whether our world is an indeterministic world with agent causation or an indeterministic world without it.[21] But as we can now see, there is observational evidence that bears strongly on the question. Only in the absence of agent causation should we, in the long run, expect observed frequencies to match the frequencies that our physical theories predict.

To this one might object that it makes sense to claim that the antecedent probabilities match up with causal factors that incline but do not determine agent-causes to act, such as reasons they have for acting. Thus the physical components of a possible action to which the causal factors strongly incline would have a relatively high antecedent probability, and the physical components of a possible action to which causal factors only weakly incline would have a relatively low antecedent probability.[22]

But this suggestion faces the same type of problem that arose for the proposals we have been considering. Consider the series of possible actions each of which has a physical component whose antecedent probability of occurring is approximately 0.87, where this probability accurately reflects the causal factors that incline the agent-cause toward the possible action. If choices are to be compatible with what according to the statistical laws is overwhelmingly likely in the long run, they would have to be made for these possible actions close to 87 percent of the time. In agent-causal libertarianism, however, the causal factors that incline the agent toward an action are not the only causal factors that contribute toward an action. There is, in addition, the agent-cause itself. That the agent-cause is a causal factor distinct from the factors that incline her is underscored by her capacity to act in opposition to them. For instance, even if her reasons incline her very strongly toward performing an action at each opportunity for performing it, she can choose to refrain every time. But what mechanism could then explain the agent-cause's conforming, in the long run, to the same frequency of choices that would be extremely likely to obtain on the basis of the

---

21. Ginet, "Freedom, Responsibility, and Agency," p. 96; Clarke claims that "there is no observational evidence that could tell us whether our world is an indeterministic world with agent causation or an indeterministic world without it . . . even highly improbable behavior could occur in a world without agent causation" ("Toward a Credible Agent-Causal Account of Free Will," p. 199).

22. Clarke makes this objection in personal correspondence.

inclining factors alone? On the agent-causal view, if the agent-cause is truly free, there is no mechanism that could provide this explanation. We would therefore have a match in frequencies without an explanation – a wild coincidence.

To put the point another way, in this model there would be no difference, in the long run, between the actual frequencies of choices and the frequencies that would hold if the choices of the agents were not free at all. There would then be no difference, in the long run, in frequencies of choices, between the situation in which the statistical laws governed all the causal factors that produce the action, and the situation in which they govern only its inclining causes and not the agent-cause. Even if the strength of the inclining causes is reflected in the antecedent probabilities, we would expect evidence of the effect of the additional causal factor, the agent-cause, to show up in the long run in the actual frequencies of choices. If the agent-causal libertarian would have it that in the long run this evidence does not show up, and the frequency of actual agent-caused free choices is close to 87 percent after all, then his proposal, again, involves wild coincidences that make it incredible.

We can now formulate more precisely the fundamental difficulty for the reconciliationist's claim that agent causation is compatible with the physical world's being governed by exceptionless physical laws. Whether such laws are deterministic or statistical, the antecedent probabilities of the physical components of human actions would be fixed. If the laws are deterministic, the antecedent probability of any such component is either 1 or 0. If the laws are those of quantum mechanics on the standard interpretation, such probabilities may span the range from 1 to 0. But regardless of which view is true, the agent-causal libertarian's proposal that the frequencies of agent-caused free choices dovetail with determinate physical probabilities involves coincidences so wild as to make it incredible.

DIFFICULTIES FOR THE OVERRIDING APPROACH

The libertarian might now hold out for the overriding strategy – for the claim that there actually do exist divergences from the probabilities that we would expect without the presence of agent-causes. These divergences are to be found at the interface between the agent-cause and that which lies beyond this entity – an interface that presumably is to be found in the brain. One major difficulty for this strategy, however, is that we have no evidence that such divergences occur. This problem, all by itself, provides a strong reason to reject this approach. One might argue that our belief in moral responsibility provides evidence for the hypothesis of agent causation, and hence for the existence of the relevant divergences. However, it is far from acceptable in physics or neurophysiology to count such a belief as evidence for a hypothesis in these sciences.[23]

On the other hand, nothing we've said conclusively rules out the ultimate success of the overriding strategy. Our knowledge of neurophysiology is limited, and we do not even approach a complete understanding of neurophysiological structures. Thus there remains the epistemic possibility that there are human neurophysiological structures that are significantly disanalogous with anything else in nature we understand. In addition, it is still epistemically possible that such structures will sustain the overriding strategy. In my view, this approach is the best one for libertarians to pursue. But at this point, we have no evidence that its claims are true.

WHY INVOKING *CETERIS PARIBUS* LAWS FAILS TO ADVANCE THE LIBERTARIAN'S CASE

A proponent of the overriding strategy might shift ground slightly and appeal to the *ceteris paribus* character of the laws as formulated by the natural sciences. He might claim that because the physical laws are *ceteris paribus* and not strict, interference of agents in the realm governed by the ordinary physical laws would not result in violations of these laws. Indeed, large bodies of laws in the various sciences are not strict, but have *ceteris paribus* — that is, "other things being equal" — clauses attached to them; they have the form

(i) L, *ceteris paribus*.

In such laws, the "L" part is violable, even though the *ceteris paribus* law itself is not. It turns out that many of the laws of physics are *ceteris paribus* laws. For example, a law for determining acceleration on the basis of gravitation would be *ceteris paribus* since it can be overridden by virtue of effects of other forces, such as electromagnetism. The agent-causal libertarian might conjecture that all physical laws are *ceteris*

---

23. Thanks to David Christensen for this point.

paribus, which leaves room for the "L" parts of all the physical laws being violable by agents, while the laws themselves are not violable.

It might well be conceivable that the "L" part of any physical law can be violated, and thus the existence of physical laws poses no conceptual barrier to agent-causal libertarianism. However, it does not follow that the *ceteris paribus* character of physical laws improves the prospects of this position. This is because

(i) L, *ceteris paribus*

is not the same as

(ii) L obtains, unless it doesn't.

(ii) is vacuously true – every sentence of this form is true. Even,

(iii) The law, *falling bodies are unaffected by gravity*, obtains, unless it doesn't

is true. Furthermore, such sentences can be known to be true independently of any special empirical evidence, since they are logically true. But sentences of the form (i), as they are conceived in scientific theory, are not vacuously or logically true. Indeed, they are conceived as testable by empirical evidence – by observation and experiment.[24] What makes these sentences testable in this way is that there are empirical scientific theories that can back up the *ceteris paribus* conditions. In our example, the *ceteris paribus* law for determining acceleration is a non-vacuous and justified law because we have a well-supported empirical theory according to which other forces can throw off a prediction based on the force of gravitation alone.

For the *ceteris paribus* character of physical laws to count in favor of agent-causal libertarianism, we would need evidence that interference that generates exceptions to physical laws strictly interpreted can be traced to agents. But we have already examined considerations that show that we have no evidence for agents' being the source of such interference. Invoking the *ceteris paribus* character of physical laws, without providing evidence that agents can generate exceptions to physical laws strictly interpreted, fails to advance the overriding strategy.

24. Jerry Fodor, "Making Mind Matter More," in his *A Theory of Content and Other Essays* (Cambridge: MIT Press, 1992), pp. 137–60; Paul Pietroski and Georges Rey, "When Other Things Aren't Equal: Saving *Ceteris Paribus* Laws from Vacuity," *British Journal for the Philosophy of Science* 46 (1995), pp. 80–110.

If the arguments I have presented here are sound, one should be skeptical about the prospects of libertarianism. But for many people, rejecting libertarianism amounts to disavowing the common-sense position. From the libertarian point of view, the alternatives typically seem unintuitive: Either no agent is ever blameworthy for wrongdoing, no matter how calmly planned and executed, or else an agent can be blameworthy for wrongdoing that results from a deterministic causal process that traces back to causal factors that he could not have produced, altered, or prevented. As in other areas in which the scientific image undermines the manifest image, we may well be forced to choose among options that our ordinary sensibilities can never completely accommodate.

4

Problems for Compatibilism

In Chapter 1, I argued that whether an agent could have done otherwise is explanatorily irrelevant to whether he is morally responsible for his action. There I also contended that this argument does not undermine incompatibilism, for there is an incompatibilist intuition that remains untouched by it. The intuition is that if all of our behavior was "in the cards" before we were born, in the sense that things happened before we came to exist that by way of a deterministic causal process, inevitably result in our behavior, then we cannot legitimately be blamed for our wrongdoing. I also remarked that in the dialectic of the debate, one should not expect compatibilists to be moved much by this incompatibilist intuition alone to abandon their position. Rather, the best type of challenge to compatibilism is that this sort of causal determination is in principle as much of a threat to moral responsibility as is covert manipulation. In this chapter, I develop this argument.

This anti-compatibilist strategy plays a pivotal role in my argument for the causal history principle:

(5) An action is free in the sense required for moral responsibility only if the decision to perform it is not an alien-deterministic event, nor a truly random event, nor a partially random event.

Not only does it have the role of establishing that agents cannot be responsible for decisions that are alien-deterministic events, but it also plays a crucial part in showing that agents cannot be responsible for decisions that are truly random or partially random events. For in discussing the latter sorts of decisions in Chapter 2, I argued (against Kane and Ginet) that agents can be no more responsible for decisions that are truly random or partially random events than they can be for those that are alien-deterministic events. Thus, to show that agents cannot be responsible for decisions that are truly random and partially random events, I still need to establish that they cannot be responsible for decisions that are alien-deterministic events.

In the Introduction, I distinguished two types of routes to compatibilism. According to the first type of route, the justification for claims of blameworthiness and praiseworthiness ends in the system of human reactive attitudes, and because moral responsibility has this type of basis, the truth or falsity of determinism is irrelevant to whether we legitimately hold agents to be morally responsible. The second type of route aims to uncover metaphysical necessary and sufficient conditions on moral responsibility that specify a kind of causal integration between agents' psychology and action, and that allow for moral responsibility when actions are causally determined. I shall argue that no proposed version of either of these two routes to compatibilism is ultimately successful, in the final analysis, for the reason that if an agent's decision is an alien-deterministic event, he cannot be its source in the way required for moral responsibility.

THE FIRST ROUTE TO COMPATIBILISM: DETERMINISM AS
IRRELEVANT TO RESPONSIBILITY

Let us begin by examining the first type of route as suggested by Hume and developed by P.F. Strawson. In §VIII of the *Enquiry Concerning Human Understanding*, Hume discusses the effect the thesis of divine determinism does and should have on the moral sentiments. He first argues for a psychological thesis: that the sentiments of approbation and blame cannot be affected by a belief in divine determinism or in any philosophical theory. He then argues for a normative thesis: that these sentiments should not be affected by a belief in divine determinism or in any philosophical theory. Regarding the psychological thesis, Hume claims that

The mind of man is so formed by nature that upon the appearance of certain characters, dispositions, and actions, it immediately feels the sentiment of approbation or blame; nor are there any emotions more essential to its frame and constitution . . . What though philosophical meditations establish a different opinion or conjecture; that everything is right with regard to the whole, and that the qualities, which disturb society are, in the main, as beneficial, and are as suitable to the primary intention of nature, as those which more directly promote its happiness and welfare? Are such remote and uncertain speculations able to counterbalance the sentiments, which arise from the natural and immediate view of the objects? A man who is robbed of a considerable sum; does he find his vexation for the loss any wise diminished by these sublime reflections?

Then, for Hume, the psychological thesis that these sentiments of approbation and blame are inevitable and unalterable leads to a normative conclusion. The passage continues:

Why then *should* his moral resentment against the crime be supposed incompatible with them [these sublime reflections]? Or why *should not* the acknowledgement of a real distinction between vice and virtue be reconcilable to all speculative systems of philosophy, as well as that of a real distinction between personal beauty and deformity? Both these distinctions are founded in the natural sentiments of the human mind: And these sentiments are *not to be controlled or altered* by any philosophical theory or speculation whatsoever.[1]

Because in certain circumstances, having the sentiments of approbation and blame is inevitable and unalterable by us, having these sentiments is compatible with and should not be controlled or altered by any philosophical theory.

Strawson's view is similar.[2] He begins his account by characterizing two opposing participants in the controversy about determinism and moral responsibility – the "optimist" and the "pessimist." The optimist is a compatibilist of the sort who justifies the practices of moral disapproval and punishment not on the ground that they express reactive attitudes, but on the basis of their social utility.[3] The pessimist is an incompatibilist who wants libertarianism to be true. Strawson rejects the incompatibilism and libertarianism of the pessimist, but he also maintains, together with the pessimist, that the optimist is missing something important in the account of moral responsibility.

---

1. David Hume, *Enquiry Concerning Human Understanding*, ed. Eric Steinberg (Indianapolis: Hackett Publishing Co., 1981), p. 68. Similar claims about the affinity between Hume's and Strawson's views are made by Paul Russell in his *Freedom and Moral Sentiment* (New York: Oxford University Press, 1995), pp. 71–84.
2. P.F. Strawson, "Freedom and Resentment," in Gary Watson ed., *Free Will* (Oxford: Oxford University Press, 1982), pp. 59–80, originally published in *Proceedings of the British Academy* 48 (1962), pp. 1–25.
3. For optimism of the sort Strawson describes, see Moritz Schlick, "When Is a Man Responsible?" and J.J.C. Smart, "Free Will, Praise, and Blame."

Rather than justifying the practice of holding people morally responsible solely on social utilitarian grounds, it is the participant reactive attitudes – the reactive attitudes to which people are subject by virtue of participation in ordinary interpersonal relationships – that play the crucial role in Strawson's account. He suggests that these attitudes supply what is missing in the optimist's explanation. It is the reactive attitudes, and the reactive attitudes alone, that provide the foundation for our holding people morally responsible. To secure his case for compatibilism, Strawson, like Hume, argues first for a psychological thesis, that the reactive attitudes *cannot* be affected by a belief in universal determinism, and then for a normative thesis, that they *should not* be affected by this belief. Consequently, what fills the role of that something the pessimist rightly sees is missing in the optimist's account of our moral life – our reactive attitudes – cannot and should not be undermined by a belief in universal determinism.

Participant reactive attitudes are "natural human reactions to the good or ill will of others towards us, as displayed in *their attitudes and actions*," for example, gratitude, moral resentment, forgiveness and love.[4] These attitudes are central features of ordinary human interpersonal relationships. Would and should they be undermined by a belief in the thesis of universal determinism?

> . . . would, or should, the acceptance of the truth of the thesis lead to the decay or repudiation of all such attitudes? Would, or should, it mean the end of gratitude, resentment, and forgiveness; of all reciprocated adult loves; of all the essentially *personal* antagonisms?[5]

According to Strawson, sometimes we can, and at times we appropriately do, forgo or suspend reactive attitudes. For example, "Type 1" considerations are those that "invite us to view an *injury* as one in respect of which a particular one of these attitudes is inappropriate," but "do not invite us to view the *agent* as one in respect of whom these attitudes are inappropriate." If someone spills his drink on your shirt but you find out that he did it by accident and not as a result of negligence, or if someone makes a gratuitously nasty remark, but you discover that she is temporarily under great stress, then you are capable of suspending normal reactive attitudes. But you do not then view the agent as generally an inappropriate subject of the reactive attitudes.[6]

---

4. Strawson, p. 67.   5. Ibid., p. 67.   6. Ibid., pp. 64–5.

"Type 2" considerations have more radical but nevertheless legitimate consequences. They invite us to view the agent as one in respect of whom these attitudes are inappropriate. This involves adopting the objective attitude toward him:

To adopt the objective attitude to another human being is to see him, perhaps, as an object of social policy; as a subject for what, in a wide range of sense, might be called treatment; as something certainly to be taken account, perhaps precautionary account, of; to be managed or handled or cured or trained; perhaps simply to be avoided . . . The objective attitude may be emotionally toned in many ways: it may include repulsion or fear, it may include pity or love, though not all kinds of love. But it cannot include the range of reactive feelings and attitudes which belong to involvement or participation with others in interpersonal human relationships; it cannot include resentment, gratitude, forgiveness, anger, or the sort of love which two adults can sometimes be said to feel reciprocally, for each other.[7]

Objectivity of attitude is befitting, for example, with regard to people who suffer from certain sorts of mental illness. But none of this shows that a belief in universal determinism would lead to a suspension of reactive attitudes:

The human commitment to participation in ordinary interpersonal relationships is, I think, too thoroughgoing and deeply rooted for us to take seriously the thought that a general theoretical conviction might so change our world that, in it, there were no longer any such things as inter-personal relationships as we normally understand them; and being involved in inter-personal relationships as we normally understand them precisely is being exposed to the range of reactive attitudes and feelings that is in question.[8]

Interpersonal relationships lie at the very core of the human way of existing. Being subject to the reactive attitudes is of a piece with participation in such relationships. Since no merely theoretical conviction could keep us from relating to each other in the ordinary interpersonal way, no such conviction could undermine our having the reactive attitudes. Because these attitudes comprise the foundation of our holding each other morally responsible, a belief in determinism is also incapable of dislodging this practice.

Strawson's answer to the "should" question, or more precisely, to someone who thinks that his answer to the "would" question leaves the "should" question unanswered is this:

---

7. Strawson, p. 66.   8. Ibid., p. 68.

First, . . . such a question could seem real only to one who has utterly failed to grasp the purport of the preceding answer . . . the commitment [to ordinary inter-personal relationships] is part of the general framework of human life, not something that can come up for review as particular cases can come up for review within this general framework. . . . [S]econd, . . . if we could imagine what we cannot have, viz. a choice in this matter, then we could choose rationally only in the light of an assessment of the gains and losses of human life, its enrichment or impoverishment, and the truth or falsity of a general thesis of determinism would not bear on the rationality of *this* choice.[9]

Thus, according to Strawson, both the optimist and the pessimist are wrong in thinking that the reactive attitudes must be justified from outside of the practice in which these attitudes are embedded. This is in fact where their deepest mistake lies. The framework of these attitudes "neither calls for, nor permits, an external 'rational' justification."[10] Against the optimist, Strawson also says: "Our practices do not merely exploit our natures, they express them."[11] This last claim echoes the anti-rationalist views of Hume and Wittgenstein, according to which all justification comes or must come to an end somewhere, and this end is (often) to be found in (the characterization of) a human practice such as induction, or mathematics, or interpersonal relationships. Demands for justification are legitimate only within such practices, and demanding justification for an entire practice is philosophical error.

Furthermore, assuming that a belief in determinism did challenge the ordinary reactive attitudes, and that we could choose to rid ourselves of these attitudes and the associated practice of holding people morally responsible, the decision would have to be made on the basis of practical considerations alone. A theoretical conviction would have no role to play in this assessment. By implication, Strawson maintains that the practical considerations would weigh very heavily in favor of retaining the reactive attitudes, and thus also retaining our practice of holding people morally responsible.

CRITICISMS OF STRAWSON'S VIEW

How should we assess the first route to compatibilism? Drawing on the ample work others have done on this issue, I will develop three points

---

9.   Strawson, p. 70.   10.   Ibid., p. 78.   11.   Ibid, p. 80.

of disagreement that have special importance for my position.[12] Two of these are pertinent to the claim that living as a hard incompatibilist is a genuine and attractive possibility. The first of these is that Strawson is mistaken to hold that the reactive attitudes cannot be affected by the belief that determinism is true. The second is that supposing a belief in determinism did issue in a theoretical or epistemic conflict with the ordinary reactive attitudes, it is not clear that rational appraisal of these attitudes would always favor retention over revision. The third point of disagreement is germane to my defense of an incompatibilist condition on the causal history of actions. I believe Strawson is wrong to maintain that a theoretical challenge to the reactive attitudes based on the thesis of universal determinism is external to the practice of holding people morally responsible, and therefore illegitimate. Rather, in my view, exemptions from moral responsibility that are widely regarded as acceptable and thus internal to the practice will generalize to an incompatibilist condition on moral responsibility.[13]

First, then, as a matter of psychological fact, it is plausible that the reactive attitudes are not immune from alteration by a belief in determinism. Gary Watson provides a compelling example that may tell against the view that Hume and Strawson defend. A man named Robert Harris brutally murdered two teenage boys in California in 1978. Watson points out that when we read an account of these murders, "we respond to his heartlessness and viciousness with loathing."[14] But an account of the atrocious abuse Harris suffered as a child "gives pause to the reactive attitudes."[15] Upon absorbing such information, not everyone relinquishes his attitude of indignation completely, but this attitude is at least typically tempered. It is not only that we are persuaded to feel pity for the criminal. Not implausibly, our attitude of indignation is mitigated by our coming to believe that there were

12. See, in particular, Jonathan Bennett, "Accountability," in *Philosophical Subjects*, ed. Zak van Straaten (Oxford: Oxford University Press, 1980), pp. 74–91; Galen Strawson, *Freedom and Belief*, pp. 84–92; Gary Watson, "Responsibility and the Limits of Evil"; Kane, *The Significance of Free Will*, pp. 83–5; and Saul Smilansky, "Can a Determinist Respect Herself," pp. 95–6. Despite the criticisms he raises, Watson defends a broadly Strawsonian perspective, as does Michael McKenna in "The Limits of Evil and the Role of Moral Address: A Defense of Strawsonian Compatibilism," *The Journal of Ethics* 2 (1998), pp. 123–42.
13. This is Wallace's formulation; cf. *Responsibility and the Moral Sentiments* (Cambridge: Harvard University Press, 1994), pp. 114–17.
14. Watson, pp. 268–71.
15. Ibid., pp. 272–4.

factors beyond his control that causally determined certain aspects of his character to be as they were.

One might argue that although belief in determinism about a particular situation can affect reactive attitudes, the more general belief in universal determinism never can. Two possible reasons for this claim might be gleaned from Hume's rhetorical question, "Are such remote and uncertain speculations able to counterbalance the sentiments, which arise from a natural and immediate view of the objects?"[16] One reason is that the thesis of universal determinism is uncertain – as is any other responsibility-threatening general proposition. But while such general propositions – for example, that all events are alien-deterministic, partially random, or truly random – are indeed uncertain, some may also be fairly well-substantiated. Moreover, some might well be no less well-grounded than other general claims that clearly can affect our attitudes and our actions, such as the proposal that if the rate of unemployment falls below 5.3 percent, significant inflation fueled by a wage-price spiral will result. Another reason for maintaining that the belief in universal determinism cannot affect the reactive attitudes is that this thesis is remote in the sense that it is not vivid. But while particular cases of determinism can be made especially vivid, the thesis of universal determinism can quite easily be made as vivid as other general propositions that can affect our attitudes and our actions, such as this last claim about inflation.

It would be implausible to maintain that in every case, the presence or the intensity of one's reactive attitudes can be affected by a belief in determinism. Sometimes a wrong committed might be too horrible for such a belief to have any effect on one's reactions. The Stoics maintained that we can always prevent or eradicate attitudes like grief and anger, regardless of their intensity, with the aid of a determinist conviction. But they surely overestimated the extent of the control we have over our emotional lives. If someone were brutally to murder your family, it might well be psychologically impossible for you ever to eradicate feelings of intense anger toward the killer. This fails to show, however, that a determinist conviction cannot affect reactive attitudes, even in typical cases.

The second criticism of Strawson is that assuming a belief in determinism would conflict with the ordinary reactive attitudes, it is not clear that a rational assessment of these attitudes would always favor

16. Hume, *Enquiry Concerning Human Understanding*, p. 68.

retaining as opposed to revising them. Suppose for the sake of argument that the practice of holding people morally responsible does make an indeterministic presupposition about human agency, and that we have a justified belief that determinism is true. Imagine that one is indignant with a friend – a normal human being – because he has intentionally betrayed a confidence. Strawson assumes that in this situation, it would typically be rational to maintain one's indignation in such circumstances, for if one did not, interpersonal human relationships would be undermined.

A determinist who acknowledged that a theoretical conviction could affect the reactive attitudes, but that adopting an objectivity of attitude would be practically irrational by virtue of being destructive of human relationships, might well override theoretical rationality by retaining her normal reactive attitudes.[17] If she acted in this way, however, she would be reduced to the uncomfortable position of maintaining attitudes that are theoretically irrational. But the determinist is not clearly forced into such a predicament. For first, some ordinary reactive attitudes that would be irrational are not obviously required for good interpersonal relationships. In addition, the reactive attitudes one would want to retain might not be undermined, or else they could have aspects or analogs that have no false presuppositions. These aspects and analogs might well not be akin to Strawson's objectivity of attitude, and they may be sufficient to sustain good interpersonal relationships. I shall develop these claims in detail in Chapter 7. For now, let us consider the examples of moral resentment and indignation.

For an interpersonal relationship to work well, is it necessary that the participants typically be morally resentful upon being wronged? An important function of resentment in such circumstances is to convey the distress suffered because of the wrongdoing. Such distress could certainly be discussed without such attitudes. But this procedure would be much too clinical, one might object. Emotional attitudes must be expressed in such circumstances if the relationship is to have significant psychological depth. However, consider again how one's attitude toward Harris might change as a result of learning his past. Indignation gradually gives way to a kind of moral sadness – a sadness not only about

---

17. One is irrational in the theoretical sense when, for example, one has a belief that has no justification, or a belief one knows to be false, or knows might well be false, and one is irrational in the practical sense if, for instance, one does something one knows will frustrate what one wants, all things considered.

his past but also for his character and his horrible actions. This kind of moral sadness is a type of attitude that would not be undermined by a belief in determinism. Furthermore, I suspect that it can play much of the role that resentment and indignation more typically have in human relationships, and that moral sadness will be at least as effective in sustaining emotional depth as its more prevalent blame-ascribing counterparts. Indeed, in the final chapter, I shall argue that human relationships and emotional depth may be improved by putting aside attitudes such as resentment and indignation, which depend on viewing agents as blameworthy for wrongdoing.

How can we deal with our ordinary reactive attitudes − those that are threatened by a belief in determinism − if they are inevitable or extremely difficult to alter, yet theoretically irrational and unfair? If we came to the conclusion that hard determinism (or hard incompatibilism) is true, and yet the ordinary reactive attitudes were inevitable or largely so, it would nevertheless seem inappropriate to maintain the way we regarded those attitudes. As Wallace points out:

> Being caught up in the practice of holding people morally responsible, and also committed to the moral norms of fairness, we might well be led to the conclusion that the practice is essentially unfair, and this conclusion would remain an important and troubling one, even if it would not lead us to cease holding people responsible.[18]

Moreover, even apart from considerations of freedom and determinism, most of us have had unfair or irrational attitudes toward others that were difficult or even impossible to eradicate. One is then sad and embarrassed that one has the attitudes in question, avoids indulging or reveling in them, does what one can to rid oneself of them, and one certainly does not justify practical decisions on their basis. This is how it would be best to deal with inescapable resentment and indignation if hard determinism is true, and this way of managing these attitudes does seem to be within our range of capability.

The third criticism is that a theoretical challenge to the reactive attitudes based on the thesis of universal determinism is not external to the practice of holding people morally responsible, and hence, contrary to Strawson's claim, is not illegitimate. First of all, analogies from other areas of ethical concern show that a system of attitudes can be subject to justificatory pressures from highly general theoretical beliefs. For example,

---

18. Wallace, *Responsibility and the Moral Sentiments*, p. 99.

some sexist and racist attitudes could be undermined by the following reflection: There is no difference across race and gender in capacities for theoretical and practical reasoning, for creative achievement, and for developing good human relationships. This reflection could and should radically alter human attitudes and practices, even if they are deeply rooted and longstanding. Despite its general and theoretical nature, the way in which such reflection affects these changes is legitimate and normative. Furthermore, as Galen Strawson emphasizes, the idea that the incompatibilist challenge to the reactive attitudes simply opposes abstract theory to deep human commitments is implausible. For "the fact that the incompatibilist intuition has so much power for us is as much a natural fact about cogitative beings like ourselves as is the fact of our quite unreflective commitment to the reactive attitudes."[19] He adds that "the roots of the incompatibilist intuition lie deep in the very reactive attitudes that are invoked to undercut it."[20] Indeed, many of us have a strong and visceral feeling that it is unfair to regard causally determined agents as deserving of blame for their wrongdoings.

In my view, the best way to challenge Strawson on this issue is by way of what Wallace calls a *generalization strategy*. An approach of this sort argues from widely accepted excuses or exemptions to the claim that there is an incompatibilist requirement on moral responsibility.[21] Since the excuses and exemptions that form the basis of the argument are widely accepted, they are plausibly features internal to the practice of holding people morally responsible. Moreover, generalization is also an internal feature of this practice. If no relevant moral difference can be found between two agents in distinct situations, it is a feature of the practice of holding people morally responsible that if one agent is legitimately exempted from moral responsibility, so is the other.

The details of my argument involve situations in which agents are manipulated to perform actions in ways that would be commonly judged to exempt them from moral responsibility, and generalizing from these situations to any case of causal determination. Since this approach will also serve as part of my argument against the sufficiency of any causal integrationist condition, I will postpone the rest of the discussion of the third criticism until after this argument is complete. There is in addition another reason to wait. Compatibilists may want to block the generalization strategy by arguing that there is a

19. Strawson, *Freedom and Belief*, p. 88; cf. Kane, *The Significance of Free Will*, pp. 83–5.
20. Ibid., p. 88.
21. Wallace, pp. 114–17.

compatibilist condition that captures the legitimate generalizations from acceptable excuses and exemptions. This is precisely Wallace's approach. In response, I contend that no principle that has been proposed provides what the compatibilist needs. If my argument is successful, this compatibilist response to the generalization strategy will be ineffective, and an incompatibilist condition should be all the more attractive.

THE SECOND ROUTE TO COMPATIBILISM: CAUSAL INTEGRATIONIST CONDITIONS

The second route attempts to formulate and defend metaphysical conditions for moral responsibility that are not threatened by determinism or its relatives. Many compatibilists have advanced their own versions as an alternative or supplement to arguing against incompatibilist conditions. These conditions, like their incompatibilist rivals, attempt to explain why we should hold agents morally responsible in certain situations, and why we should exempt them in others. But unlike the incompatibilist conditions, they are formulated so as not to exempt agents in all cases of causal determination. These compatibilist conditions tie moral responsibility to actions that are in some way or another causally integrated with features of the agent's psychology.

Let us examine four prominent compatibilist conditions of this sort – those developed by Hume and Ayer, Frankfurt, Fischer and Ravizza, and Wallace. I shall argue that each of their proposals can be undermined. In my criticisms, I will emphasize that none of these philosophers provides sufficient conditions for moral responsibility. I also maintain that except for Wallace, each fails to supply necessary conditions, but for the most part I will develop this type of argument in footnotes. I emphasize sufficiency because an incompatibilist like myself should have no issue with the existence of compatibilist necessary conditions – for example, that to be morally responsible for an action, an agent must have the ability to act on moral reasons. However, if there are compatibilist sufficient conditions on moral responsibility – in particular, if there are cases in which an agent is causally determined, and because a compatibilist condition holds, the agent is morally responsible – then incomptibilism turns out to be false.

One should note that compatibilists typically formulate their conditions as necessary but not as sufficient for moral responsibility. Still, they do not intend their conditions to function merely as necessary conditions. Suppose an incompatibilist argued that an indeterminist necessary condition is needed to supplement some compatibilist condition. The compatibilist would not respond by saying that because her compatibilist formulation was intended only as a necessary condition, her view had not been challenged. True, necessary conditions for moral responsibility do play an important role in a compatibilist account. Incompatibilists make their case by proposing necessary conditions for moral responsibility that rule out compatibilism, and compatibilists must respond by proposing alternative necessary conditions. But compatibilists also need to formulate sufficient conditions for moral responsibility, since it is essential to their case that we can attribute moral responsibility in certain standard situations. This could not be done with necessary conditions alone – sufficient conditions are obviously required.

Hume and Ayer

Perhaps the most prominent sort of causal integrationism is found in the Humean tradition.[22] This tradition actually features a family of compatibilist conditions. First, in the *Treatise of Human Nature*, Hume characterizes *liberty of spontaneity* as "that which is opposed to violence."[23] He appears to mean that an action is performed with liberty of spontaneity just in case the agent is not constrained to act as she does. A.J. Ayer's conception of free action is similar:

. . . we began with the assumption that freedom is contrasted with causality. But this assumption has led us into difficulties and I now wish to suggest that it is mistaken. For it is not, I think, causality that freedom is to be contrasted with, but constraint . . . If I am constrained, I do not act freely.[24]

Ayer's version of compatibilism can be conceived as having the following structure. It is first accepted that all actions are causally determined. A distinction is then made between the sorts of causal determination that are responsibility-undermining and those that are not. As it does for the libertarian, this distinction must reflect an intuitive division between actions that genuinely belong to the agent and those that do not. Ayer's compatibilism can be viewed as proposing that an action really belongs to the agent, and is thus free in the sense

22. Hume, *A Treatise of Human Nature*, pp. 399–412; *An Enquiry Concerning Human Understanding*, §8; A.J. Ayer, "Freedom and Necessity."
23. Hume, *Treatise of Human Nature*, p. 407.
24. Ayer, "Freedom and Necessity," p. 19.

required for moral responsibility, only if desires that genuinely belong to the agent play the right role in the causal history of the action. When an agent is under constraint, desires that genuinely belong to the agent do not play the causal role necessary for his action to be free in the sense required for moral responsibility.

As has often been pointed out, however, absence of constraint is not clearly a necessary condition for moral responsibility. One can be morally responsible when one acts under the sort of constraint that is standardly conceived as coercion. Suppose someone holds a gun to my head and threatens to kill me unless I kill five other people, and I then proceed to kill them. I could clearly be morally responsible for this action, despite the fact that I was coerced and thus constrained. Moreover, it seems that one can be morally responsible even if one acts under certain internal sorts of constraint. Kleptomania is often cited as a paradigm of such a condition.[25] But whether kleptomania undermines responsibility depends on certain characteristics of this illness. If it merely strongly inclines an agent toward stealing, and he can nevertheless resist the inclination, then this illness does not obviously undermine moral responsibility.

One response to these criticisms is to claim that responsibility-undermining constraints are those that render actions intuitively irresistible. If, for example, kleptomania makes stealing irresistible for the agent, then his moral responsibility for stealing will be undermined. Our intuitions about hypnosis also fit this picture. We think that when an agent is hypnotized so that she can no longer resist performing an action, then she is not morally responsible.[26] Accordingly, the second of the Humean family of compatibilist conditions is that an agent is morally responsible only if the desire that produces the action is not irresistible for her.

The third of this family of conditions is that an agent is morally responsible for an action only if it flows from the "durable and con-

25. Ayer, "Freedom and Necessity," pp. 20–1.
26. It might be argued that the drug addict is morally responsible for taking the drug despite the fact that he acts from an irresistible desire if his becoming a drug addict in the first place was not a result of an irresistible desire of his. Some have the intuition that under these circumstances, the addict is responsible for becoming a drug addict but not for taking the drug. If he is responsible for taking the drug, then the irresistibility theorist would have to claim something of the following sort: An agent is morally responsible for an action only if it is not the case that: the action results from an irresistible desire of his and if it (the desire) results from an action or omission of his, the action or omission in turn results from an irresistible desire of his.

stant" character of the agent.[27] One difficulty for this condition is that an agent who kills his boss for firing him could then be exempt from moral responsibility if he has been, say, law-abiding and non-abusive up to that time. In such cases, the action will be out of character, but intuitively the agent could still be morally responsible. Perhaps this condition might be revised and developed so as to eliminate this type of implausible consequence.[28]

Frankfurt

In Frankfurt's view, an action is free in the sense required for moral responsibility when the first-order desire that results in action conforms in a certain way to the agent's second-order desires.[29] Understanding Frankfurt's causal integrationist version of compatibilism depends on a clear grasp of a series of notions he develops in his article "Freedom of the Will and the Concept of a Person." Let us set them out in order.

1. **First-order desires** are identified by statements of the form "A wants to X," in which the term "to X" refers to an action.
2. The **desire** identified by "A wants to X" is (part of) A's will just in case "A wants to X" is either the desire by which he is motivated in some action he performs or the desire by which he will or would be motivated when or if he acts. The will consists in effective desires, as opposed to, for example, desires that one has that never would result in action.
3. **Second-order desires** are identified by statements of the form "A wants to X," in which the term "to X" refers to a first-order desire.
4. A **second-order volition** is a kind of second-order desire, and is identified by a statement of the form "A wants to want X," when it is used to mean that A wants X to be part of his will – that is, he wants to will X (and not that A wants merely to want X without willing X).[30]

27. Hume, *Treatise of Human Nature*, p. 411.
28. A fourth member of the Humean family invokes a conception of freedom of action: "By liberty, then, we can only mean a power of acting or not acting, according to the determinations of the will; that is if we choose to remain at rest we may; if we choose to move, we also may" (*Enquiry*, §8, p. 63). This is Hume's compatibilist attempt to develop the intuition that liberty involves having alternative possibilities. I will not consider this view here, since I have appraised the significance of alternative possibilities for moral responsibility in Chapter 1.
29. Harry Frankfurt, "Freedom of the Will and the Concept of a Person," *Journal of Philosophy* 68 (1971), pp. 5–20; reprinted in Gary Watson, ed., *Free Will* (Oxford: Oxford University Press, 1982), pp. 81–95.
30. For characterizations 1–4, see Frankfurt, "Freedom of the Will and the Concept of a Person," pp. 13–15.

5. A **person** is an agent who has first-order desires and second-order volitions (and is a type of entity "for whom the freedom of its will may be a problem").[31]
6. An agent has **freedom of the will** just in case "he is free to will what he wants to will, or to have the will he wants." A person exercises freedom of the will "in securing the conformity of his will to his second-order volitions." A person's lack of freedom of the will is manifest, for example, when he wants to will X but does not will X, or when he wants to will X and he wills X but this conformity is "not his own doing but only a happy chance." In addition, Frankfurt says "a person's will is free only if he is free to have the will he wants. This means that with regard to any of his first-order desires, he is free to make that desire his will or to make some other first-order desire his will instead."
7. A person **acts freely and of his own free will** just in case he wills X and wants to will X, and wills X because he wants to will X. (I will refer to this sort of causal integration as acting freely in Frankfurt's sense.)
8. Freedom of the will is not required for moral responsibility, but acting freely and of one's own free will is.[32]

Suppose that Ms. Peacock has killed Ms. Scarlet, and this is what she wanted to do, and that she did it because she wanted to do it, and that the will by which she was moved when she did it was her will because it was the will she wanted. According to Frankfurt, Peacock acted freely in the sense required for moral responsibility. All that is required for moral responsibility at the level of second-order desires is that she have a second-order desire that a first-order desire to kill Scarlet be effective, and that this first-order desire be effective because it is the one she desires.

Like Ayer, Frankfurt can also be viewed as attempting to capture the intuition that for an agent to be morally responsible for an action is for it to be really his. What it is for an action to really belong to an agent is, primarily, for him to have endorsed and produced his will to perform it in the right way. For him to endorse and produce his will to perform it in the right way, he must have a second-order desire to will to perform it, and his will must be his will because he has this second-order desire. What is required is identification at the level of second-order desire with his will, and that the second-order desire be efficacious in producing the will he has.

31. Frankfurt, "Freedom of the Will and the Concept of a Person," pp. 16, 19.
32. For characterizations 1–4, see Frankfurt, "Freedom of the Will and the Concept of a Person," pp. 20–24.

Frankfurt specifies two types of circumstance in which one is not free in the sense required for moral responsibility. They are, first, the "Type B situations," in which

the inner circumstances of his action are discordant with the agent's desires. What motivates his action is a desire by which, given the alternatives he confronts, he does not want to be moved to act. There is a conflict within him between a first-order desire to do what he actually does and a second-order volition that his first-order desire not be effective in determining his action.[33]

An example of this type of situation is that of the unwilling addict who, despite his second-order volition that his desire to take a drug not move him to action, is nevertheless moved to action by that desire to take the drug. In this situation, he wills to take the drug, but he does not want to will to take the drug, and he does not will to take the drug because he wants to will to take the drug. Thus in taking the drug he does not act freely in Frankfurt's sense, and thus he does not satisfy Frankfurt's necessary condition on moral responsibility.

A second circumstance in which an agent is not free in the sense required for moral responsibility is one in which the agent is coerced in a certain way without a second-order volition playing any role in the psychology of the coercion. These "Type C situations" are those in which "the agent acts because of the irresistibility of a desire without attempting to prevent that desire from determining his action." The agent "is not defeated by the desire . . . since he does not oppose a second-order volition to it," and he is not merely autonomous within an unsatisfactory set of alternatives "since his action does not result from an effective choice on his part concerning what to do." For example, suppose that an addict takes a drug because of the irresistibility of his desire to do so, and that he does not attempt to prevent the desire to take the drug from causing his action. Suppose further that he has no desire that his desire to take the drug not be effective in action, and that he has no desire that a desire not to take the drug be effective in action. Then, in Frankfurt's view, the addict is not morally responsible for taking the drug. Although he wills to take the drug, it is not the case that he wants to will to take it, nor that he wills to take the drug because he wants to will to take it.

33. Frankfurt, "Three Concepts of Free Action: II," in *Moral Responsibility*, John Martin Fischer, ed. (Ithaca: Cornell University Press, 1986), pp. 113–23, at p. 114.

The difference between Type B and Type C situations is that in Type B situations, a second-order volition – a desire that an effective first-order desire not be effective – plays an important role, whereas for an agent in a Type C situation, "no second-order volition plays a role in the economy of his desires."[34] But in both kinds of situations, the agent is not morally responsible for his action because he does not act freely in Frankfurt's sense.

Fischer and Ravizza

It is attractive to hold that the feature of human agency that under-girds moral responsibility is the capacity to regulate behavior by reasons. Moral responsibility appears closely linked to this capacity. When we take people to be the sorts of beings who are morally responsible, we expect them to govern their behavior by reasons by, for example, choosing on the basis of available reasons, considering good reasons that were previously ignored, and weighing heretofore unappreciated reasons differently. Fischer and Ravizza as well as Wallace advocate positions in

---

34. Frankfurt, "Three Concepts of Free Action: II," pp. 115–16. Frankfurt's position has been criticized by many authors; see, for example, Gary Watson, "Free Agency," in *Free Will*, ed. Gary Watson, pp. 96–110, originally published in the *Journal of Philosophy* 72 (1975), pp. 205–220; David Zimmerman, "Hierarchical Motivation and the Freedom of the Will," *Pacific Philosophical Quarterly* 62 (1981), pp. 354–68; David Shatz, "Free Will and the Structure of Values," *Midwest Studies in Philosophy* 10 (1985), pp. 451–82; Fischer, *The Metaphysics of Free Will*, pp. 208–9; Kane, *The Significance of Free Will*, pp. 61–9; Eleanore Stump, "Persons: Identification and Freedom," *Philosophical Topics* 24 (1996), pp. 183–214; Haji, *Moral Appraisability*, pp. 70–5. My criticism of Frankfurt's position is indebted to these authors. In my view, acting freely in Frankfurt's sense is also not necessary for moral responsibility. An agent can be morally responsible even in a Type B or a Type C situation. For a Type B situation, suppose that Professor Plum wants to humiliate his student, Ms. Scarlet, for a philosophical error she has made while asking a question. The professor nevertheless has a second-order volition for his desire to humiliate Scarlet not to be effective in action. However, because he could have been more resolute, he could have rendered this second-order volition effective and thus refrained from humiliating Scarlet. Here, Plum could be morally responsible. For a Type C scenario, imagine that Ms. White resolutely devotes herself to doing right. But suppose that in the process, she never forms second-order volitions for her desires to do what is right to be effective in action (cf. Watson, "Free Agency," pp. 108–9). Her desires never concern the character of her will, but rather aim directly at the good of those around her. Eventually she becomes psychologically incapable of doing wrong in normal circumstances. One day she sees a drowning child. She is at this time psychologically incapable of not attempting to save him, and accordingly an irresistible desire is formed in her to try. She jumps in, and succeeds in saving the child. White could be morally responsible, despite the irresistibility of her desire to attempt to save the child, and the absence of relevant second-order volitions.

which a capacity to regulate one's behavior by reasons is the crucial condition for moral responsibility.

In the view Fischer initially developed, what is required for moral responsibility is a particular sort of *responsiveness to reasons*.[35] He first contends that there is a strong notion of reasons–responsiveness that is clearly not required for moral responsibility:

An agent is *strongly reasons-responsive* when a certain kind K of mechanism, which involves the agent's rational consideration of reasons relevant to the situation, issues in action, and if there were sufficient reasons for her to do otherwise than she actually does, she would be receptive to these reasons and would have chosen and done otherwise by the efficacy of the same deliberative mechanism that actually results in the action.[36]

By "sufficient reason," Fischer means "justificatorily sufficient reason" – that is, a reason that is, all things considered, an agent's strongest or best reason for action.[37] If this strong kind of reasons-responsiveness were required, then someone who could fail to be aware of sufficient reasons to do otherwise, or who upon recognizing them could disregard them, would not be morally responsible, and this is all very counter–intuitive. Fischer then argues that a weaker notion of reasons-responsiveness is required for moral responsibility:

An agent is *weakly reasons-responsive* when a certain kind K of mechanism, which involves the agent's rational consideration of reasons relevant to the situation, issues in action, and in *at least some alternative circumstances* in which there are sufficient reasons for her to do otherwise than she actually does, she would be receptive to these reasons and would have chosen and done otherwise by the efficacy of the same deliberative mechanism that actually results in the action.[38]

Hence, I am morally responsible when I decide to pay the phone bill, for the usual reasons, next week rather than today if, in circumstances

---

35. Bernard Gert and Timothy J. Duggan, "Free Will as the Ability to Will," *Noûs* XIII (May 1979), pp. 197–217, reprinted in *Moral Responsibility*, ed. John Martin Fischer (Ithaca: Cornell University Press, 1986), pp. 205–24; Fischer, "Responsiveness and Moral Responsibility," in *Responsibility, Character, and the Emotions*, Ferdinand Schoeman, ed. (Cambridge: Cambridge University Press, 1987), pp. 81–106, at pp. 88–9; Fischer, *The Metaphysics of Free Will*, pp. 160–89.
36. Fischer, "Responsiveness and Moral Responsibility," p. 86; *The Metaphysics of Free Will*, p. 164.
37. John Martin Fischer and Mark Ravizza, *Responsibility and Control: A Theory of Moral Responsibility*, pp. 41–2, note 13.
38. Fischer, "Responsiveness and Moral Responsibility," p. 88; *The Metaphysics of Free Will*, pp. 166–7.

in which I knew that my phone would be disconnected if I did not pay today – and I have the ordinary sufficient reasons to want my phone to work – I would, by the deliberative mechanism that actually results in my deciding to pay next week, appreciate the different reasons and decide to pay today instead. If my practical reasoning would not differ in varying circumstances in which there are sufficient reasons to do otherwise, I am not morally responsible. An agent is not morally responsible when he steals the merchandise, if in none of the circumstances where there is sufficient reason to refrain from stealing the merchandise, he would refrain from doing so.

Fischer intends his account to capture ordinary intuitions about when people are morally responsible and when they are not. For example, according to ordinary intuitions, an irresistible urge to do something can rule out moral responsibility. Fischer considers the case of Jim, who has an irresistible urge to take a drug. There will be some physical process of kind P taking place in Jim's nervous system that accounts for his having and acting on this irresistible urge. Fischer argues:

I believe that what underlies our intuitive claim that Jim is not morally responsible for taking the drug is that the relevant kind of mechanism issuing in Jim's taking the drug is of physical kind P, and that a mechanism of kind P is not reasons-responsive. When an agent acts from a literally irresistible urge, he is undergoing a kind of physical process that is not reasons-responsive, and it is this lack of reasons-responsiveness of the actual physical process that rules out moral responsibility.[39]

In Fischer's view, the fact that irresistibility of an action is intuitively responsibility-undermining in these sorts of cases can be explained by the weak reasons-responsiveness criterion. This criterion, he claims, can do so without supplemental help from an incompatibilist condition.

Partly in response to certain kinds of counterexamples, Fischer and Ravizza have more recently advocated a revised condition for moral responsibility, which they call *moderate reasons-responsiveness*.[40] It is just like weak reasons-responsiveness, except for the following changes:

39. Fischer, "Responsiveness and Moral Responsibility," p. 97; *The Metaphysics of Free Will*, pp. 173–4.
40. Fischer and Ravizza, *Responsibility and Control: A Theory of Moral Responsibility*, pp. 69–82.

(a) In the alternative situation in which there is sufficient reason to do otherwise and the agent does otherwise, the agent performs the action for that (sufficient) reason.

(b) The agent must show regularity in recognizing reasons – the agent must be receptive to a pattern of reasons. (This condition rules out situations in which an agent is weakly reasons-responsive but recognizes only random elements in a pattern of reasons.)

(c) The agent must be receptive to a range of reasons that includes moral reasons.

In addition, Fischer and Ravizza agree that moderate-reasons responsiveness is not by itself sufficient for moral responsibility. They contend that a historical requirement – that one have taken responsibility for the springs of one's action – provides what is required, in addition to moderate reasons-responsiveness (and conditions on knowledge and the like), to generate a sufficient condition I will provide their characterization of taking responsibility in due course. As we shall see, I contend that moderate reasons-responsiveness together with taking responsibility does not supply a sufficient condition for moral responsibility.[41]

Wallace

Like Fischer and Ravizza's proposal, Wallace's focuses on our capacity for regulating our behavior by reasons.[42] First of all, in his view, *holding a person morally responsible* is defined as applying to particular acts, with essential reference to the reactive attitudes of resentment, indignation, and guilt, and to moral obligations that one, as moral judge, accepts.

---

41. Fischer and Ravizza, *Responsibility and Control: A Theory of Moral Responsibility*, pp. 210–14. For a critical evaluation of this compatibilist approach, see Eleonore Stump, "Persons: Identification and Freedom," pp. 192–4; John Howard Sobel, *Puzzles for the Will* (Toronto: University of Toronto Press, 1998), pp. 186–93; and Michael McKenna, "Assessing Reasons-Responsive Compatibilism," *International Journal of Philosophical Studies* 8 (2000). I suspect that weak reasons-responsiveness is not a necessary condition for moral responsibility, for there would seem to be situations in which agents are not weakly reasons-responsive but could be morally responsible. Effective examples are provided by actions that realize something that is of paramount value to the agent, so that there is nothing that he would not sacrifice for it, while he lacks sufficient reason for acquiring or retaining it. Suppose someone comes to your door and wants to know whether you are lodging a certain person – and you are. You are so committed to telling the truth that you would do so under any circumstances, even if, for example, you knew that the person at the door intended to murder your guest, or even if you knew that he would destroy the whole world if you told the truth. In this situation, it would seem that you could be morally responsible for your truth-telling despite not being weakly reasons-responsive.

42. Wallace, *Responsibility and the Moral Sentiments*.

What is required for legitimately holding an agent morally responsible for a particular act is that it would be appropriate to have a reactive attitude of indignation, resentment, or guilt directed toward the agent in that situation, and what would make such an attitude appropriate is the fact that the agent has violated a moral obligation.[43] Wallace distinguishes the conditions of holding someone morally responsible, which apply to a particular act, from the conditions of *accountability*, which apply to agents over an extended period. To regard someone as a morally accountable agent is "to view the person as the sort of agent whose violation of moral obligations one accepts would render reactive emotions appropriate."[44] In order for an agent to be legitimately considered morally accountable, he must possess the *powers of reflective self-control*: (1) the power to grasp and apply moral reasons, and (2) the power to control or regulate his behavior by the light of such reasons.[45]

Psychopaths, for example, are not morally accountable because they lack these powers of reflective self-control, as is the case for agents who have a particularly strong sort of drug addiction.[46] But normal agents, even if determinism is true, do possess these powers. It is important for Wallace that an agent can have the powers for reflective self-control in the sense relevant to moral responsibility even though something in a particular circumstance prevents him from applying these powers. In Wallace's terminology, the requirement of having these powers is to be understood *generally* in this respect. In making this point, he aims to preempt the incompatibilist criticism that supposing the murderer was determined to commit his crime, he did not have the capacity to regulate his behavior by moral reasons when he acted.[47] Wallace argues that even if the murderer did not have the capacity to apply the powers in this particular case, he could still be morally responsible because he nonetheless retains the powers in the general sense specified.

WHY THESE FOUR COMPATIBILIST ACCOUNTS CAN BE UNDERMINED

I shall now argue that none of these accounts provide sufficient conditions for moral responsibility. Again, it is clear that by themselves the

43. Wallace, *Responsibility and the Moral Sentiments*, pp. 51–83, for example, at p. 76.
44. Ibid., p. 70.
45. Ibid., pp. 70–1, 154–94, especially p. 157.
46. Ibid., pp. 170–8.
47. Ibid., pp. 207–21.

compatibilist conditions we have just encountered are obviously not sufficient. But, as I pointed out earlier, neither are they plausibly intended to be. The best way to understand this sort of compatibilism is that such a condition would be sufficient for moral responsibility if supplemented by implicitly understood (non-incompatibilist) conditions about agency, knowledge, and circumstance.[48] Moreover, compatibilists must require their conditions to be sufficient for moral responsibility given implicitly understood (non-incompatibilist) conditions as background, for, as I have noted, it is essential to their case that we can attribute moral responsibility in certain standard cases. I contend that the compatibilist conditions we have examined are not sufficient in this sense, and that what needs to be added is our favored incompatibilist condition, ultimately the Causal History Principle.

My argument features a deterministic situation involving an agent who meets each of the conditions we have just discussed. Professor Plum kills Ms. White for the sake of some personal advantage. His act of murder is caused by desires that flow from his "durable and constant" character, since for him egoistic reasons typically weigh very heavily – much too heavily as judged from the moral point of view. But the desire on which he acts is nevertheless not irresistible for him, and in this sense he is not constrained to act. Moreover, his desire to kill White conforms to his second-order desires in the sense that he wills to kill and wants to will to kill, and he wills to kill because he wants to will to kill. In addition, Plum's desires are modified by, and some of them arise from, his rational consideration of the relevant reasons, and his process of deliberation is moderately reasons-responsive. He is receptive to the relevant patterns of reasons – for instance, if he knew that the harmful consequences for himself resulting from his crime would be much more severe than they are actually likely to be, he would not have murdered White. But, he is not completely egoistic, and indeed he retains the general capacity to grasp, apply, and regulate his behavior by moral reasons. For example, when the egoistic reasons that count against acting morally are relatively weak, he will typically regulate his behavior by moral reasons instead. These capacities even provide him with the ability to revise and develop his moral character over time. Now, given that causal determinism is true, is it plausible that Plum is responsible for his action?

---

48. Haji's *Moral Appraisability* is especially impressive in its development of these additional conditions.

In the deterministic view, the first- and second-order desires and the reasons-responsive process that result in Plum's crime are inevitable given their causes, and those causes are inevitable given their causes. In assessing moral responsibility for his act of murder, we wend our way back along the deterministic chain of causes that results in his reasoning and desires, and we eventually reach causal factors that are beyond his control – causal factors that he could not have produced, altered, or prevented. The incompatibilist intuition is that if the action results from a deterministic causal process that traces back to factors beyond the control of the agent, then he is not morally responsible for the action.

But the compatibilist would want to resist this conclusion. In response, I will now develop a combined counterexample and generalization strategy against the causal integrationist conditions. Many compatibilists would agree that when an action comes about as a result of covert manipulation (of the right sort), the agent will not be morally responsible.[49] I will try to show, first, that an agent can be covertly manipulated and yet meet each of the causal integrationist conditions. Perhaps this counterexample all by itself would convince some compatibilists to abandon their position. For those who resist, I also aim to show, with the aid of a series of cases culminating in a deterministic situation that is ordinary from the compatibilist point of view, that an agent's non-responsibility under covert manipulation generalizes to the ordinary situation. If I am right, it will turn out that no relevant difference can be found among these cases that would justify denying responsibility under covert manipulation while affirming it in ordinary deterministic circumstances, and this would force an incompatibilist conclusion.

Each of the four cases I will describe features different ways in which Professor Plum's murder of Ms. White might be causally determined by factors beyond his control, and in each of these cases, Plum will meet the four causal integrationist conditions at issue.

Case 1. Professor Plum was created by neuroscientists, who can manipulate him directly through the use of radio-like technology, but he is as much like an ordinary human being as is possible, given this history. Suppose these neuroscientists "locally" manipulate him to undertake the process of reasoning

49. Richard Taylor discusses manipulation cases in *Metaphysics*, fourth ed., pp. 43–4; cf. Kane, *The Significance of Free Will*, pp. 65–71.

by which his desires are brought about and modified – directly producing his every state from moment to moment. The neuroscientists manipulate him by, among other things, pushing a series of buttons just before he begins to reason about his situation, thereby causing his reasoning process to be rationally egoistic. Plum is not constrained to act in the sense that he does not act because of an irresistible desire – the neuroscientists do not provide him with an irresistible desire – and he does not think and act contrary to character since he is often manipulated to be rationally egoistic. His effective first-order desire to kill Ms. White conforms to his second-order desires. Plum's reasoning process exemplifies the various components of moderate reasons-responsiveness. He is receptive to the relevant pattern of reasons, and his reasoning process would have resulted in different choices in some situations in which the egoistic reasons were otherwise. At the same time, he is not exclusively rationally egoistic since he will typically regulate his behavior by moral reasons when the egoistic reasons are relatively weak – weaker than they are in the current situation.

Plum's action would seem to satisfy all the compatibilist conditions we examined. But, intuitively, he is not morally responsible because he is determined by the neuroscientists' activities, which are beyond his control. Consequently, it would seem that none of these compatibilist conditions is sufficient for moral responsibility.

A compatibilist might resist this conclusion by arguing that although in Case 1 the process resulting in the action meets all the prominent compatibilist conditions, each of Plum's states are directly produced by the manipulators moment by moment – he is "locally" manipulated – and this is the feature of the story that is responsibility-undermining. In reply, could a time lag between the manipulators' activity and the production of the relevant states in the agent plausibly make a difference as to whether the agent is morally responsible? If all the manipulating activity occurred during one time interval and, after an appropriate time lag, the relevant states were produced in the agent, could he only then be responsible? By my intuitions, such a time lag, all by itself, could make no difference as to whether an agent is morally responsible.

The generalization strategy now requires a case more like the ordinary situation than Case 1. Case 2 alone might also serve as a counterexample to the compatibilist conditions:

Case 2. Plum is like an ordinary human being, except that he was created by neuroscientists, who, although they cannot control him directly, have programmed him to weigh reasons for action so that he is often but not exclusively rationally egoistic, with the result that in the circumstances in which he now finds himself, he is causally determined to undertake the moderately reasons-responsive process and to possess the set of first- and second-order desires that results in his killing Ms. White. He has the general ability to regulate his behavior by moral reasons, but in these circumstances, the egoistic reasons are very powerful, and accordingly he is causally determined to kill for these reasons. Nevertheless, he does not act because of an irresistible desire.

Again, although Plum satisfies each of the compatibilist conditions, intuitively he is not morally responsible because his action is determined by the neuroscientists' programming, which is beyond his control. Thus, Case 2 also shows that none of our causal integrationist versions of compatibilism supplies a sufficient condition for moral responsibility. Furthermore, it would seem unprincipled to claim that here, by contrast with Case 1, Plum is morally responsible because the length of time between the programming and the action is great enough. Whether the programming takes place two seconds or thirty years before the action seems irrelevant to the question of moral responsibility. Causal determination by factors beyond Plum's control most plausibly explains his lack of moral responsibility in the first case, and I think we are forced to say that he is not morally responsible in the second case for the same reason.

Now consider the following scenario, even more similar to the ordinary situation:

Case 3. Plum is an ordinary human being, except that he was determined by the rigorous training practices of his home and community so that he is often but not exclusively rationally egoistic (exactly as egoistic as in Cases 1 and 2). His training took place at too early an age for him to have had the ability to prevent or alter the practices that determined his character. In his current circumstances, Plum is thereby caused to undertake the moderately reasons-responsive process and to possess the first- and second-order desires that result in his killing White. He has the general ability to grasp, apply, and regulate his behavior by moral reasons, but in these circumstances, the egoistic reasons are very powerful, and hence the rigorous training practices of his upbringing deterministically result in his act of murder. Nevertheless, he does not act because of an irresistible desire.

If the compatibilist wants to claim that Plum is morally responsible in Case 3, he must point out a feature of these circumstances that would explain why he is morally responsible there but not in Case 2. But it seems that there is no such feature. In both cases, Plum satisfies all of the causal integrationist conditions, so a divergence in assessment of moral responsibility between these cases cannot be supported by a difference in meeting these conditions. Causal determination by factors beyond Plum's control most plausibly explains his lack of moral responsibility in the second case, and we seem to be forced to say that he is not morally responsible in the third case for the same reason.

So it appears that Plum's exemption from responsibility in Cases 1 and 2 generalizes to the near-normal Case 3. Does it generalize all the way to the normal case?

Case 4. Physicalist determinism is true, and Plum is an ordinary human being, generated and raised under normal circumstances, who is often but not exclusively rationally egoistic (exactly as egoistic as in Cases 1–3). Plum's killing of White comes about as a result of his undertaking the moderately reasons-responsive process of deliberation, he exhibits the specified organization of first- and second-order desires, and he does not act because of an irresistible desire. He has the general ability to grasp, apply, and regulate his behavior by moral reasons, but in these circumstances the egoistic reasons are very powerful, and together with background circumstances they deterministically result in his act of murder.

Given that we must deny moral responsibility to Plum in Case 3, what reason do we have for holding him morally responsible in this more ordinary case? There would appear to be no differences between Case 3 and Case 4 that could support the claim that Plum is not morally responsible in Case 3 but is responsible in Case 4. One distinguishing feature of Case 4 is that the causal determination of Plum's crime is not, in the last analysis, brought about by other agents.[50] However, the claim that this is a relevant difference is implausible. Imagine a further case that is exactly the same as, say, Case 1 or Case 2, except that Plum's states are induced by a machine that is generated spontaneously, without intelligent design. Would he then be morally responsible? The compatibilist might agree that this sort of machine induction is responsibility-undermining as well, and then devise a condition that stipulates that

---

50. For example, in the course of developing his compatibilist view, William G. Lycan argues that in the kinds of cases Richard Taylor discusses (in *Metaphysics*, fourth ed., pp. 43–4), the agent lacks responsibility just because he "is a puppet of another person" and not simply because he is causally determined (*Consciousness*, Cambridge: MIT Press, 1987), pp. 117–18.

agents are not responsible for actions manipulated by agents or machines. But this move is patently ad hoc. What explanation could there be for the truth of this condition other than that it gets the compatibilist the result he wants? The compatibilist might dig in and draw the line somewhere between agent manipulation and machine induction. This move seems very weak to me. The idea would be that although Plum cannot be morally responsible if he is manipulated by neuroscientists, he can be if his states are induced by the machine. If the compatibilist's suggestion is that the plausibility of this idea provides incompatibilists with some reason to reconsider their position, I think he is mistaken.

The best explanation for the intuition that Plum is not morally responsible in the first three cases is that his action results from a deterministic causal process that traces back to factors beyond his control. Because Plum is also causally determined in this way in Case 4, we should conclude that here too Plum is not morally responsible for the same reason. More generally, if an action results from a deterministic causal process that traces back to factors beyond the agent's control, then he is not morally responsible for it.

By this argument, Plum's exemption from responsibility in Case 1 generalizes to his exemption from responsibility in Case 4. Notice that this generalization strategy is not a sorites. Its force does not depend on producing a series of cases, each of which is similar to its predecessor, and then arguing that since the first has some general feature, one must draw the conclusion that the last does as well because each of the successive pairs of cases is different only in some small degree of that kind of general feature. A series of similar cases is indeed important to the argument. But its strength derives from the fact that between each successive pair of cases there is no divergence at all in factors that could plausibly make a difference for moral responsibility, and that we are therefore forced to conclude that all four cases exhibit the same kind and the same degree of an incompatibilist responsibility-undermining feature.

At this point, the compatibilist might argue that according to ordinary intuitions, Plum in Case 4 is morally responsible, and that these intuitions should be provided more weight than we have given them. But in the incompatibilist view, one consequence of determinism is that ordinary intuitions about moral responsibility in specific cases are based on a mistake. In making moral judgments in everyday life, we do not assume that agents' choices and actions result from deterministic causal processes that trace back to factors beyond their control. Our ordinary intuitions do not presuppose that determinism is true, and they may even presuppose that it is false. Indeed, in Case 4, it is specified that determinism is true, but ordinary intuitions are likely to persist regardless of this stipulation, especially if the implications of determinism are not thoroughly internalized. If we did assume determinism and internalize its implications, our intuitions might well be different.

HAJI'S RESPONSE TO AN EARLIER VERSION OF THE FOUR-CASE ARGUMENT

Haji develops a reply to the version of this four-case argument featured in my article "Determinism Al Dente." There he divides each of Cases 1 and 2 into distinct scenarios, and he argues that in these scenarios, Mr. Green (the murderer of Ms. Peacock in that example) is either morally responsible (*morally appraisable* in his vocabulary) or there is a compatibilist explanation, such as the irresistibility of the relevant desire, for the absence of moral responsibility. The scenario of Haji's that I want to address is one in which the relevant desire is not irresistible, where Haji has the intuition that Green is indeed morally responsible:

Suppose the neurophysiologists can, when they want, cause Mr. Green to form certain intentions, arrive at certain decisions, or make certain choices, and to act accordingly, by directly stimulating Green's brain: they have, that is, the ability to "locally manipulate" Green. And suppose they can do all this without the manipulations being "felt" or detected by Green. Suppose that on a certain occasion, the neuroscientists electronically manipulate Mr. Green, instilling in him various pro-attitudes, which contribute centrally to Green's killing Peacock. Assume that the instilled pro-attitudes, like the desire to kill Peacock, have strong motivational force but are *not* irresistible. Had he wanted to, Green could have resisted them by relying on his own reasoning processes. This last assumption is legitimate as, presumably, Pereboom's set of cases is meant to provide support for the "fundamental incompatibilist claim" that actions originating from factors over which one has no control are not ones for which one can be morally responsible, in a *non*-question-begging way.

If one has no prior commitment to incompatibilism, this scenario may well elicit the intuition that Green *is* morally responsible for killing Peacock. It would not be uncommon to react to the first scenario in some such way as this: "True, Green did come into existence in a rather weird way. But why should this matter? After all, Green could have been snapped into existence by God. Green *was* locally manipulated, and that's not nice at all. But though he acted on the instilled pro-attitudes, these didn't compel him to do anything. He could have resisted them, but he didn't. And that's why he bears responsibility.[51]

I might have Haji's intuition under certain incompatibilist interpretations of his sentence, "Had he wanted to, Green could have resisted them by relying on his own reasoning processes." But what readings of this sentence might Haji endorse, supposing compatibilism? Plainly, in his view a pro-attitude might not be irresistible for an agent while he is causally determined to act on it. Now, according to Haji's version of compatibilism, when moral responsibility is at issue, most crucial for a pro-attitude's being resistible is that the actions it causes be *under the agent's volitional control*, which he defines as follows:

Action A performed by agent S is under S's volitional control if and only if, holding constant the motivational precursor of A (that is, the proximal desire or pro-attitude that gives rise to A) and S's evaluative scheme, there is a scenario with the same natural laws as the actual world in which, relying on her evaluative scheme, S decides or forms an intention to do something other than A, and she successfully executes that intention or decision.[52]

For Haji, being under her volitional control is necessary for moral responsibility.[53] So let us assume that Green's action was indeed under

---

51. Haji, *Moral Appraisability*, pp. 23–4.
52. Haji, *Moral Appraisability*, pp. 75–86, at p. 76.
53. In addition, to rule out cases of induced pro-attitudes, a morally responsible action for Haji must issue from the agent's *authentic evaluative scheme*, a scheme that captures the intuition that it was developed "under the agent's own steam," and is not alien. For example, to be authentic, the scheme cannot be "beaten into" an agent or psychosurgically induced into her against her will. (But of course here Haji must be careful not to allow determinism to undermine a scheme's authenticity; *Moral Appraisability*, pp. 124–39.) Haji's compatibilist theory of moral responsibility is in some respects similar to Fischer and Ravizza's. Indeed, the sort of counterexample I raised against the necessity for moral responsibility of Fischer's condition (note 41) would also challenge Haji's view, but Haji denies that agents are morally responsible in these sorts of cases. Suppose that a woman saves a child as a result of a moral commitment that is so strong that, holding this commitment fixed, there is no relevant alternative scenario in which she does not save the child. Such an agent would not, by Haji's definition, have volitional control over her action, and could not be morally responsible (pp. 96ff). Could he be right? Haji's view has the consequence that an agent whose action is produced by an unshakeable and overriding moral commitment could not be praiseworthy, while if the action issued from a weaker commitment, the agent could be praiseworthy for it. Consider Martha, who is hiding a family of innocent refugees. The secret police at the door ask her if she is hiding anyone, and she knows that they intend to kill the refugees. Suppose she has such a strong commitment to preserving the lives of people who are persecuted that holding fixed this commitment there is no relevant scenario in which

his volitional control. Let us also suppose, however, that his action is under his volitional control only because holding fixed the desire that is the proximal cause of his killing Peacock, there are alternative scenarios in which the egoistic reasons to refrain from killing her are more vividly presented to him. For example, if he were more vividly presented with the probability of his being caught, and with an account of the subsequent punishment, his disposition to weigh reasons would have resulted in his refraining from killing Peacock. But now imagine that the manipulators carefully shield Green from any such vivid presentation of egoistic reasons, thereby assuring that as a result of their manipulations, he kills her. I don't see how he could be morally responsible under these circumstances.

Or suppose that Green has volitional control over his action only because his disposition to weigh reasons is somewhat flexible, that under certain types of conditions – after the home team wins several games in a row, or after a substantial gain in his stock portfolio, for example – moral reasons weigh more heavily for him and egoistic reasons less. (Haji does require that the alternative scenarios be unexceptional for the agent.[54]) Imagine that in these circumstances, Green, holding the proximal-cause desire fixed, would refrain from killing Peacock. But now suppose that the neuroscientists are careful to prevent such circumstances from occurring, or at least (where this is pertinent) from Green's becoming aware of any such circumstances. As a result, they are assured that despite his having volitional control, their manipulations will nevertheless inevitably cause him to kill Peacock. Again, I don't see how Green could be morally responsible in this scenario either.

As a result, there are ways of embellishing Cases 1 and 2 so that Green acts on a desire that, in Haji's view, is not irresistible for him because the subsequent action is under his volitional control, and yet it is intuitive that he is not morally responsible because of the way in which he is manipulated. Consequently, Haji's alternative explanation as to why Green would not be morally responsible in certain cases of

she tells the police the truth. Even if she believed that not telling the truth and being found out would result in her torture and death, she would not act differently. Ann is also hiding a family of refugees, and the secret police are also at her door. But although she has a very strong commitment to preserving the lives of persecuted people, and she acts on this commitment, it is not unshakeable and overriding for her, because she would tell the police the truth if she felt that the threat to her if she did not tell and were found out were severe enough. It would seem implausible that Ann could be praiseworthy while Martha could not be.

54. Haji, *Moral Appraisability*, p. 82.

manipulation – that his action is not under his volitional control – will not do the work it needs to. I suggest again that an incompatibilist explanation for Green's lack of responsibility in these cases is the only one left standing.

FISCHER AND RAVIZZA'S PROPOSED SUFFICIENT CONDITION

Fischer and Ravizza would argue at this point that their account nevertheless supplies a sufficient condition for moral responsibility. Indeed, as they acknowledge, moderate reasons-responsiveness by itself is not sufficient for moral responsibility because one might be moderately reasons-responsive and nevertheless be manipulated so as to preclude moral responsibility.[55] But they contend that the historical requirement that one have *taken responsibility* for the springs of one's action provides what is required, in addition to moderate reasons-responsiveness (and conditions on knowledge, and the like), to generate a sufficient condition. Someone's taking responsibility for these springs of action has three ingredients:

(a) The individual must see himself as an agent; he must see that his choices and actions are efficacious in the world. This condition includes the claim that the individual sees that if he were to choose and act differently, different upshots would occur in the world.
(b) The individual must accept that he is a fair target of the reactive attitudes as a result of how he exercises this agency in certain contexts.
(c) The individual's view of himself specified in the first two conditions must be based, in an appropriate way, on the evidence.[56]

Fischer and Ravizza argue that by proceeding through these steps, it is the mechanisms that produce action, in particular, for which the agent takes responsibility. These mechanisms include practical reasoning and unreflective habit.[57] Fischer and Ravizza also contend that agents who are manipulated do not take responsibility for the manipulating mechanism, and this is why they are not morally responsible.

55. Fischer and Ravizza, *Responsibility and Control: A Theory of Moral Responsibility*, pp. 230–1.
56. Ibid., pp. 210–14.
57. Ibid., pp. 215–17.

But this strategy does not work against the kinds of cases I've presented. Note first that according to Fischer and Ravizza, to take responsibility for a mechanism one does not need to know everything about it, and indeed this is what they must say for their account to be plausible. When someone takes responsibility for ordinary practical reasoning, he need not know the details of the neural machinery that underlies the mental states that comprise his practical reasoning. On Fischer and Ravizza's view of taking responsibility, an agent need not know these details, but in taking responsibility for a kind of mechanism, he takes responsibility for these details.[58] However, if a normal agent takes responsibility for the neural mechanisms that generally underlie his mental states, despite not knowing much about them, why couldn't Professor Plum of Case 1 take responsibility for the mechanisms of manipulation that generally underlie his mental states despite not knowing much about them?

Fischer and Ravizza reply to this sort of suggestion by claiming that a person like Plum of Case 1 would not be "a coherent self... That is, under the envisaged circumstances, there is no self or genuine individual at all – from the beginning, there has been no opportunity of a genuine self to emerge and develop."[59] But one might imagine that Plum's mental states in Case 1 or Case 2 are qualitatively identical over time to those of a non-manipulated person. For example, one might envisage him to be manipulated to respond to evidence and to alter his self-conception in response to relevant experiences in just the way that a reasonable, non-manipulated person would. On what grounds could one claim that Plum is not a coherent self while the non-manipulated person is? Furthermore, in Case 2, the programmers do not directly manipulate Plum, and so, given plausible principles of mechanism-individuation, manipulation might well not be a feature of the mechanisms that result in action. Thus when he, in the ordinary course of events, takes responsibility for his mechanisms, he takes responsibility for ordinary neurophysiological structures. It would seem that Plum in Case 2 could as easily take responsibility for his action-producing mechanisms as an ordinary agent. But intuitively he is not morally responsible.

58. Fischer and Ravizza, *Responsibility and Control: A Theory of Moral Responsibility*, pp. 230–5.
59. Ibid., pp. 234–5, note 26.

Fischer and Ravizza develop a response to the case in which someone's taking responsibility itself is electronically manipulated.[60] They suggest that such an individual has not formed his view of himself as an agent subject to the reactive attitudes on the basis of the evidence in the appropriate way. But one might imagine that Plum in Cases 1 and 2 is manipulated to possess the very same types of neural states as some ordinary agent has – even both actually and counterfactually – while he is in the process of taking responsibility. Some of the ordinary agent's neural states realize his formation of a view of himself based on the evidence in the appropriate way. Why then couldn't Plum's formation of his view of himself be appropriately based on the evidence? Yet Plum is not morally responsible. Taking responsibility in conjunction with moderate reasons-responsiveness appears not to generate a sufficient condition for moral responsibility.

Many compatibilists have hoped to secure their view by showing that what undergirds moral responsibility is a kind of causal integration between agent and action, and that whether causal determinism is true is irrelevant to the issue. But now we can see that the various attempts to develop this strategy are unsuccessful. Although the proposed forms of causal integrationism might initially seem to capture intuitive judgments in specific situations, for each approach there are cases in which the condition is satisfied but the agent is not morally responsible. In particular, when the causal determination of an action is brought to the forefront in an ordinary situation, as in Cases 1 and 2, the sense that it is responsibility-undermining becomes especially powerful. Consequently, these causal integrationist varieties of compatibilism do not provide credible ways to show how agents might be morally responsible supposing that causal determinism is true.

Have we now developed a group of arguments that tells against any possible causal integrationist version of compatibilism? Our argument against the sufficiency of causal integrationist conditions holds promise for this sort of extension. The sufficiency of all the conditions we considered can be undermined by examples like Cases 1 or 2, in which the agent meets the proposed condition but is causally determined by other agents. In each situation, making the agent's causal determination particularly vivid undermines the sense that he is morally responsible. It is quite plausible that other causal integrationist proposals would fall to the same strategy.

60. Fischer and Ravizza, *Responsibility and Control: A Theory of Moral Responsibility*, pp. 235–6.

Reflection on the generalization strategy against the sufficiency of any prominent compatibilist condition allows us to amplify the third criticism of Strawson's position – that he is mistaken to claim that a challenge to the reactive attitudes based on the general metaphysical thesis of determinism is external to our practice of holding people morally responsible, and therefore illegitimate. The argument allows us to see that the challenge determinism poses to moral responsibility and the associated reactive attitudes is not based on justificatory requirements external to the practice of holding people morally responsible. For the crucial elements of the argument are features of this very practice. First, it is this practice that mandates that in Cases 1 and 2, Plum is not morally responsible. If an agent is causally determined by manipulators (or by a machine or a brain tumor) to act as he does, then our practice exempts him from moral responsibility. Second, the argument involves a procedure of generalizing from these cases of manipulation. We generalized to a claim about the agent in Case 4 by arguing that there are no differences relevant to an assessment of moral responsibility between him and the agents in the previous cases. But generalization of this sort is also a characteristic of our practice of holding people morally responsible, indeed a thoroughly central characteristic of that practice.

A prominent feature of Wallace's position is the claim that a generalization strategy of this sort will not provide support for incompatibilism. By his characterization, a generalization strategy argues from accepted reasons for excuses or exemptions to the claim that moral accountability in general requires alternative possibilities for action. It would then conclude that incompatibilism is confirmed because agents would lack such alternative possibilities in case determinism is true.[61] Indeed, Wallace argues for his compatibilist position by attempting to show that neither acceptable excuses – which, by his characterization, aim to establish that it is not fair to consider an agent blameworthy for a particular act – nor acceptable exemptions – which indicate that it is not fair more generally to hold an agent accountable for his actions – ever need to appeal to the claim that an agent lacks alternative

---

61. Wallace, *Responsibility and the Moral Sentiments*, pp. 114–17.

possibilities for action.[62] Wallace's counter-strategy is to establish, first, that ordinary excuses should be understood as aiming to demonstrate that the agent did nothing wrong, and second, that ordinary exemptions need appeal only to a deficiency in the general powers to grasp, apply, and regulate behavior by moral reasons. In his view, the need for alternative possibilities, and vulnerability to the generalization strategy, would thereby be avoided.

The incompatibilist condition for determinism that I favor makes no reference to alternative possibilities for action, but instead claims that for an agent to be morally responsible (accountable), her action cannot result from a deterministic causal process that traces back to factors beyond her control. Let us examine Wallace's contentions about excuses and exemptions as they bear on this condition. First, there are indeed many sorts of excuses that aim to show that the agent did nothing that is morally impermissible. But some excuses do not seem to fit this mold. Wallace discusses cases of what Frankfurt calls coercion, in which the motive on which the agent acts is irresistible and thus beyond her ability to control, and its being beyond her ability to control is what explains her acting on this motive (Frankfurt's Type C situations).[63] One can imagine a case in which Colonel Mustard is threatened with torture if he fails to divulge the whereabouts of his comrades. He knows that if he talks, at least two hundred of them will be killed, but because his desire not to be tortured is irresistible, he does indeed divulge the information. It would not be unnatural to describe this case as one in which what the Colonel does is indeed wrong, there are factors beyond his control that determine him to act as he does, and for this reason he is not morally responsible. Hence, this case nicely generalizes to the incompatibilist condition that precludes agents from being morally responsible for actions with deterministic causal histories.

Wallace wishes to deal with such cases as instances of exemptions rather than excuses.[64] But given that the distinction between excuses and exemptions is mainly a matter of short-term versus long-term reprieve, this analysis seems forced. The effect of the threat may after all be only very short-term. More significantly, Wallace claims that all legitimate exemptions can be accounted for by a lack of general powers to grasp, apply, and regulate behavior by moral reasons. But we can

---

62. Wallace, *Responsibility and the Moral Sentiments*, pp. 118–94.
63. Ibid., pp. 145–7.
64. Ibid., pp. 146–7.

imagine that Mustard retains these general powers, but fails only to be able to make full use of them in his current predicament. He might well have the general capacity to grasp the reasons why divulging the relevant information in these circumstances is morally impermissible, have the general ability to apply these reasons in his predicament, and have the general power to act on such moral reasons, but only be unable in this particular situation to make use of this last general power. As a result, Mustard's exemption from moral accountability cannot be explained by his lacking these general powers. However, in this case there are factors beyond the agent's control that determine him to act as he does, and this fact potentially sustains an incompatibilist generalization strategy.

One tactic for avoiding incompatibilism at this point would be simply to add the irresistibility of the relevant desires as an exempting condition. But as we have now seen, there are possible situations in which an agent retains the general powers for reflective self-control, the relevant desires are not irresistible, and yet the agent is not morally responsible. For a case that might be especially effective against Wallace's position, we might imagine that an external manipulator operates not by impairing the ability to grasp, apply, and regulate an agent's behavior by moral reasons, but rather by adjusting the phenomenological weight of the countervailing reasons so that they always seem strongly to outweigh the moral reasons. This might be done by rigid training, or by direct manipulation of the brain. Under these circumstances the general powers of reflective self-control and the resistibility of relevant desires can be retained while the agent is not morally responsible. This sort of case provides new support for the generalization strategy. For now it seems false that in all cases of legitimate exemption, it is the lack of the general powers of reflective self-control alone or the irresistibility of the relevant desires that sustains the exemption. As a result, we seem to be driven back to an incompatibilist condition to account for absence of moral accountability.

CONCLUSION

In summary, Strawson's route to compatibilism fails to appreciate, among other things, the kinds of theoretical presuppositions made by holding people morally responsible, and therefore mistakenly regards this practice as immune from a determinist or similar threat. Furthermore, none of the proposed causal integrationist approaches provides sufficient conditions for moral responsibility, and at the same time we have found good reason to believe that there could be no successful strategies of this sort. Thus, we have good reason to believe that an agent cannot be responsible for decisions that are produced by a deterministic process that traces back to causal factors beyond her control – decisions that are alien-deterministic events. Moreover, given the result of Chapter 2 that agents can be no more responsible for decisions that are truly random or partially random events than they can be for those that are alien-deterministic events, we now have good reason to believe that they indeed cannot be responsible for decisions that are truly random or partially random events.

This completes my case for my version of causal history incompatibilism, and in particular for the Causal History Principle:

(5) An action is free in the sense required for moral responsibility only if the decision to perform it is not an alien-deterministic event, nor a truly random event, nor a partially random event.

This principle is underlain, in my view, by:

(O) If an agent is morally responsible for her deciding to perform an action, then the production of this decision must be something over which the agent has control, and an agent is not morally responsible for the decision if it is produced by a source over which she has no control.

If an agent is to be morally responsible for her decisions, then she must be their source in a way incompatible with those decisions being events found on the continuum described in (5).

5

The Contours of Hard Incompatibilism

My version of hard incompatibilism consists of two main theses. The first is that all of our actions and choices are either alien-deterministic events — events such that there are causal factors beyond our control by virtue of which they are causally determined, or truly random events — those that are not produced by anything at all, or partially random events — those for which factors beyond the agent's control contribute to their production but do not determine them, while there is nothing that supplements the contribution of these factors to produce the events. The second thesis is that incompatibilism defined by the Causal History Principle is true. Traditionally, incompatibilism is the view that freedom of the sort required for moral responsibility is incompatible with determinism. I have expanded the notion to mean that freedom of this sort is incompatible with our actions and choices being events that lie on the continuum from alien-deterministic through partially random to truly random events. Together, these two theses yield the conclusion that we do not have the kind of free will required for moral responsibility.

The justification for each of these claims is implicit in the case I've made against libertarianism and compatibilism. The argument for the first thesis — that all of our actions and choices are events that lie on the responsibility-undermining continuum — arises from the arguments developed in Chapter 3 (Empirical Objections to Agent-Causal Libertarianism). According to our best physical theories, all events governed by physical laws are to be found on this continuum, and if our actions and choices are identical to such events, or are wholly constituted of such events on the ordinary nonreductivist model, they will also fall on this continuum. Libertarian proposals without agent-causation do not deny that our actions and choices are events of this sort. It is only the agent-causal version of libertarianism that places our actions and choices beyond the continuum. But empirical objections provide good (albeit not conclusive) reasons to believe that we are not agent-causes. We therefore have good reasons to believe that our actions and choices are not agent-caused events, but are rather either alien-deterministic, or partially random, or truly random events.

The second hard incompatibilist thesis is that incompatibilism defined by the Causal History Principle,

(5) An action is free in the sense required for moral responsibility only if it is not an alien-deterministic event, nor a truly random event, nor a partially random event,

is true. The arguments for this claim were developed in Chapters 4 (Problems for Compatibilism) and Chapter 2 (Coherence Objections to Libertarianism). In Chapter 4, we saw that there are good reasons for claiming that agents cannot be responsible for actions and choices that are alien-deterministic events. Furthermore, I argued in Chapter 2 that there is no more reason to hold that agents can be responsible for truly random or partially random events than there is to maintain that they can be responsible for alien-deterministic events. Thus, there are good reasons to believe that agents cannot be responsible for actions and choices that are events anywhere on the continuum. Consequently, we have found significant support for each of the two hard incompatibilist theses, and for the conclusion that hard incompatibilism is true.[1]

CONTRASTS WITH SIMILAR VIEWS

I have contended that although it is not clear whether determinism is true, the claim that we lack the sort of free will required for moral

1. C.D. Broad (cf. "Determinism, Indeterminism, and Libertarianism") is an example of a philosopher who also thinks that incompatibilism is true, and opts for a hard incompatibilist position because both event-causal libertarianism and agent-causal theory seem implausible. Like me, he denies event-causal libertarianism on the basis of Humean considerations, although his reason for rejecting agent-causal theory is different from mine: it is the timing objection that Ginet develops (see Chapter 2).

responsibility has strong support. Consequently, my position differs in an obvious respect from the classical hard determinism advocated by Spinoza, Holbach, and Priestley, according to which we do not have free will because determinism is true.[2] That is, it is incumbent on the hard determinists, but not on me, to show that determinism is true. At the same time, while I must show that all events lie on the continuum I've described, and that event-causal libertarianism is implausible, these tasks are inessential to their project.

Bruce Waller argues, as I do, that whether determinism is true or whether microphysical events are fundamentally indeterministic, we are not morally responsible.[3] He contends, and I agree, that important notions of freedom can yet survive. He also provides insightful analyses of what it would be like to live without the belief that we are morally responsible, aspects of which we will examine. Waller and I differ in our strategies for establishing our views. Whereas his arguments are often psychological and social, I do not pursue this approach. We also diverge in the degree to which we are attracted to behavioristic models – he is more inspired by theorists such as B.F. Skinner than I am.

Galen Strawson also maintains that we lack the free will required for moral responsibility, but unlike me, he affirms that whether determinism or indeterminism is true is irrelevant to whether we have this sort of free will. As we have seen, he contends that moral responsibility requires a conception of agency that human beings could not satisfy, and thus its impossibility for us can be established independently of an examination of the truth of determinism.[4] Strawson, then, is a no-free-will-either-way theorist – that is, he maintains that for us, moral responsibility is incompatible with both determinism and indeterminism. I have argued, by contrast, that there is one indeterminist position – agent-causal libertarianism – that yields a coherent conception of human morally responsible agency, and that it might well be possible for us to be agent-causes.[5]

---

2. Baruch Spinoza, *Ethics*, Appendix to Part I. For further indications of his hard determinism, see *Ethics*, Part II, Proposition 48, Part III, Scholium to Proposition II; Paul Holbach, *Système de la Nature*, Amsterdam, 1770; Joseph Priestley, *A Free Discussion of the Doctrines of Materialism and Philosophical Necessity, In a Correspondence between Dr. Price and Dr. Priestley* (1788); reprinted in Joseph Priestley, *Priestley's Writings on Philosophy, Science, and Politics*, ed. John Passmore (New York: Collier, 1965).
3. Bruce Waller, *Freedom Without Responsibility* (Philadelphia: Temple University Press, 1990).
4. Galen Strawson, *Freedom and Belief*, pp. 25–60; "The Impossibility of Moral Responsibility," *Philosophical Studies* 75, pp. 5–24.
5. Clarke, "On the Possibility of Rational Free Action."

Strawson carefully develops a subjectivist notion of free agency, according to which "it is true that x is a truly responsible agent, given that x believes that it is true, although it is not true if x does not believe it is true."[6] He then argues that the price for accepting this position is very high, for it would require abandoning the unity of truth, of splitting truth in two in accordance with two forms of life – "doing science" and "experiencing ourselves and others as free and truly responsible agents." This price is higher than the price one pays "when one grants that true responsibility is impossible, and then patently continues to believe in it without question in one's daily thought and action (continuing to think and act as if one believed in it without question)."[7] For Strawson there is a third alternative – being a fully consistent hard determinist, who is under no illusions. He thinks that achieving this status may be possible, but it would be very difficult.[8] As will soon emerge, I do believe that we can shed much of our conception of human beings as truly responsible, and that this change can have a profound effect on how we regard ourselves and others. But I do not dispute the claim that as a matter of psychological fact it would be difficult for us to abandon every aspect of this view.

Saul Smilansky concurs with Strawson's argument that the sort of free will required for moral responsibility is impossible for us, and thus he too, in my estimation, is a no-free-will-either-way theorist.[9] Nevertheless he believes that he can at the same time accept a "dualistic" picture, which combines aspects of both hard determinism and compatibilism, since what he calls *The Assumption of Exhaustiveness* – that one must either be a compatibilist and not an incompatibilist, or an incompatibilist and not a compatibilist – is false.[10] I agree with what Smilansky intends by his denial of this principle, given that he thinks it is sufficient for it to be false that "some of morality is tenable without libertarian free will (or even requires its absence), while some of morality would be hurt by the lack of libertarian free will."[11] But assuming my own definitions, to maintain this last claim does not amount to compromising one's hard determinism, for one can justifiably maintain

6. Strawson, *Freedom and Belief*, p. 314.
7. Ibid., pp. 315–16.
8. Ibid., pp. 281–2, 317.
9. Smilansky, "Can a Determinist Respect Herself?" p. 86.
10. Smilansky, "Does the Free Will Debate Rest on a Mistake?" *Philosophical Papers* 22 (1993), pp. 173–88; "Can a Determinist Respect Herself?" p. 85.
11. Smilansky, "Does the Free Will Debate Rest on a Mistake?" p. 175.

that we lack the free will required for moral responsibility while affirming that much of morality remains intact. I oppose defining "incompatibilism" as the view that determinism in incompatible with all of morality, because philosophers have only seldom argued for this contention, and it is difficult to see how it might be supported. Rather, what they have very frequently argued is that determinism is incompatible with moral responsibility, a claim that can readily be made intuitive.

Given my definitions, for a hard determinist to endorse what a compatibilist can agree to about issues like deliberation and rationality of action does not necessarily make her in part a compatibilist, and therefore a "dualist" in Smilansky's sense. For what the compatibilist can affirm about these sorts of issues need not involve moral responsibility. Another way Smilansky defends "dualism" is by arguing that a valuable type of self-respect would be undermined if determinism were true, and that "illusion may well be needed to fill in the gap" since "the truth on free will and respect is perhaps too dangerous to leave to human nature."[12] But even if he is recommending here that we retain the view we ordinarily hold, and that this view indeed combines aspects of compatibilism and hard determinism, it is nevertheless clear that by virtue of this fact, his *philosophical position* is not "dualistic." After all, according to his philosophical position, having the sort of self-respect at issue requires an *illusion* of free will, and not its reality. Despite these differences of opinion, there is much in Smilansky's analysis of the consequences of determinism with which I concur.

Richard Double contends that the claim that we have the free will required for moral responsibility, given that this claim assumes that there is a mind-independent feature of human agency that is necessary and crucial for moral responsibility, cannot be true.[13] His fundamental reason for believing this is that the concept of free will is internally incoherent, and thus cannot be realized. One supporting argument he advances is that the debate between compatibilists and incompatibilists is irresolvable, and hence both compatibilist and incompatibilist notions of free will are part of the concept of free will. Another argument defends an irrealist position such as Mackie's about moral judgments in general, according to which they cannot be true, then contends that 'moral responsibility' and 'the sort of free will required for moral responsibi-

---

12. Smilansky, "Can a Determinist Respect Herself?" pp. 97–8.
13. Double, *The Non-Reality of Free Will, Metaphilosophy and Free Will.*

131

lity' are moral notions, and concludes that claims that agents exemplify these notions also cannot be true.[14]

One might distinguish three general classes of moral irrealist. *Noncognitivists* claim that moral judgments have no truth value, and they typically argue that these judgments are used to express attitudes of approval and disapproval rather than to (attempt to) state facts. *Subjectivists* claim that there are no moral facts per se, but that moral judgments nevertheless make factual claims about psychological states. A subjectivist might argue that for someone to judge that killing is wrong is for him to claim that he himself disapproves of killing. *Error theorists* affirm that when an agent makes a moral judgment, he is attempting to make a factual claim about morality, but that since there are no moral facts, all such claims are false.

Of these three, Double endorses the error theory.[15] Propositions of the sort "X has free will" will in fact be necessarily false because free will is a conceptual impossibility. By analogy, "X is a round square" is also necessarily false because a round square is a conceptual impossibility. Moreover, a conjunction of "X is a round square" with any other proposition will be false, and thus X's being a round square is incompatible with any state of affairs. Similarly, if A's having free will is conceptually impossible, then A's having free will is incompatible with any state of affairs, including both a deterministic world and an indeterministic world. Double is thus committed to a no-free-will-either-way theory of an especially strong sort.[16] Strawson's position is in a sense weaker, since he is a no-free-will-either-way theorist, not for the reason that free will is conceptually impossible, but because it is metaphysically impossible that beings like us have it. My view is weaker yet, for I hold that free will might well be both conceptually and metaphysically possible, although there are good empirical reasons to believe that we do not in fact have it.

14. One of Mackie's main arguments for irrealism is that only very bizzare properties could have the descriptive and prescriptive aspects that moral properties would have if moral judgments were true (J.L. Mackie, *Ethics: Inventing Right and Wrong* (Harmondsworth, England: Penguin, 1977). Hence, if Mackie is right, moral properties would be in a sense incoherent, and if indeed 'moral responsibility' and 'the sort of free will required for moral responsibility' are moral concepts, these concepts too would be incoherent in the same sense.

15. Double's terminology may make it sound as if he would endorse subjectivism or, at times, non-cognitivism, but despite this, he assures me (in personal correspondence) that he is a resolute error theorist.

16. In personal correspondence, Double indicates that this is indeed his position.

How plausible are Double's contentions? I suspect that he is right to argue that if irrealism about moral judgments were true, then the same sort of position would hold for attributions of moral responsibility and the sort of free will required for moral responsibility, for these notions are in fact moral. I am not currently willing, as Double is, to cast my lot with moral irrealism, and thus I am not willing to endorse the soundness of this type of argument. Nevertheless, moral irrealism is clearly a contender, and thus his argument has force.

There is reason to doubt Double's claim that his conceptual-impossibility irrealism about free will gains powerful support from the irresolvability of the debates that separate compatibilists and incompatibilists. Examples of such debates Double cites are the dispute about the consequence argument from determinism to the claim that we could not have done otherwise, and the controversy over Frankfurt-style cases. I agree that the consequence argument will not settle the issue between compatibilists and incompatibilists, for the familiar reason that it is open to the two sides to opt for different analyses of "could have done otherwise" and that it hasn't been possible for either side to convince the other of the superiority of its favorite version. Partly for this reason, I place the weight of my anti-compatibilism on the counterexample and generalization strategy of Chapter 4. I believe that this strategy successfully challenges compatibilism, and for this reason I resist the claim that the issue between compatibilists and incompatibilists is irresolvable. Predictably, I also deny that the controversy over Frankfurt-style cases cannot be decided. Moreover, as Fischer points out, this debate should not be conceived as a contest between compatibilists and incompatibilists, since, as I too have argued, incompatibilism can survive the success of Frankfurt-style arguments.[17] Thus, even if that debate could not be settled, it would not show that the issue between compatibilists and incompatibilists is irresolvable.[18]

17. Fischer, review of Richard Double, *Metaphilosophy and Free Will*, *Philosophy and Phenomenological Research* 59 (1999), pp. 1083–6; see also Yakir Levin and David Widerker, review of Richard Double, *Metaphilosophy and Free Will*, *The Philosophical Review* 107 (1998), pp. 630–4.

18. Part of Double's case for the irresolvability of these disputes is based on the claim that people bring different metaphilosophical positions about the point of philosophy to these issues. I would want to set out the counterexample and generalization strategy as a challenge to anyone, no matter what metaphilosophy he or she favors, and to argue that viewing the issue from the perspectives of various metaphilosophies does not substantially affect the force of this strategy.

Honderich advocates a sophisticated version of non-cognitivism about moral judgments generally, and in particular about judgments that attribute moral responsibility. In his view, such judgments essentially express attitudes, do not report moral facts, and do not have truth values. But they nevertheless do involve propositional content in a distinctive way. For example, one might morally disapprove of a vicious politician for some action, where this disapproval includes a retributive desire. On Honderich's conception, the attitude then takes the action to have been both voluntary and originated, and it thereby involves a commitment to this propositional content.[19]

It will not be logically inconsistent to have a retributive desire toward the politician and at the same time believe she did not originate her action. But according to Honderich, given our human nature, someone who has retributive desires for the politician will also believe that she originated the action, and the belief will function as a reason in support of the attitude. Moreover, given human nature, rejection of the belief will serve as a reason to relinquish the attitude. At the very least:

> . . . it is agreed on all hands that *some* factual belief about an action's having been free is required by us for holding an agent responsible and of course for blaming or punishing her. If I lose the belief, I cannot persist in the attitude or the behavior. Currently, at any rate, that is a psychological impossibility.[20]

Determinism is a threat to retributive desires, and more generally to the reactive attitudes connected to the practice of holding people morally responsible, because determinism is incompatible with origination, and given human nature, determinism will serve as a reason to relinquish these attitudes. Honderich presents a long and careful empirical argument for the conclusion that determinism is in fact true.[21] As a result, he thinks we should reassess our commonly held attitudes about moral responsibility.

Nonetheless, Honderich disavows incompatibilism – and compatibilism as well. In his view, incompatibilism incorrectly dismisses the significance of mere voluntariness as opposed to voluntariness together with origination, while compatibilism dismisses the significance of vol-

---

19. Honderich, "Compatibilism, Incompatibilism, and the Smart Aleck," *Philosophy and Phenomenological Research* 56 (1996), pp. 855–62, at pp. 856–9; cf. *A Theory of Determinism.*
20. Ibid., p. 861.
21. Honderich, *A Theory of Determinism,* p. 156.

untariness with origination. He argues that voluntariness can rescue a significant amount of what in human life is affected by determinism, which in his view includes not only moral disapproval, but also our life-hopes – the aspirations we have for achievement and meaning (which I will examine in Chapter 7).

I do not currently endorse Honderich's non-cognitivist version of moral irrealism, and I reserve judgment on his argument for determinism. While I call myself an incompatibilist, Honderich does not, but the apparent disagreement is largely verbal. As we shall see, I concur with Honderich's substantive claim that voluntariness is not at all insignificant for morality and life-hopes. I believe that there is a great deal in Honderich's analysis of the consequences of determinism that is truly valuable, but my views also differ from his in certain key respects.

AGENCY

Philosophers have expressed many worries about hard determinism that also apply to hard incompatibilism. Hard incompatibilism would undermine our self-conception as deliberative and rational agents and destroy our view of ourselves as morally responsible beings. It would make morality incoherent, leave no reason to be moral, render unjustifiable our policies for dealing with wrongdoers, and it would threaten the emotions and attitudes that lie at the core of human interpersonal relationships. The rest of this book is devoted to dealing with these issues. Chapters 6 and 7 examine criminal punishment and the possibility of meaning in life, respectively, and the remainder of this chapter explores the other challenges to living as a hard incompatibilist.

Let us begin by considering the difficulties that hard incompatibilism might raise for our views of ourselves as deliberative agents. These problems have been posed for determinist conceptions of agency more generally, and as a result many compatibilists have responded to them. What I have to say adds little to their contributions, but these issues are raised often enough for me to provide a synopsis. From there on, we will proceed to territory that is not so thoroughly mapped out.

Obviously undermined is the natural view of ourselves as agent causes, according to which we are not restricted to choices that are alien-deterministic, partially random, or truly random events. This means, in my view, that a pervasive conception of ourselves as agents is lost. Our actions do not result from the sort of power of agency that many naturally believe to be their source, a power that is indeterministic and features a robust capacity for control. But clearly, compatibilists are also forced to make this acknowledgement.

Another aspect of our self-conception as agents that could be threatened by hard incompatibilism is a feeling about ourselves that we typically have when we deliberate. It is undeniable that when we deliberate about what to do, we almost always feel that more than one option for choice is open to us. You surely feel that it is now possible for you to decide to continue or to decide to stop reading this book. Now if our actions are truly random or partially random events, this sense might not in fact be an illusion – although even then it would be an illusion if the feeling we have is that we could do otherwise by an agent-causal power. This feeling would more clearly be an illusion if our actions are alien-deterministic events.

Kant provides a reason not to discount this feeling of freedom. He suggests that engaging in a process of deliberation requires that one suppose that more than one choice for action is (causally) possible.[22] This view seems compelling: Could one deliberate about which of two roads to take if one believed that as a matter of causal fact one was capable of making only one of the two choices? But if determinism is true, one could not choose otherwise than as one actually does. Accordingly, Hector-Neri Castañeda contends that whenever one engaged in a process of deliberation, one would be making a false supposition: "We are, thus, condemned to presuppose a falsehood in order to do what we think practically." Similarly, van Inwagen argues that "anyone who denies the existence of free will must, inevitably, contradict himself with monotonous regularity."[23]

This challenge would be most clearly directed against the determinist version of hard incompatibilism. Two sorts of reply are available to an adherent of this view. The first grants that when we deliberate, at the moment of choice we must indeed make what might well be the false and unjustified assumption that more than one course of action is available to us. It then claims that it is legitimate to assume this cognitive posture because the practical gains of engaging in deliberation are significant enough to outweigh the losses of having false and unjustified

22. Kant, *Groundwork of the Metaphysics of Morals*, tr. Mary Gregor (Cambridge: Cambridge University Press, 1997), Part III, Ak IV, 448.
23. Hector-Neri Castañeda, *Thinking and Doing* (Dordrecht: D. Reidel, 1975), p. 135; van Inwagen, *An Essay on Free Will*, pp. 153–61. The quote is on p. 160.

beliefs. We are left with the following choice: either deliberate and have a belief that you know might well be false whenever you do, or cease to deliberate. In this case, practical rationality would appear to have the upper hand.

It is nevertheless disturbing to maintain that we would be theoretically (epistemically) irrational whenever we deliberate. Fortunately, there is a more attractive alternative that does not require us to override the requirements of theoretical rationality. The hard determinist might well be forced to deny that at the moment of choice, the agent must assume that more than one option is causally possible. But suppose that although she believes that only one option is metaphysically or causally possible, she does not know in advance of deliberation which option she will choose. It would seem that under these conditions, there would be no interference with her deliberative process. Tomis Kapitan provides an interesting embellishment of this suggestion.[24] In his view, the fact about open alternatives that is plausibly required for deliberation is that more than one option is epistemically contingent or possible for the agent, in the sense that more than one option for which choice she will make is possible relative to an appropriate subset of her beliefs.[25] While engaged in deliberation, it will in fact typically be the case that more than one option is epistemically possible for the agent in this sense.[26] Thus, to deliberate, one need not deny causal determinism or its consequences. For deliberation does not require that more than one option be causally possible, but rather only that more than one option be epistemically possible for the agent in the sense outlined.

Thomas Nagel poses a further difficulty for a determinist conception of agency. He argues that when we move away from our individual point of view and consider our own actions and those of others simply as part of a course of events in a world that contains us among other creatures and things, it begins to look as though we as agents never really contribute anything.[27] Indeed, an instinctive reaction to

24. Tomis Kapitan, "Deliberation and the Presumption of Open Alternatives," *The Philosophical Quarterly* 36 (1986), pp. 230–51.

25. It is difficult to specify the right subset, as Kapitan's discussion indicates; "Deliberation and the Presumption of Open Alternatives," pp. 241–3.

26. Philip Pettit presents this sort of solution in a slightly different way. In his view, instead of believing of each of two incompatible options considered in deliberation that it is metaphysically or causally possible, the agent need only fail to believe for each of these options that it necessarily will not be realized ("Determinism with Deliberation," *Analysis* 49 (1989), pp. 42–4).

27. Nagel, *The View From Nowhere*, pp. 113ff.

determinism, and by extension, to hard incompatibilism, is that if it were true, we would have no reason to attempt to accomplish anything – to try to improve our lives or the prospects of society – because our deliberations and choices could make no difference. One way to spell out this view is by the claim that determinism or hard incompatibilism would have the following consequence for our conception of agency: Our deliberations and actions could not have an effect on the future, because the future is fixed or produced independently of our deliberations and choices.

This challenge has also been directed toward compatibilists, and they have responded persuasively. Ayer and Dennett, among others, have pointed out that the determination of our deliberations, choices, actions, and their consequences does not undermine their causal efficacy.[28] The hard incompatibilist can legitimately appropriate this position. It is true that according to hard incompatibilism, we are not free in the sense required for moral responsibility, and therefore what happens cannot be affected by choices that are free in this sense. But what happens may nevertheless be caused by the deliberations we engage in and the choices we make. The future could be produced as it is by way of our deliberations and decisions, which, if determinism is true, are also determined. The view suggested by the objection is one in which agents are overpowered by causal factors external to their capacities for deliberation. However, this is not a picture that the hard incompatibilist is forced to accept.

One also finds a widespread tendency to assume that determinism, and thus the deterministic version of hard incompatibilism, would have the following consequence: we could not be genuinely responsive to reasons, because in any particular situation we would be determined to deliberate and act as we do even if the reasons for acting were different. But, as Dennett persuasively argues, there is no good argument for believing that determinism has this consequence either.[29] Determinism allows our actions to be different had the causes of those actions been different from what they actually were. Given that reasons can be causes of action, determinism allows that if the reasons had been otherwise, our actions could have been different as well. Thus, our deliberations and actions can vary with the reasons if determinism is true.

28. Ayer, "Freedom and Necessity," p. 23; Dennett, *Elbow Room*, pp. 100–30; Pettit, "Determinism with Deliberation," pp. 42–4.
29. Dennett, *Elbow Room*, pp. 20–49.

Moreover, hard incompatibilism can easily accommodate the legitimacy of holding people accountable to reasons. Indeed, on this view, agents are not blameworthy when they fail to act in accord with the best reasons. But the hard incompatibilist can still maintain that it could legitimately be demanded of agents to explain whether their actions accord with the best reasons, and to assess what their behavior reveals about their rationality. We might call someone for whom these demands are legitimate *rationally accountable*. Making these demands of agents might be justified by its effectiveness in improving rationality – we humans are manifestly susceptible to being causally influenced by rational admonition of this sort. Indeed, the more nearly rational an agent is, the more likely it will be that such a process will affect his behavior. None of this is threatened by hard incompatibilism.

Hard incompatibilism also does not endanger the legitimacy of holding people accountable to moral reasons. True, the hard incompatibilist must deny that an agent can be morally blameworthy when he fails to act in accord with such reasons. But there is no adequate support for believing that if this position were correct, we could not in fact regulate our behavior by moral reasons. Recall Wallace's powers of reflective self-control – the power to grasp and apply moral reasons, and the power to control or regulate one's behavior by the light of such reasons.[30] Hard incompatibilism does not threaten the claim that we possess these capacities. Furthermore, on this view, it can also be demanded of agents to explain how their decisions accord with the moral reasons, and to consider what their decisions reveal about their moral character and dispositions. The legitimacy of making such demands might be grounded in their value for generating moral improvement. Hilary Bok provides a thorough and impressive development of this sort of moral accountability.[31] She argues that this conception is compatible with determinism, and I think she is clearly right. Moreover, I don't believe any further aspect of hard determinism or of hard incompatibilism fails to harmonize with this type of view.

DISPENSING WITH BLAMEWORTHINESS AND PRAISEWORTHINESS

The feature of our ordinary conception of ourselves that would most obviously be undermined if hard incompatibilism were true is our belief

---

30. Wallace, *Responsibility and the Moral Sentiments*, pp. 70–1, 154–94, especially p. 157.
31. Bok, *Freedom and Responsibility*, pp. 122–98.

that people are typically praiseworthy when they perform morally exemplary actions, and that they are typically blameworthy when they perform actions that are morally wrong. To be blameworthy is to deserve blame just because one has chosen to do wrong. Hard incompatibilism rules out one's ever deserving blame just for choosing to act wrongly, for such choices are always alien-deterministic events, or truly random events, or partially random events.

Susan Wolf has argued that whereas such deserved blame cannot be justified if determinism is true, the analogous sort of deserved praise does not collapse along with it.[32] As she puts it, she is "committed to the curious claim that being psychologically determined to perform good actions is compatible with deserving praise for them, but that being psychologically determined to perform bad actions is not compatible with deserving blame."[33] Wolf, in effect, endorses the hard incompatibilist's view about deserved blame, but not about deserved praise. She cites the following example in support of her view:

Two persons, of equal swimming ability, stand on equally uncrowded beaches. Each sees an unknown child struggling in the water in the distance. Each thinks "The child needs my help" and directly swims out to save him. In each case, we assume that the agent reasons correctly – the child *does* need her help – and that, in swimming out to save him, the agent does the right thing. We further assume that in one of these cases, the agent has the ability to do otherwise, and in the other case not.[34]

Wolf says that whereas according to the libertarian, only the first of these agents is responsible, "there seems to be nothing of value that the first agent has but the second agent lacks." Perhaps the second agent does not have the ability to do otherwise because "her understanding of the situation is so good and her moral commitment so strong." Wolf concludes that the fact that the second agent is determined to do the right thing for the right reasons does not make her any less deserving of praise than the first agent.

But, Wolf's argument is susceptible to an objection inspired by a point Fischer raises in connection with a Frankfurt-style example.[35] Given the way Wolf presents her lifesaver case, the reader might yet presuppose that the swimmer who cannot do otherwise is not causally determined to

---

32. Wolf, *Freedom Within Reason* (Oxford: Oxford University Press, 1990), pp. 79–85; see also her "Asymmetrical Freedom," *Journal of Philosophy* 77 (1980): pp. 151–66.
33. Wolf, *Freedom Within Reason*, p. 79.
34. Ibid., pp. 81–2.
35. Fischer, "Responsibility and Control," p. 176.

deliberate and act as she does. If it were specified that her action results from a deterministic causal process that traces back to factors she could not have produced, altered, or prevented – perhaps by adding that she is controlled by neuroscientists – the intuition that she deserves praise might well vanish. Wolf's case may indicate that an agent might deserve praise even if she could not have done otherwise, but it fails to show that an agent deserves praise even if her action results from a deterministic causal process that traces back to factors beyond her control.

But suppose that the intuition that the second swimmer deserves praise persists even if it is specified that she is causally determined. The hard incompatibilist can now argue that while according to ordinary intuitions, both swimmers deserve praise, the second swimmer really does not. Ordinarily, we consider persons praiseworthy for their great intelligence, good looks, or native athletic ability, even though these qualities are not due to any agency of theirs and even though they in no sense really deserve praise for these qualities. Thus, it comes as no surprise that we would ordinarily consider the second swimmer, who is determined to do the right thing for the right reasons, praiseworthy. She may be considered praiseworthy because she is a good person, and has acted in pursuit of the good, but as in the case of the person of great intelligence, we need not conclude that she is genuinely deserving of praise.

Sometimes it may well be a good thing to praise someone despite her not deserving it, perhaps because praise can at times simply be an expression of approbation or delight about the actions or accomplishments of another. By contrast, blaming someone who does not deserve it would seem always to be (at least prima facie) wrong. The explanation for this disanalogy might be that because blaming typically causes pain, it must be wrong unless it is deserved, whereas since praise is far from painful, it can be appropriate beyond cases in which it is deserved. Whatever may be the case here, the intuition that the determined swimmer is praiseworthy fails to undermine the hard incompatibilist view – that not only deserved blame but also deserved praise is incompatible with determinism.

DOES HARD INCOMPATIBILISM UNDERMINE MORALITY?

It has at times been suggested that if we can never be praiseworthy or blameworthy for our actions, then all of morality collapses. For judgments of moral obligation would not survive, and it wouldn't make sense to call certain actions right and others wrong. Spinoza, for example, intimates that judgments of moral responsibility and those of right and wrong are undermined at once; he remarks that because human beings mistakenly "believe that they are free, the following abstract notions came into being: – praise, blame, right, wrong."[36] In opposition to a view of this sort, Honderich maintains that although determinism is in his distinctive sense incompatible with retributive attitudes, since these attitudes typically presuppose that agents causally originate actions, determinism is not incompatible with judgments of right and wrong, goodness, and badness.[37] In a similar vein, Smilansky contends that it is difficult to see why denying moral responsibility should entail rejecting these other moral notions.[38] His scheme divides morality into two distinct components. The first concerns what "morally ought to be done (or not done)," and the second, agents' blameworthiness or praiseworthiness for their actions. In Smilansky's view, ordinarily moral agents have both components in mind when contemplating what to do. Hard determinism undermines the second component. But, he argues, it does not thereby undermine the first as well. I am sympathetic with views such as Honderich's and Smilanksy's, although their defense will have to contend with an important objection, as we shall now see.[39]

It could be that central kinds of moral "ought" judgments would be threatened in a determinist picture.[40] For the following "ought implies can" principle is indeed attractive: If one ought to do something, then it must be the case that one can do it.[41] Thus, if because one is causally

36. Spinoza, *Ethics*, Appendix to Part I.
37. Honderich, *A Theory of Determinism*, pp. 525–30.
38. Smilansky, "The Ethical Advantages of Hard Determinism," *Philosophy and Phenomenological Research* 54 (1994), pp. 355–63, at p. 358.
39. Haji, *Moral Appraisability*, pp. 42–64; "Moral Anchors and Control," *Canadian Journal of Philosophy* 29 (1999), pp. 175–203.
40. See Broad, "Determinism, Indeterminism, and Libertarianism" for a defense of the claim that determinism undermines central judgments of moral obligation. Broad also describes types of 'ought' judgments that are not threatened by determinism, for example: "When we say that a man ought not to cheat at cards we often mean to assert two things. (a) That the average decent man does not do this, and that anyone who does falls in this respect below the average. And (b) that a man who does this either has a very low ideal of human nature or a very weak and unstable desire to approximate the ideal which he has. So in this further respect, he falls below the average" (pp. 159–60).
41. For a sensitive discussion of these issues, see Walter Sinnott-Armstrong, "'Ought' Conversationally Implies 'Can'," *The Philosophical Review* 93 (1984), pp. 249–61, and "'Ought To Have' and 'Could Have'," *Analysis* 45 (1985), pp. 44–8.

determined one can never do otherwise, then it seems false that one ever ought to do otherwise. Furthermore, one might also claim that if our choices and actions are partially or truly random events, then we could never do otherwise by the sort of agency required for it to be true that we ought to do otherwise. But if it is never true that one ought to do otherwise, then what would be the point of a system of moral "oughts"? The first thesis of hard incompatibilism – that all of our actions lie on the continuum from alien-deterministic to truly random events – might then imperil this system, because it would seem that if "A ought to do x" is true at all, it must be true not only when A does x, but also when A fails to do x.[42]

Even if moral "ought" judgments are never true, it would seem that moral judgments such as "it is morally good for A to do x" and "it is morally bad for A to do y" still can be. Thus, for example, even if one is causally determined to refrain from giving to charity, and even if it is therefore false that one ought to give to charity, it still might be good to do so. Cheating on one's taxes might be a bad thing to do, even if one's act is causally determined, and thus, even if it is false that one ought not to do so. These alternative moral judgments would indeed lack the deontic implications they might be assumed to have, but nevertheless, it would seem that they can be retained when moral "ought" statements are undermined.

Haji does not dispute the claim that causal determinism is compatible with the truth of judgments of moral goodness and badness. But he does argue that causal determinism undermines judgments of moral rightness and wrongness, and that it does so for the same sorts of underlying reasons that it undermines moral "ought" judgments. His argument begins with an "ought implies can" principle:

K: S has a moral obligation to perform [not to perform] A only if it is within S's power to perform [not to perform] A.

He then adds "a standard principle of moral obligation":

OW: S has a moral obligation to perform [not to perform] A if and only if it is morally wrong for S not to perform [to perform] A.

Haji defends these principles by saying:

---

42. See Haji, "Moral Anchors and Control" for a more thoroughly developed argument along these lines.

143

It is hard to contest these principles. In fact, it is reasonable to suppose that the mark of *any* adequate theory of moral obligation – any theory that specifies necessary and sufficient conditions for the obligatoriness of actions . . . – should "validate" these principles. We might think of **K** and **OW** as deontic axioms.

He also cites the fact that these principles serve as axioms or theorems in several prominent moral theories, and hence enjoy an impressive level of theoretical support.[43] But **K** and **OW** entail:

WAP: It is morally wrong for S to perform [not to perform] A only if it is within S's power not to perform [to perform] A.

In accord with these claims, Haji argues that if causal determinism is true in a world, and therefore no person can do anything other than what he or she does in that world, then no action of this person in such a world is obligatory, and no action of this person in such a world is wrong.[44] Haji's argument has considerable force, but I shall explore the possibilities for resisting it.

First, the degree to which Haji's conclusions are unintuitive must be weighed against how unintuitive it is to reject one or more of his premises. If a theory that uses certain principles as premises has components derived from these principles that are unintuitive, the principles would thereby be to some degree disconfirmed. It would be implausible to claim that in a theory that uses **K** and **OW** as premises, these principles would have a justificatory status so strong that it immunizes them against disconfirming pressures from their unintuitive consequences. This is true even if **OW** and **K** are conceived as axioms in a moral theory. One might begin with principles such as **K** and **OW**, and regard them as axioms because they are intuitively true and because they appear central to the theory. If the components of the theory derived from these principles conform to our intuitions, that would provide theoretical support for them. But if such derived components do not conform to our intuitions, that would to some extent disconfirm these principles. I don't see how a principle's being an

---

43. "Moral Anchors and Control"; Haji cites Fred Feldman, *Doing the Best We Can* (Dordrecht: D. Reidel, 1986) and Michael Zimmerman, *The Concept of Moral Obligation* (New York: Cambridge, 1996).
44. Haji, *Moral Appraisability*, pp. 53–4; cf. p. 12.

axiom in a moral theory would immunize it from such disconfirming pressures.

Moreover, the claim that actions are never obligatory, right, or wrong (which has the consequence, for example, that nothing Hitler ever did was wrong) is not the only unintuitive result of the argument that crucially depends on **K** and **OW**. The line that Haji is constrained to draw – because he endorses this argument – between judgments about goodness and those about rightness is also unintuitive. The following principle seems true:

GR: Sometimes, actions that bring about the greatest good overall in worlds accessible to S are right for S.[45]

However, given that Haji wants to retain judgments about goodness, he must disavow **GR**, assuming causal determinism, and it is the argument based on **K** and **OW** that explains why he is committed to this result. Furthermore, Haji holds that blameworthiness survives determinism, while wrongness does not. Thus, in his view, when agents are blameworthy in a deterministic world (and they can indeed be), it is never because they have done anything wrong.[46] In the context of a deterministic world, Haji must therefore deny another very intuitive principle:

BW: Sometimes, when S is blameworthy for performing A, it was morally wrong for S to perform A.

It is again the argument that crucially depends on **K** and **OW** that explains why Haji is committed to denying **BW**. Now, it may very well be that in the final analysis, any view on these issues will have unintuitive consequences. But it is not clear that a position that denies **GR**, **BW**, and that actions are sometimes morally obligatory, right or wrong, while maintaining **K** and **OW** is superior to a view that, say, rejects **OW** and the claim that actions can be morally obligatory but accepts **GR**, **BW**, **K**, and that actions are sometimes right or wrong.

---

45. Another intuitively true principle that Haji must reject is: **GR′**: There is some correlation between an action's bringing about the greatest good overall in worlds accessible to S and that action's being right for S.

46. Haji says: "I argue, in addition, that if the 'ought' implies 'can' principle – that is, the principle that one ought (morally) to perform an action only if one can perform that action – is true, and if the principle that one has a moral obligation to perform an action only if it is morally wrong for one not to perform that action is also true, then, once again, no action to which there are no alternatives can be wrong. One may well be appraisable for performing such an action, but even if one is so, one will not thereby be appraisable for performing a *wrong* action" (*Moral Appraisability*, p. 12).

Furthermore, in this discussion it is important to keep in mind that we humans commonly presume that our actions are typically not causally determined. If this presumption were true, then **K**, **OW**, **GR**, and **BW** could all be maintained without any unintuitive consequences. But if we were to discover that causal determinism is true instead, then our easy acquiescence in these principles might need to be reconsidered. However, supposing that they cannot all be maintained, it seems arbitrary to privilege absolutely **K** and **OW** over **GR** and **BW** – and over the claims that actions are sometimes right and wrong and that judgments of moral obligation are sometimes true.

Despite all of this, it may be that Haji's position wins out in the end. But, as I have mentioned, an alternative – supposing the truth of causal determinism (or the first thesis of hard incompatibilism) – is to deny:

OW: S has a moral obligation to perform [not to perform] A if and only if it is morally wrong for S not to perform [to perform] A,

and to maintain judgments of rightness and wrongness, but to disavow the central judgments of moral obligation. This would allow us to preserve these three principles:

K: S has a moral obligation to perform [not to perform] A only if it is within S's power to perform [not to perform] A,

GR: Sometimes, actions that bring about the greatest good overall in worlds accessible to S are right for S,

and

BW: Sometimes, when S is blameworthy for performing A, it was morally wrong for S to perform A.

Perhaps the strongest challenge to this conception, provided by the intuitions and theoretical considerations that support **OW**, can be mitigated by the sense that while one half of this biconditional –

If S has a moral obligation to perform [not to perform] A then it is morally wrong for S not to perform [to perform] A

is extremely plausible, the other half –

If it is morally wrong for S not to perform [to perform] A, then S has a moral obligation to perform [not to perform] A is not quite so obviously true. (Reflecting on the bracketed version of the biconditional), I cannot think of a case in which intuitively an agent has a moral obligation not to perform an action and it is not morally wrong for the agent to perform it. Yet there are cases in which it seems quite intuitive that it is morally wrong for the agent to perform the action, but not that the agent has a moral obligation not to perform it. For example, suppose you say to an animal-abuser, "You ought not to abuse that animal," but then you find out that he has a psychological condition (which he could have done nothing to prevent) that makes animal-abusing irresistible for him, so that he cannot help but abuse the animal. From my point of view, there is an appreciably strong pull to admitting that the "ought" judgment was false, but there is relatively little to denying that abusing the animal is morally wrong for him.

Can central moral "ought" judgments be true given hard determinism, as Smilansky suggests? I'm not sure. Another alternative preserves **GR**, **BW**, and a version of **OW**, provides a limited defense of the idea that not only judgments of rightness and wrongness but also judgments of moral obligation could be maintained if causal determinism were true, and challenges **K** only for one central function of the moral "ought." This approach has the advantage that it preserves the truth of some central moral "ought" judgments, but it contravenes the intuition that for these judgments "ought" implies "can."

One clear role that moral "ought" judgments have is to guide actions. We tell people that they ought not to steal in order to keep them from stealing. Whether an action-guiding function exhausts the legitimate role of these moral judgments would be controversial – such judgments arguably have other purposes as well. Does **K** harmonize with an action-guiding point of view? Not so nicely, perhaps, with at least one such perspective. Suppose that causal determinism is true, and that hence no agent could ever have done otherwise. Nevertheless, we do not typically know in advance – before deliberation is complete or a decision has been made – which choice for action has been causally determined. Rather, as we have already pointed out, it is almost always true that from the epistemic point of view of the agent at the time of deliberation, more than one option for which choice she will make is possible. That is, more than one such option is possible relative to an appropriate subset of what she believes (or of what she should believe), in the sense that it is at least not ruled out by what she believes (or by what she should believe). Often, when one attempts to guide an agent

147

by means of a moral "ought" judgment, it is the range of options for action that are in this sense epistemically possible for the agent at the time of deliberation that one addresses. Frequently, it is significantly probable that expressing a moral "ought" judgment will causally influence action, and thus there is a good moral reason to do so – even if it turns out that because causal determinism is true, the agent could not have complied with the judgment.

Now **K** is indeed consistent with the practical rationality of any such use of "ought" judgments, since it could be practically rational to employ them in this way while they are false. However, one might think that in these sorts of situations, "ought" judgments might well not only be practically rational to express but also generally true. If this is right, then **K** would be false for these uses of "ought." One might hypothesize that **K** stands as a principle governing certain roles for moral "ought" judgments, but for this action-guiding function of moral judgment, **K** is best disavowed.

Against this solution, one might argue that although "ought" judgments in these action-guiding roles would retain practical value, so that it might often be practically rational to express them, they must nevertheless be false, if, say, causal determinism were true. This claim could be supported by the strength of our intuition that such "ought" judgments would be false if the agent were causally determined to do what he did, and more generally, by the force of the intuition that these judgments would be false if the agent could not have acted as recommended (due to no fault of his own). I am somewhat sympathetic with this objection, and for this reason I prefer the previous solution to this last one.

WHY HARD INCOMPATIBILISM IS NOT RESTRICTED TO CONSEQUENTIALISM IN ETHICS

It has sometimes been supposed that relinquishing deserved praise and blame restricts hard determinism to a consequentialist position in ethics. Indeed, hard determinists have historically argued for consequentialist positions. In developing his account of praise and blame, Priestley recommends that our understanding of these notions be revised along utilitarian lines:

In common language we say a man is praiseworthy and has merit. The philosopher says that a man has acted from or been influenced by good principles, or such principles as will make a man happy in himself and useful to others; that he is therefore a proper object of complacency and fit to be made happy; that is, the general happiness will be promoted by making him happy. So also when in common language a man is said to be blameworthy and have demerit, the philosopher says that he has acted from or been influenced by bad principles, or such as will make a man unhappy in himself and hurtful to others; that he is therefore a proper subject of aversion, and is fit to be made unhappy; that is, the making him unhappy will tend to promote the general happiness.[47]

At first glance, one might be tempted by the claim that although rejection of moral responsibility is consistent with the goodness of certain consequences and, derivatively, with the goodness of actions that bring about such consequences, abandoning moral responsibility rules out principles of right that are based on non-consequentialist considerations.

But setting aside the problems raised by Haji, the plausibility of the view that hard determinism, and by extension, hard incompatibilism, is restricted to consequentialist ethics diminishes under scrutiny. Michael Slote agrees. He points out that although Spinoza maintains that determinism undermines moral responsibility, he is nevertheless willing to speak of certain character traits as virtues and vices.[48] About Spinoza's position, Slote says: "A person who frequently turns on people unexpectedly – someone who acts angrily and aggressively toward people without provocation – can be regarded as vicious (as having a vicious temper or disposition) and may be avoided as such independently of any commitment to blame the person for being vicious and acting/interacting badly with others in certain

---

47. Priestley, *Priestley's Writings on Philosophy, Science, and Politics*, ed., Passmore, pp. 96–7. Just prior to these passages Priestley writes: "In common speech we say that we are accountable creatures, justly liable to rewards and punishments for our conduct. The philosopher says that justice ought to be called propriety or usefulness, or a rule of conduct adapted to answer a good purpose, which in this case is the good of those who are the subjects of government or discipline; and therefore, instead of saying, We are justly liable to rewards and punishments, he says, We are beings of such a constitution that to make us happy upon our observance of certain laws and to make us suffer in consequence of our transgressing those laws, will have a good effect with respect to both our own future conduct and that of others; i.e. tending to our own amelioration, and operating to the amelioration of others."

48. Michael Slote, "Ethics Without Free Will," *Social Theory and Practice* 16 (1990), pp. 369–83.

ways . . ."[49] He goes on to argue that most of the evaluative dimensions of virtue ethics are consistent with hard determinism. We can legitimately make moral criticisms of others even if hard determinism undermines evaluations of agents as blameworthy or praiseworthy.

Slote's claims, I believe, are correct, but as Waller also contends, a more general version of this position can be defended.[50] In my view, most of the descriptive and prescriptive content of any normative ethical system is consistent with hard determinism, and more inclusively, with hard incompatibilism. The reason for this is that the metaphysical bases for non-consequentialist positions in general, insofar as they have been developed, do not clearly involve an essential appeal to notions of freedom unavailable to the hard incompatibilist. For example, absolutist restrictions on consequentialist principles do not entail that we are free in the sense required for moral responsibility or that we can be praiseworthy and blameworthy. The doctrine of double effect's prohibition on intentional violations of certain rights, for instance, does not entail that those who violate this prohibition are blameworthy, as opposed to their actions simply being morally wrong. The hard incompatibilist can legitimately accept this range of non-consequentialist ethical views.[51]

Is Kantian ethics compatible with hard incompatibilism? True, the hard incompatibilist would have to deny one important component of Kant's view – that agents are morally responsible – and he might need to reject the Kantian "ought" implies "can" principle or else the claim that moral "ought" judgments are of crucial importance to ethics. But is the content of Kantian normative ethics inconsistent with hard incompatibilism? Significantly, all by themselves, the legitimacy of neither the first formulation of the Categorical Imperative,

Act only on that maxim which you can at the same time will that it become a universal law,

49. Slote, "Ethics Without Free Will," pp. 375–6.
50. Waller, *Freedom Without Responsibility*, pp. 152, 170–4.
51. Smilansky also argues that hard determinists are not restricted to consequentialist ethics. "One might be a hard determinist and see substantial moral requirements in utilitarian terms. But one might also be a hard determinist and think that morally one must not break a promise or kill another human being, irrespective of the consequences" ("The Ethical Advantages of Hard Determinism," p. 360).

nor the second,

> Act so that you treat humanity, whether in your own person or in the person of any other, always at the same time as an end, never merely as a means,

entails that the agents to whom they apply are free in the sense required for moral responsibility, or even that they ever be praiseworthy or blameworthy.[52] Perhaps a more threatening conflict is suggested by Fischer's claim that on the hard determinist position, we cannot retain a conception of ourselves as persons.[53] The Kantian conception of morality provides one interpretation of this thesis: If hard determinism is true, then the basis for respecting human beings will be undermined, and thus any claim to moral dignity will have to be relinquished. For Kant, moral dignity is ascribed to human beings because they possess certain kinds of capacities. First, humans have dignity insofar as they are capable of rationality – in particular, rationality of the practical sort. In Thomas Hill's interpretation of Kant, practical rationality allows us to set ends or goals for ourselves, to reason about means for achieving those goals, to set goals and choose means in accord with principles that specify respect for all humanity, to formulate such principles and to make a commitment to them.[54] But none of these capacities is threatened by hard determinism, nor, for similar reasons, by hard incompatibilism. If hard incompatibilism is true, then agents are not morally responsible for setting ends and choosing means, for formulating principles and making commitments to them. Nevertheless, the capacities for these activities can remain intact.

A second sort of capacity that in Kant's view confers dignity is autonomy. In fact, he sometimes says that it is autonomy, specifically, that is the ground of dignity.[55] One might think that hard incompatibilism obviously undermines autonomy, and that hence hard incompatibilists are barred from adopting the most central component of Kantian ethics. However, at least the core feature of Kantian autonomy – "positive freedom" – does not presuppose free will of the sort required for moral responsibility. To have positive freedom is to have a capacity to commit oneself to certain principles of conduct as rationally binding, principles that are not adopted to satisfy any contingent desires and are

52. Kant, *Groundwork of the Metaphysics of Morals*, Ak IV 421, 429.
53. Fischer, *The Metaphysics of Free Will*, pp. 1–3.
54. Thomas E. Hill, Jr., "Humanity as an End in Itself," *Ethics* 91 (1980), pp. 84–90, reprinted in his *Dignity and Practical Reason* (Ithaca: Cornell University Press, 1993), pp. 38–57.
55. Kant, *Groundwork of the Metaphysics of Morals*, Ak IV 436, 440.

necessarily imposed on oneself as a rational agent.[56] No feature of hard incompatibilism is incompatible with positive freedom, for having this capacity is clearly consistent with lacking free will.

MORAL WORTH

Smilansky argues that hard determinism actually has an ethical advantage over the competing positions. In his conception, hard determinism allows for the possibility of an ethical life of greater purity than is possible if one believes that one is morally responsible.[57] If one believes that one is morally responsible, one will believe that one's own moral worth is at stake whenever one makes a morally relevant decision. Hence, a kind of self-concern arises for such a moral agent in situations of moral decision-making. In fact, according to Smilansky, such a moral agent "is inherently concerned with himself, and what action would make him praiseworthy or blameworthy in the eyes of others or of himself." Smilansky does not claim that in this respect the agent who believes in moral responsibility is egoistic. But in his view, for such an agent "a concern with the self's moral stature is however at least tacitly present."[58] By contrast, the hard determinist moral agent is potentially not concerned with himself at all. Rather, "he is solely focussed on determining what he ought to do."[59] Furthermore, "the hard determinist agent we are considering enquires after the right thing to do and goes on to do it *despite* realizing that he is not praiseworthy for doing so, and would not be blameworthy were he to act differently ... If you like, he does not care about saving his moral soul, but about morality alone."[60]

One might doubt Smilansky's claim that for an agent who believes in moral responsibility, a concern with one's blameworthiness or praiseworthiness is always present. To me it seems possible that one believes in moral responsibility, but that this belief plays no role in one's moral decision-making. Furthermore, for the hard incompatibilist agent, an analog to concern for one's own praiseworthiness or blameworthiness seems as likely to be present as does this concern itself for the agent

---

56. Hill, "The Kantian Conception of Autonomy," in his *Dignity and Practical Reason* (Ithaca: Cornell University Press, 1993), pp. 76–96.
57. Smilansky, "The Ethical Advantages of Hard Determinism," pp. 356ff.
58. Ibid., p. 358.
59. Ibid., p. 358.
60. Ibid., pp. 358–9.

who believes in moral responsibility. This analog can also be characterized as a concern that one be a morally worthy person. Although hard
incompatibilism denies that human beings can have moral worth in the
sense that they are morally praiseworthy for their actions, it need
not renounce the notion of an agent's moral worth altogether (as
Smilansky himself argues elsewhere).[61] An agent can have moral worth
by, for example, persistently doing what is right, even in situations in
which there are strong countervailing pressures, by regulating her
behavior by moral reasons, by having dispositions to examine her past
behavior from the moral point of view, and by possessing a willingness
to change her behavior when tendencies to immorality are recognized.
These features of moral worthiness would not be illegitimate or impossible if hard incompatibilism were true. Moreover, perhaps from the
moral perspective, it is these features of the ordinary concept of moral
worthiness that are most significant, while praiseworthiness has a com-
paratively diminished role. Indeed, if one is a hard incompatibilist, a
concern for one's moral worth in this sense might be more or less continuously present.

Smilansky affirms that in the hard determinist view, agents can be
more or less morally attractive. An agent "could be seen as a 'fine moral
specimen'," and "a determined human being can behave in an 'ethically
noble' way."[62] As hard determinists, we might appreciate agents for
having these qualities. This seems right to me. Smilansky does say that
such appreciation "would border on the aesthetic" even though it still
has deeply moral aspects. In my view, perhaps such appreciation is more
like the aesthetic sort than is often thought because it does not involve
blameworthiness or praiseworthiness, but it is no less moral for that
reason.

It is nevertheless important to emphasize that the notion of moral
worth that hard incompatibilism can retain differs significantly from the
ordinary conception. Hard incompatibilist moral worth is indeed moral,
but it is more similar to the value we might assign to an automobile
or a work of art. Moral accomplishments would not genuinely be an
agent's own in a sense strong enough to sustain judgments of fundamentally deserved credit or praise. More generally, no matter what of
value about human life hard incompatibilism can legitimately retain, it
must relinquish a component of the ordinary conception of what sets

61. Smilansky, "Can a Determinist Respect Herself," pp. 88–92.
62. Smilansky, "The Ethical Advantages of Hard Determinism," p. 361.

human beings apart from the rest of the world. My claim is that this conception would not be diminished to the degree that many would fear, and that the resulting view of ourselves is one with which we can live.

WRONGDOING

The hard incompatibilist position implies that human immoral behavior is much more similar to earthquakes and epidemics than it would be if we were morally responsible. The justification we assume for regarding moral offenses as deeply different from natural disasters is that persons are typically responsible for their actions. But according to hard incompatibilism, because a person's actions are the result of processes over which he has no control, we cannot consider him responsible for them, just as we cannot hold earthquakes or epidemics responsible for their effects. One still might legitimately have a feeling of moral concern about what persons do, or about what persons who are reasons-responsive do, which would differ from one's attitudes to earthquakes and epidemics. Nevertheless, attitudes that presuppose the cognitive component that persons are morally responsible would be theoretically unjustified.

Honderich rightly contends that in the face of determinism, we must eschew retributive attitudes toward wrongdoers, but he also argues that

we can persist in certain responses to the desires and intentions of others, and hence to them. There is no obstacle to my abhorrence of the desires and intentions of the treacherous husband foreseeing his divorce, or, more important, to my abhorrence of him, a man whose personality and character are consistent with these desires and intentions, and support them.[63]

But the hard incompatibilist must be more abstemious here. Moral abhorrence of a person because of the actions he has performed at least typically involves blaming him for those actions, which, in turn, presupposes that his actions and character did not result from processes beyond his control. If one were to discover that an especially immoral action was caused by some non-psychological, physiological reaction in the agent, one's moral abhorrence would tend to vanish, and this would suggest that this abhorrence was founded on a presupposition of free

63. Honderich, *A Theory of Determinism*, p. 533.

will. From the hard incompatibilist perspective, it is legitimate to feel moral concern in response to an immoral action, and to be deeply saddened that there are agents with immoral character, but most often one's response of moral abhorrence, because it presupposes moral responsibility, is unjustified.[64]

Perhaps one can learn to abhor people because of the immoral actions they perform without regarding them as blameworthy, just as one might abhor soggy corn flakes because of their sogginess without considering them blameworthy. But it is doubtful that developing such an attitude toward people could be justified on moral grounds if hard incompatibilism were true. One might then be able to abhor people for their immoral actions without being theoretically irrational, but it seems unlikely that one would advance the good by fostering this attitude, by contrast, for example, with attitudes such as moral concern or sadness.

However, what should we say to someone who regularly and deliberately does wrong, refuses to make a commitment to morality, and offers hard incompatibilism and his consequent lack of freedom as an excuse for his behavior? Wouldn't the hard incompatibilist have little to say to such a person? Jean-Paul Sartre would impugn such denial of freedom as a form of "bad faith," a kind of self-deception, and he is clearly describing a form of thought and behavior that we would want to avoid.[65]

There are cases of this sort in which the hard incompatibilist can agree that the agent is self-deceived, but not because he is denying the free will he knows himself to have, but rather because he is telling a specific causal story that he knows to be untrue. There are also situations in which the agent is not self-deceived, but his specific causal story is nevertheless false. However, especially for those cases in which the agent does not specify a specific causal story, the hard incompatibilist must admit that the agent's lack of free will provides a legitimate excuse. The hard incompatibilist would have to reject the view that this excuse betrays a form of self-deception, whereas the proponent of moral responsibility would not. But the hard incompatibilist would not need to accept the claim that the causal history that produced the agent's past actions will determine him to be similarly immoral in the future. Moreover, even if the wrongdoer is causally determined to persist in

---

64. Thanks to Rachel Wertheimer for convincing me to make this point.
65. Jean-Paul Sartre, *Being and Nothingness* (New York: Philosophical Library, 1956).

his bad behavior, in most circumstances no one, including the agent, will know this to be the case. Typically, it is epistemically possible for an agent in this situation that he avoid similarly immoral actions in the future, and then morality would require that he commit himself to refraining from such actions, no matter what the character of his past life.

One might propose that even if hard incompatibilism were true, it would still be best to behave as if people were morally responsible. Even if the claim that we are morally responsible cannot be justified, there may be a practical argument for nevertheless treating ourselves and others as if it were true. Dennett suggests a position of this kind:

Instead of investigating, endlessly, in an attempt to *discover* whether or not a particular trait is of someone's making – instead of trying to assay exactly to what degree a particular self is self-made – we simply *hold* people morally responsible for their conduct (within limits we take care not to examine too closely). And we are rewarded for adopting this strategy by the higher proportion of "responsible" behavior we thereby inculcate.[66]

In the final analysis, whether Dennett is right would have to be decided by careful empirical investigation. But his suggestion might initially be found attractive on the ground that acting as if people sometimes deserve blame is typically necessary for effectively promoting moral reform and education. If we were to act as if people were not morally responsible, then it might well seem that we would have insufficient leverage to change people's immoral ways of behaving.

It is nevertheless important to keep in mind that this option would have the hard incompatibilist treating agents as blameworthy – by, for example, expressing indignation toward them – when they do not deserve this sort of treatment, which would seem to be morally wrong. As Waller also argues, if people are not responsible for their wrongdoing, treating them as if they were would be unfair.[67]

However, there are practices for promoting moral reform and education that would not suffer from this sort of unfairness, and a strong case can be made that at least in ordinary situations, they could be as effective as those that assume moral responsibility. Instead of treating people as if they were blameworthy, the hard incompatibilist can appeal

---

66. Dennett, *Elbow Room*, p. 164.
67. Waller, *Freedom Without Responsibility*, pp. 130–5.

156

to the practice of moral admonishment and encouragement. One could explain to an offender that what he did was wrong, and then encourage him to refrain from performing similar actions in the future. The hard incompatibilist can maintain that by admonishing and encouraging a wrongdoer one might communicate a sense of what is right, and a respect for persons, and that these attitudes can lead to salutary change. Likewise, instead of treating oneself as deserving of blame, one could admonish oneself for one's wrongdoing, and resolve to refrain from similar actions in the future. It is not obvious that the hard incompatibilist's resources for moral education and imparting respect for persons are less effective than those that would be legitimate if we were morally responsible.

But what resources does hard incompatibilism have for legitimately dealing with genuinely criminal behavior? It might seem that here, hard incompatibilism is at a clear disadvantage, and that practical considerations should force us to treat criminals as if they were morally responsible. We shall turn to this issue in the next chapter, in which I will argue that hard incompatibilism does not obviously diminish the morally acceptable options for dealing with criminals, and that the policies that are justifiable from this perspective are in fact sufficient.

6

Hard Incompatibilism and Criminal Behavior

Perhaps the most frequently and urgently voiced criticism of the type of view I am developing is that the responses to criminal behavior it will allow are insufficient for acceptable social policy. The way matters actually lie, however, is more complex than this objection suggests. Some of the most prominent justifications for punishing criminals will be undermined by hard incompatibilism, and thus in some respects it may appear to permit fewer policies for opposing crime than the alternative positions. But, as we shall see, each of these justifications faces significant difficulties independent of hard incompatibilist considerations. At the same time, hard incompatibilism leaves other methods for responding to such behavior intact, and arguably, these methods are sufficient for good social policy. As a result, we need not extend Dennett's advice to criminals and treat them as if they were morally responsible (with a possible exception, as we shall see). Let us discern which justifications for dealing with criminal behavior are legitimate and which are not, given hard incompatibilism, while taking care to note whether this view is left with fewer tenable policies than the alternative positions.

The problem for the hard incompatibilist position is that without the robust conceptions of agency that are ruled out if hard incompatibilism is true, it would appear unacceptable to blame criminals for what they have done, and we would therefore seem to have inadequate justification for punishing them. Hard incompatibilism would then render unjustified what is arguably a core feature of justice and morality. Moreover, we would appear to be left with no legitimate and effective method for preventing people from doing horrible things to others. These opinions challenge the claim that it is practically rational to act as if hard incompatibilism is true. A hard incompatibilist who hopes that he can justifiably maintain the view both theoretically and practically must answer these worries.

Some methods for dealing with criminal behavior are punitive, others are rehabilitative. The central cases of punishment impose on an offender serious harm, such as long-term loss of liberty by confinement in the sorts of prisons we have in our society, significant physical or psychological pain, or death, because he has done wrong. The central cases of rehabilitation attempt to improve the criminal morally and psychologically, and any significant pain or deprivation of liberty that occurs is a side-effect of the method and not its goal or its means. There are three standard methods for justifying a punitive response to criminal behavior – the retributivist, moral education, and deterrence theories. Let us examine each of these to ascertain how the justification of punishment fares from the hard incompatibilist perspective, and to assess whether this position must relinquish a justification for punishment that would otherwise have been sound. Thereafter, we will consider non-punitive methods for dealing with criminals.

HARD INCOMPATIBILISM RULES OUT RETRIBUTIVISM

According to the retributivist position, punishment of a wrongdoer is justified for the reason that he deserves something bad to happen to him – pain, deprivation or death, for example – just because he has done wrong.[1] Hence, a wrongdoer's deserving to be harmed is not reducible to a component of a scheme justified solely on the basis of its consequences. This claim is typically subjected to qualifications such as that the agent had to have committed the wrong intentionally or knowingly. But we can set these niceties aside, for what is crucial to our discussion about the retribution theory is that according to the retributivist, it is the desert attached to the criminal's wrongful action alone that provides the justification for punishment. The retribution

---

1. Immanuel Kant, *The Metaphysical Elements of Justice* (New York: Bobbs-Merrill), tr. John Ladd, pp. 99–107; Michael Moore, "The Moral Worth of Retribution," in *Responsibility, Character, and the Emotions*, ed. Ferdinand Schoeman (Cambridge: Cambridge University Press, 1987), pp. 179–219, reprinted in *Punishment and Rehabilitation*, third edition, ed. Jeffrie G. Murphy (Belmont, CA: Wadsworth, 1995), pp. 94–130.

theory does not appeal to a good such as the safety of society or the moral improvement of the criminal in justifying punishment. Rather, the good to be achieved by punishment, by means of which retributivism justifies punishment, is that an agent receive what he deserves as a result of his having done wrong.

This position would be undermined if hard incompatibilism were true, since if agents do not deserve to be blamed just because they have done wrong, neither do they deserve to be punished just because they have done wrong. Because retributivism justifies punishment solely on the grounds of a basic notion of desert, hard incompatibilism is incompatible with retributivism for the reason that it rejects this notion of desert. Hard incompatibilists must therefore abandon the retributivist justification for punishment.

One might suppose that retributivism constitutes an intuitive justification for punishment that would be powerful and resilient absent hard incompatibilism. However, there are rather substantial arguments for the claim that retributivism turns out to be unacceptable even disregarding the hard incompatibilist considerations, although it is also not clear that these arguments are decisive.[2] Perhaps the deepest problem for this theory derives from the skeptical hypothesis that retributivist sentiments are at root vengeful desires, and that therefore retribution has little more plausibility than vengeance as a morally sound policy for action.[3] Acting on vengeful desires might be wrong for the following sort of reason. Although acting on such desires can bring about pleasure or satisfaction, no more of a moral case can be made for acting on them than can be made for acting on sadistic desires, for example. Acting on sadistic desires can bring about pleasure, but in both cases, acting on the desire aims at the harm of the one to whom the action is directed, and in neither case does acting on the desire essentially aim at any good other than the pleasure of its satisfaction. But since retributivist motivations are disguised vengeful desires, acting for the sake of retribution is also morally wrong.

One counter-strategy involves pointing out salient differences between vengeance and retribution. For example, by contrast with

---

2. For such criticisms, see C.L. Ten, *Crime, Guilt, and Punishment* (Oxford: Oxford University Press, 1987), pp 38–65; John Braithwaite and Philip Pettit, *Not Just Deserts* (Oxford: Oxford University Press, 1990), pp. 156–201; Philip Montague, *Punishment as Societal Defense* (Lanham: Rowman and Littlefield, 1995), pp. 11–23, 80–90.
3. See Moore, "The Moral Worth of Retribution," for a discussion of this sort of objection to retributivism.

vengeance, retribution is in principle limited in its severity, and while vengeance often engenders further vengeance, retribution brings about closure. One might respond that the core motivation in retribution is vengeful, and that retribution is at root a controlled form of vengeance. On another retributivist response, in central cases, the sentiment of vengeance is an emotional expression of the sense of retributivist justice.[4] In such cases, the sense of retributivist justice is explanatorily prior to the sentiment of vengeance, and thus if retribution has an independent justification, it might well not be threatened by the objection from vengeance.

But suppose it is unclear which prevails – retributivism or the objection. Then a case might be made that the plausibility of the objection makes it illegitimate to justify actual punishment policy retributivistically. Punishment – in particular, punishment designed to satisfy the retributivist goals – harms people. If one aims to harm another, the justification must meet a high epistemic standard. If it is not beyond reasonable doubt that retributivist justifications are disguised vengeful justifications, and vengeful justifications are illegitimate, then there is reason to believe that it is immoral to justify punishment policy retributivistically. More generally, where there is a substantial likelihood that one's justification for harming someone is illegitimate, then harming that person on the basis of that justification could well be morally wrong.

If hard incompatibilism were true, the retributivist justification for punishment would be undermined. But independently of grounds deriving from hard incompatibilism there are reasons for rejecting a punishment policy based on a retributivist justification. However, we have certainly not decided this issue here, and it is the appropriate subject of a much longer discussion. We can conclude that although hard incompatibilism might forgo a justification for punishment that would otherwise have been morally legitimate, it does not clearly do so.

HARD INCOMPATIBILISM AND THE MORAL
EDUCATION THEORY

There are further ways of justifying punishment that do not appeal to a notion of basic desert, and as a result they could be acceptable to the

4. George Sher once made this suggestion in conversation.

hard incompatibilist. Consider the proposal to morally educate criminals by punishing them. We typically do not punish children for retributivistic reasons, but to educate them morally. Hence, the punishment of children provides a model for justifying criminal punishment that the hard incompatibilist can potentially accept.[5] There are several ways in which punishment or threat of punishment might serve to educate a child. The first way, as Herbert Morris suggests, is by indicating to the child the consequences of the wrongdoing for himself and for others. To use his example, if a child cheats, one might exclude him from playing the game for a time, thereby informing him of the possible game-destroying consequences of cheating for both himself and others.[6] Jean Hampton proposes that a wrongdoer might be "made to endure an unpleasant experience designed, in some sense, to 'represent' the pain suffered by her victim(s)."[7] Second, Hampton also argues that punishment might morally educate a child by conveying to him the seriousness of the wrongdoing.[8] Different levels of severity can communicate distinct levels of seriousness of wrongdoing and important moral boundaries. A third way, which Morris also points out, is by communicating the strength of the parents' attachment to the moral rules that have been violated. A fourth is by coercing a child into behaving in accord with morality, and thereby helping to acquaint him with the benefits of a morally virtuous lifestyle, which he might subsequently come to adopt for reasons less mercenary than fear of punishment.

However, it is not at all clear that punishing adult criminals, by contrast with children, is especially likely to produce moral improvement. A serious difficulty for the moral education theory is that children and adult criminals are relevantly disanalogous in several respects. First of all, criminals, unlike children, typically know the moral rules generally accepted in their society. Contrary to Hampton's view in particular, one could hardly justify punishment on the ground that it would convey

---

5. Herbert Morris, "A Paternalistic Theory of Punishment," *American Philosophical Quarterly* 18 (1981); reprinted in *Punishment and Rehabilitation*, third edition, ed. Jeffrie G. Murphy (Belmont, CA: Wadsworth, 1995), page numbers are from the latter source; Robert Nozick, *Philosophical Explanations* (Cambridge: Harvard University Press, 1981), pp. 363–97; Jean Hampton, "The Moral Education Theory of Punishment," *Philosophy and Public Affairs* (1984), pp. 208–38.
6. Morris, "A Paternalistic Theory of Punishment," p. 160.
7. Hampton, "The Moral Education Theory of Punishment," p. 227.
8. Ibid., pp. 225–6.

to the criminals that their actions are morally wrong, and to communicate to them "that there is a barrier of a very special sort against these kinds of actions," given that criminals typically already understand the moral code. Some criminals, to be sure, do not comprehend that their actions are morally wrong, but we have a strong disposition not to punish them for reasons of mental incompetence. Indeed, in both the British and American traditions, it is precisely when the criminal does not know that his actions are morally wrong that he is judged insane and therefore not liable to punishment.

Consequently, a moral education theory of adult criminal punishment would have to claim that punishment is likely to aid in motivating or inducing criminals to improve morally. But disanalogies between children and criminals threaten this proposal as well. Children are much more psychologically malleable than criminals are. Moreover, where punishment might be successful in morally educating children, it is typically administered in the context of a caring environment. Punishment outside of such a context arguably tends to create resentful attitudes and behavior rather than moral improvement. Here again, the analogy between children and adult criminals is weak in relevant respects, and thus the claims for punishment as a likely vehicle for moral improvement based on this analogy are insufficiently plausible.

Especially because criminals differ in significant respects from the only agents for whom the success of punishment as moral education might be reasonably thought to have been established, one would require empirical evidence to substantiate the claims of a moral education theory for criminals. Indeed, without substantial empirical evidence that punishment can successfully educate criminals morally, it would be thoroughly wrong to punish criminals for the reason that it can realize this outcome. If one proposes to harm someone in order to achieve a salutary result, one must have very good evidence that harming him in this way can have the intended effect.

Hampton makes several suggestion for types of punishment that can help realize the moral education of a criminal.

One way the moral education theorist can set punishments for crimes is to think about "fit." Irrespective of how severe a particular crime is, there will sometimes be a punishment that seems naturally suited to it; for example, giving a certain youth charged with burglarizing and stealing money from a neighbor's house the punishment of supervised compulsory service to this neighbor for a period of time, or giving a doctor charged with cheating a government medical insurance program the punishment of compulsory unre-munerated service in a state medical institution.[9]

First, service requirements of this sort are certainly not paradigms for criminal punishment. Indeed, one might question whether they should be classified as punishment at all, and not as programs for moral reha-bilitation. Hampton would reply that these types of service include a punitive aspect – the restriction of an offender's freedom.[10] Also, for some, actually working through such a program might involve psycho-logical discomfort. But all compulsory rehabilitative programs will involve some restriction of freedom, and often some pain or inconve-nience in working through the program.

Second, exactly what is it about service requirements that might produce moral improvement? Could it be the punitive aspect – the restriction of freedom or the pain of service? More likely, the feature that would produce moral change is involvement with the people or the kind of people the criminal has harmed. A tax evader who is sen-tenced to helping those who require government assistance could as a result come to care more for them, and hence be motivated to pay his taxes in the future. The restriction of freedom and the pain of service that such a program might involve is best regarded as a side-effect of the method, and not as its goal or its means. This provides a further reason for classifying such approaches as programs for moral rehabilita-tion rather than cases in which punishment morally educates.

Moreover, suppose that punishment can morally educate criminals. Even then, all other things being equal, if there exist non-punitive methods of achieving the moral education that one might also attain through punishment, those methods should be preferred. If a criminal can be as effectively morally educated through a fairly painless rehabil-itative program, that method should be favored over the punitive option. By analogy, if a neurophysiological problem such as insufficient serotonin production explains a lack of moral motivation, then it might well be that drug therapy is to be preferred to punishment, even if pun-ishment or threat of punishment can achieve the same goals. All other things being equal, if two methods achieve the same goal for an agent, but one harms him while the other does not, the one that does not harm the agent should be preferred.

9.   Hampton, "The Moral Education Theory of Punishment," pp. 227–8.
10.   Ibid., p. 224.

164

Morris claims that an important feature of moral rehabilitation – the wrongdoer's retaining of his self-respect – requires that he be punished. This is because

punishment "rights the wrong." It has, in contrast to blame and disapproval, the character of closure, of matters returning to where they were before, of relationships being restored. Just as a limit being placed upon conduct serves to provide a bounded, manageable world for the child, so the punitive response to the breach defines a limit to separation that is occasioned by wrongdoing. The debt is paid, life can go on.[11]

In fact, Morris claims that "a general practice of pardoning persons who claimed that they were repentant would destroy the principal means of reestablishing one's membership in the community."[12]

There is more than one way to interpret Morris's claim. Perhaps the idea that punishment "rights the wrong" presupposes retributivism. If so, a hard incompatibilist would have to reject much of what Morris argues here. If hard incompatibilism is true, then there is no abstract and basic requirement of desert, and so punishment cannot right the wrong by the offender's receiving what he deserves for it. However, Morris might also be read as not presupposing retributivism, but as maintaining that the psychological and social well-being of victims and criminals alike depends on punishment. Even then, there are reasons independent of hard incompatibilism for believing that Morris's claim is implausible. If a criminal brutally murders your child, it is thoroughly unintuitive to claim that the criminal's suffering or death could in any sense right the wrong. Horrendous acts of this sort cannot be "righted" by the perpetrator's punishment. To think that a wrong of this sort can be righted by punishment fails to appreciate the degree to which the effects of the wrongdoing persist after punishment.

If the criminal repents of his wrongdoing, and he is forgiven, relationships and community membership might be restored. But it is not clear how punishment should have a role in this process. Perhaps the criminal might sense that relationships or community membership cannot be fully restored until he has been made to feel appropriate pain or deprivation. The only good that such pain or deprivation could plausibly realize is a self-directed retributivistic good. It is not only from

11. Morris, "A Paternalistic Theory of Punishment," p. 160.
12. Ibid., p. 165.

the hard incompatibilist perspective that this notion of a good is to be viewed as a moral and metaphysical misconception.

One objective that societies have in punishing criminals is to prevent those criminals and other prospective criminals from committing crimes. On deterrence theories, it is the prevention of criminal wrongdoing that serves as the good by means of which punishment is justified. Initially, it would seem that there is no feature of hard incompatibilism that makes deterrence theories less acceptable to it than to libertarianism or to compatibilism. As we shall see, deterrence theories are not clearly immune to a hard incompatibilist challenge. Furthermore, deterrence justifications of paradigmatic sorts of punishment face difficult objections that do not rely on hard incompatibilism for their force.

The classic deterrence theory is Jeremy Bentham's. In his conception, the state's policy toward criminal behavior should aim at maximizing utility, and punishment should be administered if and only if it does so.[13] The pain or unhappiness produced by punishment results from the restriction on freedom that ensues from the threat of punishment, the anticipation of punishment by the person who has been sentenced, the pain of actual punishment, and the sympathetic pain felt by others such as the friends and family of the criminal.[14] The most significant pleasure or happiness that results from punishment derives from the security of those who benefit from its capacity to deter both the criminal himself as well as other potential criminals. No feature of hard incompatibilism, specifically, challenges this view.

But several more general objections have been raised against the utilitarian deterrence theory.[15] Three of these objections are especially threatening. The first is that this approach will justify punishments that are intuitively too severe. For it would seem that in certain cases,

---

13. Jeremy Bentham, *An Introduction to the Principles of Morals and Legislation* (1823); a good excerpt on punishment can be found in *Punishment and Rehabilitation*, third edition, ed. Jeffrie E. Murphy (Belmont, CA: Wadsworth, 1995), pp. 22–35.

14. Bentham, in Murphy, *Punishment and Rehabilitation*, third edition, p. 27.

15. For criticisms of this kind, see C.L. Ten, *Crime, Guilt, and Punishment*, pp. 7–37; Philip Montague, *Punishment as Societal Defense*, pp. 6–11.

extremely severe punishments would be more effective deterrents than much milder forms would, while such punishments are intuitively too severe to be fair. For example, if society were threatened by a crime wave, administering penalties of this sort might well maximize utility. The utilitarian could reply that if we are careful to include the pain of punishment in the calculation, the resulting severity will typically or always be intuitively unacceptable. He might also claim that in certain uncommonly dangerous situations, extremely severe penalties might indeed be justified. Nevertheless, one might reasonably fear that utilitarian recommendations will often fail to conform to our intuitions about fairness..

Second, the theory would seem to justify punishing the innocent.[16] If the perpetrator of a series of horrible crimes is not caught, potential criminals might come to believe that they can get away with serious wrongdoing. Under such circumstances, it might maximize utility to frame and punish an innocent person. Utilitarians might reply that the probability of such a scheme's being discovered is always significant, and that as a result, punishing the innocent is unlikely to maximize utility in any situation. However, it is far from obvious that this response is convincing. John Rawls offers a different reply on behalf of the utilitarian. There exist good utilitarian reasons for a punishment policy to be general, stable, and public – in short, to be institutionalized. Given this, there will be solid utilitarian reasons against deceptively punishing the innocent.[17] As a matter of practical fact, it is doubtful that a general, stable, and public scheme that would allow deceptively punishing the innocent could achieve the envisioned maximization of utility. Indeed,

16. A classic version of this objection is presented by H.J. McCloskey in "A Non-utilitarian Approach to Punishment," *Inquiry* 8 (1965), pp. 239–55.

17. Rawls writes about an institution, "telishment," that would allow for punishing the innocent: "Once one realizes that one is involved in setting up an *institution*, one sees that the hazards are very great. For example, what check is there on the officials? How is one to tell whether their actions are authorized? How is one to limit the risks involved in allowing such systematic deception? How is one to avoid giving anything short of complete discretion to the authorities to telish anyone they like? In addition to these considerations, it is obvious that people will come to have a very different attitude toward their penal system when telishment is adjoined to it. They will be uncertain as to whether a convicted man has been punished or telished. They will wonder whether or not they should feel sorry for him. They will wonder whether the same fate won't at any time fall on them. If one pictures how such an institution would actually work, and the enormous risks involved in it, it seems clear that it would serve no useful purpose. A utilitarian justification for this institution is most unlikely" (Rawls, "Two Concepts of Rules," *The Philosophical Review* 64 (1955), pp. 3–32).

an institution of this sort could easily engender massive disutility in society. A concern about Rawls's reply is that this practice would seem to be more deeply wrong than can be accounted for by the utilitarian reasons he presents.

Perhaps the most serious misgiving raised against utilitarian deterrence theory is the "use" objection. A general problem for utilitarianism is that it allows people to be harmed severely, without their consent, in order to benefit others, and this is often intuitively wrong. Punishing criminals for the security of society would appear to be just such a practice. Even if this problem fails to undermine utilitarian deterrence theory decisively, it should challenge one's confidence in this approach. Again, in assessing justifications for punishment, it is crucial that for a theory to be legitimately applicable in practice, we must be reasonably confident that it can withstand the objections that have been raised against it. Criminal punishment involves treating people severely – often it has very harmful short- and long-term consequences for the person being punished. If we are only mildly confident about the justification for such punishment, it would be morally wrong to administer it. Thus, we have solid reasons not to employ the classical utilitarian deterrence theory in justifying actual punishment policy – whether or not hard incompatibilism is true.

DETERRENCE JUSTIFIED BY THE RIGHT TO SELF-DEFENSE

One of the finest non–utilitarian developments of the deterrence theory can be found in "The Justification of General Deterrence" by Daniel Farrell.[18] Farrell's theory is impressive if only because it rests punishment on grounds most would accept – the right to harm in self-defense or defense of another (Warren Quinn advocates a theory that is similar in important respects[19]). Since it would seem that hard incompatibilism

---

18. Daniel M. Farrell, "The Justification of General Deterrence," *The Philosophical Review* 104 (1985); reprinted in *Punishment and Rehabilitation*, third edition, ed. Jeffrie E. Murphy (Belmont, CA: Wadsworth, 1995), pp. 38–60.
19. Quinn's theory differs from Farrell's in the following way. While Farrell contends that it is legitimate to threaten to harm an aggressor in certain circumstances because one may harm him in those circumstances, Quinn argues that one may harm him just because one may threaten to harm him. Accordingly, Quinn aims to establish that punishing criminals is legitimate because threatening to punish them is legitimate (Warren Quinn, "The Right to Threaten and the Right to Punish," *Philosophy and Public Affairs* 14 (1985), pp. 327–73).

could endorse this right, a theory of this sort promises to provide it with an acceptable justification for criminal punishment. But, as we shall see, there are reasons independent of hard incompatibilism to doubt the soundness of this type of view.

Farrell first distinguishes between special deterrence – punishment aimed at preventing the criminal himself from committing crimes – and general deterrence – punishment aimed at preventing people other than the criminal from committing crimes. A central feature of Farrell's account is that special deterrence is significantly easier to ground in the right to harm another in self-defense or defense of others than is general deterrence. He also differentiates between the right of direct self-defense and defense of others – your right to harm an unjust aggressor in order to prevent him from harming you or someone else – and the right of indirect self-defense and defense of others – your right to threaten an unjust aggressor with a reasonable amount of harm in order to prevent him from harming you or someone else.

In broad outline, Farrell's justification of special deterrence is this. Each of us has the right of direct self-defense (let us omit the "and defense of others" for short) and thus each of us also has the right of indirect self-defense. Furthermore, if each of us has the right of indirect self-defense, each of us also has the right to carry out the threat against the criminal once its condition has been violated. In addition, if each of us has the right of indirect self-defense, then an impartial agency such as the government has the right to issue a general threat to harm unjust aggressors, and also to carry out the threat once its condition has been violated. Thus, our possession of the right to self-defense justifies punishment as special deterrence.

This special deterrence theory promises to overcome the objections to its utilitarian counterpart. Intuitively, there is a limit to the severity of acceptable punishment, and Farrell's conception seems to generate this result. Quite clearly, one may not, on grounds of indirect self-defense, issue a threat to inflict a penalty more severe than is required to prevent the criminal himself from attacking. So if a threat of five years in prison would be sufficient to deter, one may not issue a death penalty threat. Further, the theory arguably does not justify punishing the innocent. Plausibly, one may not harm anyone other than an unjust aggressor in self-defense, or carry out a threat to harm anyone other than an unjust aggressor for these reasons. For example, one may not kill or threaten to kill an aggressor's innocent children even if this would prevent or stop an attack.

But harming an unjust aggressor does involve harming him without his consent for the benefit of others, and insofar as this characterization captures the notion of using someone, one does use the unjust aggressor when one harms him in order to prevent harm to oneself. Perhaps this is a legitimate kind of use because its target brings it upon himself by his unjust aggression – he deserves this kind of use. Significantly, Farrell thinks the right of self-defense assumes a form of retributivism.[20] In his view, the justification for direct and indirect self-defense and for special deterrence is a "weakly retributive" principle of distributive justice:

If an aggressor forces one to make a choice between harming the aggressor or allowing him/herself or others to be harmed, then one may harm the aggressor to the degree that preventing the harm to oneself or others requires

(within bounds – if the harm threatened is minor, but killing the aggressor would be required to prevent it, then killing the aggressor is wrong.) Note, however, that Farrell is not obviously correct to call this principle "retributive," since it, and the right to harm in self-defense more generally, arguably extend to individuals who are threats but are not morally responsible, such as people who are brainwashed or are psychopaths.

Farrell argues that the theory he develops cannot justify full-fledged general deterrence, for that would involve preventing aggression by harming someone not just to prevent *his* aggression, which again gives rise to a strong "use" objection. A person is illegitimately being used merely as a means for the benefit of others when he is punished in order to prevent people other than himself from committing crimes. Farrell believes, however, that some general deterrence can be justified on the basis of his principle of distributive justice. When someone, as a result of his action, makes you more vulnerable than you otherwise would be to the attacks of others, then you are justified in countering just this degree of added vulnerability by harming him. For example, suppose that you are being abused by a schoolyard bully, and that inflicting 100 units of pain is needed to prevent him from harming you. But suppose it is also true that had the bully not abused you, no one else would have been interested in harming you, but now that you have

20. Farrell, in *Punishment and Rehabilitation*, third edition, ed. Jeffrie E. Murphy, p. 43.

been abused, the interest of others in abusing you has been ignited. In addition, were the other potential bullies to see you inflicting merely 100 units of pain on the first bully, they would not be discouraged from abusing you, since you would then be perceived to be a soft touch when harmed. But inflicting 150 units of pain on the first bully would not only prevent him from harming you, it is also the minimum harm you could inflict on him that would effectively deter the other potential aggressors.

Farrell thinks that one is justified in inflicting 150 units of pain on the first bully in certain circumstances. For as a result of his action, this bully makes you more vulnerable than you otherwise would be to the attacks of the other potential bullies, and thus you are justified in countering just this degree of added vulnerability by harming him. According to Farrell, the deepest reason for this is also expressed by the "weakly distributive" principle of justice. The bully forces you to make a choice between harming him or allowing yourself to be harmed by himself as well as by others, and thus you may harm the aggressor to the degree that preventing all this harm requires.

One might suggest that a more ambitious sort of general deterrence can be justified by embellishing the "retributivist" component of the theory. Just because the criminal has done wrong, one might argue, we can punish him to show others what would happen to them if they were to commit a crime, and the amount of harm we may inflict on the criminal is not limited by the harm to which he makes the victim vulnerable as a result of his action. But such a view cannot be justified on the basis of the strong moral intuitions that undergird the plausibility of the right to harm in self-defense. Moreover, it still suffers from the major problem for retributivism that we first encountered – it might well be grounded in the desire for vengeance – and for this reason it cannot clearly serve as a legitimate foundation for criminal punishment.

By contrast, a Farrell-style deterrence theory is grounded in the powerful moral intuitions that underlie the right to harm in self-defense. Since – at least initially – this right would seem to be ours even if hard incompatibilism were true, it would appear that the hard incompatibilist could avail himself of Farrell's theory in arguing for the legitimacy of criminal punishment. Then he might not be at a disadvantage with respect to the competing positions in justifying an effective response to criminal behavior.

But although our right to defend ourselves and others by harming a threatening agent would seem not to be contingent on whether he is morally responsible, we have encountered a reason why this appearance may be deceptive. It may be, as Farrell suggests, that the right to harm in self-defense depends on a retributivist principle. Our intuitions about the legitimacy of harming in self-defense do derive mainly from cases in which we believe the threatening agent to be blameworthy. Typically, examples of criminal behavior are used in support of such a right, and it could be that the intuition that the threat is blameworthy is playing a crucial role in forming our intuitions.

Perhaps, then, the right to harm in self-defense is significantly weaker, assuming hard incompatibilism, than it would be if we were morally responsible. My own sense is that it is not much weaker, but establishing this claim would require a careful argument.[21] But if the right to harm in self-defense indeed turns out to be significantly weaker given hard incompatibilism, then an otherwise compelling way to develop the deterrence theory would be threatened if hard incompatibilism were true. The hard incompatibilist would have to question a justification and correlative policy for punishment that would seem well-anchored if we had moral responsibility.

It is a mistake to suppose that Farrell's theory would clearly be sound even if hard incompatibilism were false. In my view, this theory makes the incorrect assumption that the threats we can legitimately carry out against a criminal in the custody of the law are those that we can legitimately carry out against an aggressor who poses an immediate danger. In our society, the circumstances of criminals when deterrent threats toward them would typically be carried out – being in the custody of the law – are very different from those in which criminals pose an immediate danger. When in the custody of the law, criminals usually pose no immediate danger to anyone.

Examination of two analogies will indicate why it is often illegitimate to carry out a threat against a criminal in custody that would legitimately be carried out in circumstances in which the criminal poses an immediate danger. First, let us assume that threats that can legiti-

---

21. Otsuka provides an interesting case for the claim that the right to kill someone in self-defense requires that he be morally responsible. "Killing the Innocent in Self-Defense," *Philosophy and Public Affairs* 23 (1994), pp. 74–93.

mately be carried out against a potential aggressor who is immediately dangerous specify what one would reasonably believe to be the minimum harm required to prevent aggression. Now suppose that a potential aggressor clearly aims to kill you, and that to avoid being killed you may hit him on the head with a blunt instrument in order to render him unconscious. You may inflict this damage because it is reasonable to believe that it is the minimum harm that would prevent your being killed. As a result, it is legitimate for you to threaten him as follows: "If you attack me, I will hit you over the head with this weapon." Suppose he does attack you, clearly with the intent to kill, but in the process he slips in the mud, which allows you to pin him to the ground and tie him up. At this point, is it still legitimate for you to hit him on the head with the weapon to knock him out? To do so would clearly be immoral. Moreover, it is obvious that one could not justify hitting him by the right of self-defense and defense of others. All that this right justifies is that one inflict on the criminal what one would reasonably believe to be the minimum harm required to protect against him in his actual situation.

Second, imagine that the aggressor clearly aims to kill your child, and that to protect him it is legitimate for you to hit him on the head with the weapon and to threaten to do so. Suppose that despite your efforts, he kills the child, but that subsequently he slips in the mud and you tie him up. Is it then legitimate for you to hit him with the weapon? Certainly not because of the right of self-defense or defense of others, since he no longer poses an immediate threat. One surely retains the right to protect oneself and others against him, but not by carrying out the threat designed to prevent a harm that has already occurred.

But then, a threat that one could justifiably make and carry out to protect against someone who is immediately dangerous cannot legitimately be carried out against a criminal in custody, even if he would be dangerous if released. For the minimum harm required to protect oneself from someone who is immediately dangerous to oneself and others is typically much more severe than the minimum harm required to protect against a criminal in custody. If our guide is the right of self-defense, what we can legitimately do to a criminal in custody to protect ourselves against him will be determined by the minimum required to protect ourselves against him in his actual situation. If one would want to harm him more severely – say in the interests of providing plausibility for a system of threats – the right of self-defense could not provide the requisite justification, and one would again be in danger of endorsing a view that is subject to the "use" objection.

What is the minimum harm required to protect society against a criminal in custody? It seems clear that nothing more severe would be required than isolating the criminal from those he would endanger. Consequently, it is not obvious that theories like Farrell's can justify punishment of criminals, given that punishment involves the intentional infliction of significant harm, such as death or severe physical or psychological pain, as opposed to, for example, "quarantining" them. But, as we shall see, a justification for isolating criminals does not have to proceed by way of the right to harm an aggressor who is immediately dangerous, and for that reason it will be less encumbered by difficulties.

QUARANTINE AND CRIMINAL DETENTION

A much more resilient theory for justifying policies for protecting society from criminals, and one that is not threatened by hard incompatibilism, proceeds precisely by an analogy with the right to quarantine. Ferdinand Schoeman has argued that if in order to protect society, we have the right to quarantine people who are carriers of severe communicable diseases, then we also have the right to isolate the criminally dangerous to protect society.[22] For the carriers, it is morally acceptable to restrict their activities and even keep them isolated from anyone else in order to protect society. If the danger to society is great enough, it is acceptable to deprive carriers of their liberty to the degree that the safety of society requires. This is true irrespective of the carriers' moral responsibility for the disease. If a child is a carrier of the Ebola virus by its being passed on to her at birth from her parent, quarantine is nevertheless intuitively legitimate.

Suppose a person poses a danger to society by a sufficiently strong tendency to commit murder. Even if he is not in general a morally responsible agent, society would nevertheless seem to have as much right to detain him as it does to quarantine a carrier of a deadly communicable disease who is not responsible for being a carrier. One must note, however, that it is morally wrong to treat carriers of a disease more severely than is necessary to keep them from being dangerous to society. Thus, if the quarantine analogy provides our only justification

---

22. Ferdinand D. Schoeman, "On Incapacitating the Dangerous," *American Philosophical Quarterly* 16 (1979), pp. 27–35.

for criminal detention, it will be morally wrong to treat those with violent criminal tendencies more harshly than is required to keep them from being dangerous to society. Furthermore, the less dangerous the disease, the less invasive the legitimate prevention methods would be, and similarly, the less dangerous the criminal, the less invasive the legitimate prevention methods would be. For seriously violent criminals, detention until the threat has ended would seem justified. But for shoplifters, perhaps only some degree of monitoring could be defended.

What should we say of those who have committed serious crimes, but demonstrably no longer have any criminal tendencies as a result of being reformed during a long interval between crime and apprehension? After being convicted of murder in Tennessee in 1969, Robert Lee Curtis served two years of his ten-year sentence, and then escaped. From 1971 until 1997, he lived peacefully in a small New Hampshire village, earning the trust and respect of the local residents.[23] The quarantine analogy clearly provides no right basis for his continued detention. And if the quarantine analogy provides our only justification for significant detention of criminals, then Curtis must remain free. This result contravenes ordinary intuitions about the appropriateness of criminal punishment. Nevertheless, perhaps it must be accepted if hard incompatibilism is true, and perhaps even if it is not.

One might be tempted to think that on the quarantine view, it will regularly be the case that perpetrators of serious crimes will not be required to undergo detention. For example, some people who out of anger murder their spouses are very unlikely ever to murder again. Would the quarantine view recommend that such criminals simply go free? Not obviously. For even if such spousal murderers are unlikely to kill again, they often have seriously abusive tendencies against which society has the right to protect itself. In such cases detention would seem justified. Moreover, as we shall see, by the quarantine analogy, society may also protect itself against threats of this sort by therapeutic programs.

Yet there are cases of unlawful killing in which the killer has no unusual tendency toward any sort of serious abusive behavior. For example, if someone were in the process of brutally harming one's child, one might treat the criminal much more severely than would be required for the defense of the child. Rather than simply knocking him unconscious with a baseball bat, one's anger might instead motivate

23. *USA Today*, April 8, 1997.

175

beating him to death. Yet it might well be that many who are motivated to beat the criminal to death in such a situation are not generally abusive at all. Wouldn't the quarantine view require us to advocate not detaining such an individual?

I suspect that the quarantine view would, in some such cases, fail to justify detention. But we can live with such a position. In fact, many have intuitions about these sorts of cases that support this result. Such intuitions are sometimes underlain by vengeful sentiments. However, they are sometimes also motivated by the view that given the way the human being works, violent tendencies are not easily controlled when the lives of one's family and friends are threatened. Since such tendencies are difficult for the state to control, and since controlling them isn't obviously advantageous, it might well be unjustified to bring the resources of the criminal justice system to bear on such cases. Those who have severely harmed others under such circumstances may well need therapy, but, on the quarantine view, not necessarily therapy motivated by the desire to prevent crime. Therapy may be required to help the person come to terms with violent tendencies that perhaps most of us have, or to come to terms with the trauma involved in killing someone.

Schoeman's article explores the acceptability of preventative detention for those who have not yet committed crimes, reflection on which occasions the following objection to the quarantine view. If justification of detention by this analogy is tenable, must it not then be legitimate to detain those who have not committed a violent crime, if by some means it has been ascertained that they are quite likely to do so? Here, Schoeman points out that while the kinds of testing required to determine whether one is a carrier of a communicable disease may often not be unacceptably invasive, the kind of screening necessary for determining whether one has a violent criminal tendency might well be invasive in ways that raise serious moral difficulties. Furthermore, there exist thoroughly objectionable bases on which it might be decided that one is likely to be a violent criminal. Given our current measures for prediction, instituting a policy of attempting to predict who will commit crimes and detaining them is likely to do much more harm than good.[24] To avoid this problem, it seems that invasive preventative

---

24. If someone actually threatens to commit a violent crime by words and actions, one can determine the likelihood of violence without objectionably invasive measures, and in such cases preventative detention might be legitimate. However, our current legal system already criminalizes threatening violence – it is simple assault.

measures should be restricted to those who have committed crimes. The right to liberty should count heavily here. This right would yield a strong reason not to detain someone even if there were some reason to believe that he is likely to commit a crime.

Furthermore, if we have the right to "quarantine" criminals, we have the right to tell people in advance that they will be isolated from society if they commit crimes. Publicizing the detention policy is justified and in fact required by the standards of an open society. This publicity itself has a powerful general deterrent effect. People generally have a strong aversion to being detained or watched or forced to undergo preventative psychological treatment, even if the administration of these measures is as humane as it can be.

In our discussion so far, we have found no persuasive justification for punishment. The paradigmatic kinds of punishments we had in mind, however, were confinement in our sort of prison and the death penalty. What should we say of depriving criminals of property, for instance of imposing a fine on tax evaders? First, imprisonment and the death penalty are prima facie violations of the rights to liberty and life. Such rights violations are generally much more serious than violations of property rights, in particular if the property loss leaves sufficient means for a reasonably good life. Furthermore, even though the intent of quarantine is not to inflict significant deprivation and serious psychological pain either as an end or as a means, it will often have such pain and deprivation as a foreseeable side-effect. In many cases, the pain or deprivation resulting from a fine would be much less severe. For instance, most people would rather pay a hefty fine than be detained even for a year. But, a fine does amount to pain or deprivation imposed as a means to deter, and therefore it has the core characteristics of punishment, whereas detention justified on the quarantine analogy does not.

In my view, deprivation of property is a type of punishment that is justifiable on largely consequentialist grounds, whether or not hard incompatibilism is true. If we can be justified in "quarantining" criminals, we should also be justified in administering a less painful and invasive deterrent for some sorts of crimes. Furthermore, the deterrent benefit of a policy of imposing fines for certain kinds of crimes plausibly outweighs any relevant property right, especially if the loss of property at issue does not undermine the likelihood of living a reasonably good life. Since none of these considerations would be undermined by hard incompatibilism, it can endorse a policy of imposing fines on some types of criminals.

When a person with cholera is quarantined, she is typically made to experience deprivation she does not merit. Society benefits by this deprivation. It is plausibly a matter of fairness that society should do what it can, within reasonable bounds, to make the victim safe for release as quickly as possible. If a society quarantined cholera victims but was unwilling to provide medical care for them because it would require a modest increase in taxation, that society could well be acting unfairly. Similarly, when a criminal is "quarantined," supposing that hard incompatibilism is true, then he is also made to experience a deprivation he does not merit, and from which society benefits. By analogy with the cholera case, here also it is a matter of fairness for society to do what it can, within reasonable bounds, to make the criminal safe for release. For society to repudiate programs for criminal rehabilitation because it is unwilling to pay for them could well involve serious unfairness.

Policies for making a detained criminal safe for release would address a condition in the offender that results in the criminal behavior. These conditions include psychological illness, but also problems that are not plausibly classified as illness, such as insufficient sympathy for other people, or a strong tendency to assign blame to others for whatever goes wrong. In my conception, what binds these policies together is not that they treat the criminal as mentally ill and therefore in need of psychiatric treatment. Rather, they are all policies that attempt to bring about moral change in an offender by non-punitively addressing conditions that underlie criminal behavior.

Indeed, it is often argued that rehabilitative views are objectionable because they treat an offender as suffering from an illness and not as an immoral agent.[25] But this is a false opposition. Some rehabilitative policies, as I have argued, do not treat the offender as suffering from an illness. Furthermore, an offender may be ill and in need of therapy, and at the same time correctly regarded as an immoral agent. The reha-

---

25. Morris, "Persons and Punishment," *The Monist* 52 (1968), pp. 475–501, reprinted in *Punishment and Rehabilitation*, third edition, ed. Jeffrie E. Murphy, pp. 74–93; Hampton, "The Moral Education Theory of Punishment," p. 214. A frequent target of such criticisms is Karl Menninger, who develops his position in "Verdict Guilty, Now What?" *Harper's Magazine*, August 1959, pp. 60–4, and in *The Crime of Punishment* (New York: Viking Press, 1968). My view is similar to Menninger's insofar as we both advocate the idea that protection of society and rehabilitation be the primary aims for criminology.

bilitative view is committed to the claim that there are criminal tendencies that can be remedied by non-punitive means. It need not deny the notion that those who possess such tendencies are in fact immoral agents.

An objection that is often raised for views of the sort I am developing is that they would justify forms of therapeutic treatment that would violate human dignity. Recall that Strawson warns that if the thesis of universal determinism were to affect our reactive attitudes, objectivity of attitude would be in place, by which human beings would be regarded as machines to be manipulated and controlled.[26] But, as we have seen, hard incompatibilism does not imperil the reasons we have for holding that human beings have dignity, and neither does it undermine the respect that would invalidate certain forms of control and manipulation. Hard incompatibilism therefore does not underwrite objectionable therapeutic procedures.

Morris adduces Kantian reasons in his argument against policies for criminal therapeutic rehabilitation.[27] In his view, among the human qualities we value most is the capacity to regulate actions autonomously and rationally. The problem for typical forms of therapy proposed for altering criminal tendencies is that they circumvent, rather than address, these capacities. For example, consider the Ludovico method, made famous by Anthony Burgess's book and Stanley Kubrick's film *A Clockwork Orange*. Alex, a violent criminal, is injected with a drug that makes him nauseous while at the same time he is made to watch films depicting the kind of violence to which he is disposed. The goal of the method is eliminating the violent behavior by generating an association between violence and nausea. Morris's objection to therapy of this sort is that the criminal is not changed by being presented with reasons for altering his behavior that he would autonomously and rationally accept. As an alternative, Morris argues for treatment that presents the criminal with a conception of the good that he could accept in this way. As he conceives it, this treatment must involve punishment, for by this means it would communicate to the criminal how his wrongdoing had adversely affected himself and others, and the appropriateness of guilt and repentance.[28]

However, the fact that a mode of therapy circumvents rather than addresses the capacities that confer dignity on us cannot all by itself

26. Strawson, "Freedom and Resentment," p. 66.
27. Morris, "Persons and Punishment," pp. 75ff.
28. Morris, "A Paternalistic Theory of Punishment," pp. 157–8.

make it illegitimate. Imagine someone who is beset by bouts of violent and explosive anger. Some recent studies suggest that this tendency is due to deficiencies in serotonin, and that it can sometimes be alleviated by taking a drug such as Prozac.[29] It would be peculiar to claim that such a mode of treatment is illegitimate because it circumvents capacities for rational and autonomous response. In fact, this sort of treatment often produces responsiveness to reasons where it was previously absent. A person beset by violent and explosive anger will typically not be responsive to certain kinds of reasons, to which he would be responsive if he were not suffering from this problem. Therapy of this sort can thus enhance autonomy (as Morris himself acknowledges). By analogy, one standard form of treatment for alcoholism – which many alcoholics voluntarily undergo – involves the use of a drug, Antibuse, which makes one violently ill after the ingestion of alcohol. By counteracting addictive alcoholism, this drug can indeed produce increased reasons-responsiveness.

Furthermore, suppose that despite serious attempts at moral rehabilitation that do not circumvent the criminal's rational capacities, and despite procedures that mechanically increase the agent's capacities for reasons-responsiveness, the criminal still displays dangerously violent tendencies. Imagine that the choice is now between indefinite confinement without hope for release, and behavioristic therapy that does not increase the agent's capacity for reasons-responsiveness. It is not obvious that in this situation, the behavioristic therapy should be ruled out as morally illegitimate. One must assess the appropriateness of therapy of this kind by comparing it with the other options. Suppose, for example, that the only legitimate alternative to confinement for life is application of the Ludovico method. It seems quite clear that under such circumstances, the moral problems for this method are outweighed.

Types of therapy that have classically raised grave worries include processes such as electro-shock treatment and lobotomy.[30] Indeed, methods such as these have often been used without sufficient evidence that they will be of therapeutic value, while they typically cause suf-

29. *Burlington Free Press* (Associated Press), December 15, 1997, p. 1.
30. Such difficulties for therapeutic criminology have also been raised by Francis A. Allen, "Criminal Justice, Legal Values, and the Rehabilitative Ideal," *Journal of Criminal Law, Criminology, and Police Science* 50 (1959), pp. 226–32, and by Richard Wasserstrom in "Punishment," in *Philosophy and Social Issues* (Notre Dame, IN: University of Notre Dame Press, 1980).

fering and permanent disability. They are often employed just to make the patient easier to manage, without any regard for his well-being. A very serious problem for electro-shock treatment is that sometimes it is nothing more than a form of torture. Lobotomy has significant permanent ramifications for a person's mental functioning, and hence there are strong reasons not to perform this operation regardless of the positive benefits. But electro-shock treatment and lobotomy need not be our paradigms for therapy.

Objections to rehabilitative programs for criminals also arise from the claim that such procedures are ineffective. Such objections were common in the 1970's. The most influential article that is skeptical about such programs is Robert Martinson's "What Works," published in 1974.[31] This article set the tone for widespread public abandonment of support for rehabilitative programs in the 1970's and 1980's. But Martinson's review has more recently been widely criticized; one author remarks, "the research upon which Martinson's review is based was so flawed as to defy meaningful analysis and interpretation."[32] In fact, Martinson himself has retracted his claims. In 1979, he acknowledged that under various conditions there are many examples of successful rehabilitative efforts . . . "such startling results are found again and again . . . for treatment programs as diverse as individual psychotherapy, group counselling, intensive supervision, and what we have called individual help."[33] About the same time, Paul Gendreau and Robert Ross reviewed ninety-five psychological intervention programs for criminals, and found that 86 percent were successful, with reductions in recidivism from 30 percent to 60 percent.[34] The claims of their landmark study have been supported by more recent findings.[35]

31. Robert Martinson, "What Works? – Questions and answers about prison reform," *The Public Interest* 35 (1974), pp. 22–54.
32. Glenn D. Walters, *Foundations of Criminal Science* (New York: Praeger, 1992), v. 2, p. 228.
33. Robert Martinson, "New Findings, New Views: A Note of Caution Regarding Sentencing Reform," *Hofstra Law Review* 7 (1979), pp. 242–58.
34. Paul Gendreau and Robert Ross, "Effective Correctional Treatment: Bibliography for Cynics," *Crime and Delinquency* 25 (1979), pp. 463–89; my information about therapeutic programs comes from Kris R. Henning and B. Christopher Frueh, "Cognitive-Behavioral Treatment of Incarcerated Offenders," *Criminal Justice and Behavior* 23 (1996), pp. 523–41.
35. Paul Gendreau and Robert Ross, "Revivification of Rehabilitation: Evidence for the 1980's," *Justice Quarterly* 4 (1987), pp. 349–407; T. Palmer, "The 'Effectiveness Issue Today'," *Federal Probation* 46 (1983), pp. 3–10; P. Greenwood and F. Zimring, *One More Chance: The Pursuit of Promising Intervention Strategies for Chronic Juvenile Offenders* (Santa Monica: RAND, 1985).

These studies indicate that certain types of programs for criminal rehabilitation have been especially successful. Anti-criminal family interventions provide a good example. The Oregon Learning Center has developed widely discussed behavioral management programs for families of problem and delinquent children. These programs are designed to train parents and families to establish clear rules, monitor behavior, and establish fair and consistent procedures for positive and negative reinforcement. In one study on the Oregon program, youth in ten families showed reductions of 60 percent in aggressive behavior compared with a 15 percent drop in untreated control families.[36] Several studies show that behavioristic therapy for certain select disorders is very effective. Therapy of this sort for exhibitionism is especially successful, even in the long term. Gendreau and Ross describe B.M. Maletzky's program:

In the authors' opinion, the most impressive data come from a long-term series of clinical evaluations by Maletzky (1980), beginning in 1974. He treated a total of 155 exhibitionists with follow-ups of one to nine years. His program relied principally on assisted covert sensitization and, to a secondary extent, on counseling for related problems, such as marital therapy. Subjects were treated twice weekly for up to five months. Then, most important, "booster" sessions were provided at home for a further year to those requiring additional treatment. Maletzky reported that 87 percent of his clients eliminated all exhibitionist behaviors.[37]

Assisted covert sensitization is the procedure featured in the Ludovico method. In a variety used in contemporary programs, clients are instructed to imagine the relevant deviant sexual act, at which time a strongly noxious odor is used to produce a response of nausea.[38] Those skeptical of the moral appropriateness of this type of behavioral therapy

36. G.R. Patterson, P. Chamberlain, and J. Reid, "A comparative evaluation of a parent training program," *Behavior Therapy* 13 (1982), pp. 638–50, cited in Walters, *Foundations of Criminal Science*, v. 2, p. 143, and in Gendreau and Ross, "Revivification of Rehabilitation," p. 363; cf. G.R. Patterson, *A Social Learning Approach: Coercive Family Process 3* (Eugene: Catalia, 1982), J.F. Alexander and B.V. Parsons, *Functional Family Therapy* (Monterrey: Brooks/Cole, 1982). For a review of studies on family therapy, see Gendreau and Ross, "Revivification of Rehabilitation," pp. 358–64.
37. Gendreau and Ross, "Revivification of Rehabilitation," p. 383; cf. B.M. Maletzky, "Assisted Court Sensitization," in D.J. Cox and R.J. Daitzman, eds. *Exhibitionism: Description, Assessment, and Treatment* (New York: Garland, 1980).
38. Robert G. Meyer, *Abnormal Behavior and the Criminal Justice System* (New York: Macmillan, 1992), pp. 102–3.

for violent offenders. In addition, although this sort of therapy involves coercing people to adopt certain beliefs about themselves, it is arguably more respectful of the offender's dignity than are most behaviorist methods, for the reason that it addresses rather than circumvents the agent's capacity for reasoning and autonomous choice. Far from treating an offender mechanically, it aims to change the offender by presenting him with problems for his ways of thinking and with ways to change them.

Moreover, the hard incompatibilist can endorse this type of therapeutic procedure. It requires that criminals be able to improve their behavior by changing the way they think, and for criminals themselves to recognize that improvement can be effected by this method, none of which hard incompatibilism would imperil. This sort of procedure also demands that criminals recognize that their ways of thinking are causally efficacious in producing their criminal behavior, and that different ways of thinking would produce behavior that is not criminal. The hard incompatibilist can agree to all of this.

Furthermore, there are additional moral reasons for endorsing rehabilitative programs for criminals generally. Such programs promise to enhance the lives of criminals subjected to treatment, and indirectly the lives of their friends and relatives. These programs will reduce crime, and thereby enhance safety in society. As we have now seen, objections against a broad array of rehabilitative programs for criminals can be answered. Contrary to popular misconceptions prominent in the 1970's and 1980's, many such programs have demonstrated an impressive degree of success.[43] In addition, there is ample room for devising better programs and improving those that are in use. Hard incompatibilism can legitimately adopt the rehabilitative model for criminal treatment. Indeed, on the hard incompatibilist view, we have a special reason to establish programs for rehabilitating criminals, for the alternatives are that they be closely monitored or forcibly separated from society, which they do not deserve.

---

43. There may be reasons based on considerations of human dignity for ruling out therapy for certain kinds of crimes. For example, as a result of sincere consideration of reasons, someone might have become a very strong supporter of animal rights, or an opponent of nuclear power, or an opponent of certain foreign policy initiatives, so that he engages in protests that violate the law. Therapeutic treatment in such cases would typically be illegitimate. This proscription might be justified on a utilitarian basis, or on unclarity about whether the offenders are genuinely wrongdoers.

If hard incompatibilism is true, criminal punishment for retributive reasons is ruled out. Hard incompatibilism must therefore relinquish one of the most prominent ways for justifying criminal punishment, although there are independent objections to this position. By contrast, the moral education theory of punishment is not challenged by hard incompatibilism specifically. Nevertheless, doubts must be resolved about whether punishment can be an effective moral educator of criminals. In the absence of good empirical evidence that punishment can help produce moral education, it would be wrong to punish criminals for the sake of this aim. For it is wrong to harm someone for the sake of some good if one has little or no evidence that the harm can realize the good. Moreover, even if punishment can produce moral improvement, we should prefer non-punitive methods for such improvement – whether or not agents are morally responsible.

Although it might well be that the two most prevalent versions of the deterrence theory are not undermined by hard incompatibilism, they are independently dubious. The utilitarian deterrence theory is beset by familiar difficulties – arguably it sometimes mandates punishment that is too severe, it prescribes punishing the innocent, and it endorses using people merely as means. A deterrence theory of the sort that Farrell advocates, based on the right to harm in self-defense, is also objectionable – for typically, when criminals are in custody, they pose no immediate danger, and threats designed to defend against someone who is immediately dangerous may not in general be carried out against someone who is not.

A theory of crime prevention that would be acceptable whether or not hard incompatibilism is true can be developed by analogy with our rationale for quarantining carriers of dangerous diseases. Such a theory would not justify the sort of criminal punishment whose legitimacy is most dubious, such as death or confinement in the most common kinds of prisons in our society. More than this, it demands a certain level of care and attention to the well-being of criminals that would radically change our current practice. Just as society has a duty to attempt to cure those who are quarantined for its protection, so it has a duty to attempt to morally educate or cure the criminals it detains for its protection. When this is not possible, and a criminal must be confined indefinitely, his life should not be made unnecessarily unpleasant.

7

Hard Incompatibilism and
Meaning in Life

INTRODUCTION

When people are first confronted with hard determinism, initial reactions are often apprehensive. Frequently, the first response is that lives would then have no purpose, and a dispirited resignation to one's fate would be inevitable. Indeed, philosophical critics have contended that if hard determinism were true, we would lack the sort of control over our lives that would allow us to derive fulfillment from the projects we pursue. The power to affect our futures would not be ours in a sense sufficiently strong for our projects to count as our achievements, and as a result the possibility of meaning in life would be jeopardized.

Another common first response to hard determinism is that it would endanger the rich emotional texture of our relationships with others. We have seen that P.F. Strawson has developed a philosophical elaboration of this reaction. For him, a hard determinist conviction would imperil the other-directed reactive attitudes essential to the interpersonal relationships that make our lives meaningful. It could also jeopardize self-directed attitudes such as guilt and repentance, crucial not only to good relationships with others but also to personal moral development.

Philosophers have also contended that determinism can make a significant contribution to meaning in life. The Stoics argued that affirming determinism while taking a broader perspective can result in a profound sort of equanimity. If determinism is true, everything that happens in one's life can be attributed to God or the universe, and then through one's identification with this entity one can attain an acceptance of anything that happens. The hard determinist might aspire to this sort of view. Moreover, it has been suggested that a hard determinist conviction can serve to calm attitudes such as anger and dissatisfaction, thereby making one's emotional life less turbulent and more serene.

I shall develop the claim that our commonplace initial response of apprehensiveness toward hard determinism – more broadly, toward hard incompatibilism – is an overreaction. Although hard incompatibilism would diminish the sense in which we can have genuine achievements, and the sense in which we can be worthy as a result, it would by no means thoroughly undermine the fulfillment in life that our projects can provide. Moreover, far from threatening good interpersonal relationships, hard incompatibilism holds out the promise of better relationships through release from the anger that underlies so much human misery. Hard incompatibilism could indeed encourage an equanimity that would offer a significant benefit for us.

LIFE PROJECTS: SARTRE AND HONDERICH

According to existentialist philosophy, the possibility of meaning in life is closely connected with our capacity for freedom of choice. Jean-Paul Sartre claims, famously, that for human beings, existence is prior to essence, and that it is up to each of us to create an essence for ourselves through our free choices. The notion of a human essence includes that of a meaning or purpose for one's life. We create purpose and meaning for ourselves through our projects – life-defining plans that we freely choose.[1]

Sartre argues that we possess libertarian freedom, and one might readily assume that if meaning in life is to be realized through choice of projects, these choices would have to be free in this sense. Certain kinds of examples might support Sartre's case. Discovering that one's choice of profession was determined by one's home environment to realize a parent's career fantasies could threaten the possibility of fulfillment through that profession. Finding that one's choice of spouse was determined by a tendency to persist in familiar but unhealthy patterns of interaction could undermine the fulfillment that an intimate relationship might supply. But to this proposal the hard incompatibilist might reply that causally determined choices for projects could as easily

---

1. Jean-Paul Sartre, "The Humanism of Existentialism," in *Existentialism and the Human Emotions*, tr. Bernard Frechtman (New York: Philosophical Library, 1957).

provide meaning for our lives. For example, suppose one discovered that one's career choice was determined by a deep interest, produced by the circumstances of one's upbringing, in finding solutions for some of the problems facing humanity. Or that the choice of one's spouse is explained by the salutary features of one's childhood environment, which one was determined to replicate because of the happiness it produced. These discoveries might well enhance the fulfillment provided by these projects.

More generally, the hard incompatibilist might reply that it could matter for meaning that the project one chooses be appropriate, that one chooses reasonably after reflection on various options, or that one is not coerced when one chooses. But whether we have free will is irrelevant to meaning in life. Furthermore, the absence of moral responsibility would not hinder the capacity of a choice to give one's life meaning. Moral responsibility is required for a choice to be blameworthy or praiseworthy, but not for it to provide one's life with purpose or value.

Still, this hard incompatibilist response might be insufficiently reflective. As we have seen, Honderich advocates a position similar in some respects to hard incompatibilism, and he argues that determinism (which he endorses) generates both losses and gains for our sense of meaning in life. In his discussion he fixes on what he calls *life-hopes*, hopes for what would make one's life fulfilled, happy, satisfactory, or worthwhile.[2] Our life-hopes are not primarily focused on what will happen to us, but rather on our achievements. Life-hopes are thus dependent on one's capacity to initiate actions, for this capacity is integral to the notion of achievement. Determinism calls into question the extent to which we are capable of initiating our actions, and therefore provides a potential challenge to our life-hopes.

Honderich believes that when confronted with determinism, people often have a pre-philosophical sense that their life-hopes are adversely affected. In his conception, there is in addition a pre-philosophical picture that generates the sense that determinism is detrimental to one's life-hopes. This picture has two components. The first is the thought that our futures are open, alterable, or unfixed.[3] The second is the belief that our futures are not the products of our dispositions, but that instead we can mold our futures by overcoming these dispositions.

2. Honderich, *A Theory of Determinism*, p. 382.
3. Ibid., p. 385.

Pre-philosophically, we think that we can overcome our dispositions by means of a "determinate center" that can initiate actions. This "center" is readily identified with a self that is distinct from its dispositions and has the ability to overcome them without being causally determined in how it does so. Accordingly, determinism's pre-philosophical challenge to one's life-hopes is that it undermines the claim that we are selves, distinct from our dispositions, who can indeterministically initiate actions, and who by this capacity can overcome any of these dispositions.

Honderich characterizes three philosophical responses to the determinist challenge. The first, which he calls *dismay*, is that our life-hopes are completely undermined by determinism. The second, *intransigence*, is that determinism makes no difference to our life-hopes.[4] The third, *affirmation*, is that there is an aspect of our life-hopes that is undermined by determinism, but nevertheless determinism does not destroy them. Honderich endorses this third response. He argues that the aspect of our life-hopes that does not survive determinism is the hope "for an unfixed future, a hope for a future in which we are not creatures of our environments and our dispositional natures."[5] An important part of the pre-philosophical view is that no matter what dispositions to action or inaction one may have, and no matter what environment one finds oneself in, the self has a power for action-initiation that is not reducible to disposition and environment. If determinism is true, then this part of the pre-philosophical picture must be rejected. Consequently, the intransigent response is inaccurate.

At the same time, Honderich maintains that a large part of the pre-philosophical perspective does survive the determinist challenge.[6] We have desires and intentions for the future that are potentially or actually opposed by features of the world such as a struggling economy, or people who aspire to domination, or bodily disabilities, or factors internal to the person such as addictions or compulsions.[7] Life-hopes in this respect are hopes that my desires will not be effectively opposed by any such internal and external factors, and that I will therefore achieve their satisfaction. By contrast with those that are undermined by determinism, such hopes do not involve "a hope for a future in which we are

---

4. Honderich, *A Theory of Determinism*, pp. 391–400.
5. Ibid., p. 390.
6. Ibid., pp. 516–17.
7. Ibid., p. 397.

not creatures of our environments and our dispositional natures," and thus they can withstand determinism. The response of dismay, according to which nothing of our life-hopes survives determinism, is therefore mistaken.

AFFIRMATION

Honderich is right to claim that the responses of dismay and intransigence are unwarranted. Assuming that the three responses he describes are jointly exhaustive, affirmation is therefore the view left standing. However, the variant on this position that I endorse diverges from Honderich's in several ways.

Rejecting the response of dismay is justified for several reasons. Determinism does not challenge the causal efficacy of the deliberations and decisions by which we aim to mold our futures. Nor does it endanger the prospect of overcoming challenges that result from the kinds of external and internal impediments Honderich mentions. For example, determinism does not imperil the view that if others wish to make one's life miserable, one might achieve a happy life for oneself despite their efforts, nor the claim that if one has a proclivity to laziness that threatens to frustrate one's career aims, one might be able, through one's efforts, to surmount this tendency.

In my view there is a significant difference between the determinist and pre-philosophical perspectives on the possibility of overcoming these sorts of obstacles. In the determinist view, if one will not overcome one's laziness, there will be factors beyond one's control – which one could not have altered or prevented – that yield this consequence. If one will overcome one's laziness, there will be factors beyond one's control that produce this result. Typically, a person hoping to overcome his laziness does not know in advance which of these two epistemic possibilities will be actual. For him, it will often be epistemically possible that the former will be realized. He will then be correct to acknowledge that some aspect of the universe completely beyond his control may make it true that he will not overcome his laziness.

Acknowledgments of this sort mark a divergence from the pre-philosophical stance in how one regards one's life-hopes. From the pre-philosophical point of view, it is typically true that if one envisions the possibility of failing to overcome one's laziness, one will also see oneself as nevertheless having been able to succeed by expending more effort. For although one then imagines that one would not actually expend sufficient effort, one also supposes that one could have been able to provide enough by an indeterministically self-caused effort of will. Consequently, the pre-philosophical view would encourage the following reflection on the prospect of overcoming one's laziness. "Reaching genuine fulfillment depends on overcoming my laziness. Whether I do so is wholly within my power. If I fail, it will be because I did not expend effort that I genuinely could have expended. So whether I attain my life-hope is truly up to me." The determinist would think differently: "Reaching genuine fulfillment in life depends on my overcoming my laziness. It might be that there are factors beyond my control that will produce this failure. So, whether I succeed is in one significant respect not up to me." In the determinist perspective, if one is to overcome one's laziness, one's efforts to do so will typically be causally efficacious in bringing it about. Nevertheless, achieving one's life-hopes is in an important respect outside of one's control, a respect in which it is not outside one's control on the pre-philosophical view.

According to Honderich, the intransigent response is also mistaken, for important aspects of our life-hopes are undermined by determinism. The aspect he emphasizes is the dependence of our life-hopes on the notion of a self with an indeterministic causal power. He maintains that if the notion of such an indeterministic self is rejected, we are left with the position according to which our actions are caused solely by our environment and dispositions. In his view, "a hope for a future in which we are not creatures of our environments and our dispositional natures" must be rejected if determinism is true. Here I believe Honderich is mistaken. He argues, correctly I believe, that an aspect of our ordinary self-conception is that we are selves distinct from our mental states and dispositions to act, and that these selves have causal powers. Indeed, on one conception, we are selves of this sort and they have indeterministic causal powers. But such selves might also be components of a deterministic system. In fact, the Stoics and Descartes maintain that we are selves that are distinct from our dispositions, and at the same time that determinism is true.

The thesis that such a self can initiate action independently of dispositions and environment fares as well in the deterministic picture as it does in the indeterminist scheme. Suppose, for example, that a person had a life-hope that she would behave morally despite all of her dispositions and her environment, and that she would do so by the causal power of a self motivated solely by moral principles she had adopted independently of the influence of her dispositions. This life-hope is amenable to either a determinist or an indeterminist view. Nothing about determinism per se rules out the view that a self can select principles of action and initiate action on their basis independently of the influence of her dispositions and environment. Perhaps a Humean psychological determinism would rule out this sort of eventuality, but determinism isn't restricted to its Humean variety.

Accordingly, in one respect the intransigent response fares better than Honderich thinks. The determinist must reject the notion of a self that has the power to overcome its dispositions and the effects of its environment indeterministically, but she need not deny that we are determined selves with the power to overcome these factors. This is an important concession to the intransigent response. One can be a determinist and deny that we are creatures of our dispositions and environment in the way that Honderich envisions. But the pre-philosophical position does include the assumption that factors beyond our control do not generate our futures, because we have selves whose choices are not produced by factors beyond their control. Perhaps this assumption is tied to the belief that there is an intrinsic value to shaping aspects of our lives that were not determined prior to our decisions, and that there are such aspects of our lives.[8] The determinist is forced to relinquish these assumptions, and in these respects the intransigent response is mistaken.

Nevertheless, the degree to which we have found the intransigent response deficient so far is not as substantial as one might have feared. For in the determinist view, given that we lack knowledge of how our futures will turn out, we can still reasonably hope for success in achieving what we want most even if our prospects are hindered by dispositions or environment. In fact, such hopes will often be reasonable even if we are fully creatures of our environments and our dispositions. For we do not have thorough knowledge of what our environments and dispositions are or will be. Thus, it is often true of any disposition or difficulty in an agent's environment that might prevent the realization of a life-hope that it is epistemically possible that he does or will possess a disposition that allows him to overcome it. For example, someone might think that his laziness could frustrate his aim to become a successful doctor, but at the same time it might be epistemically possible for him that he possess a disposition that provides him with the ability

8. Ginet makes a similar suggestion (in personal correspondence).

193

to overcome this laziness. As a result, he might reasonably hope that he will overcome his laziness and succeed in his aspiration. In the determinist view, if he does overcome his laziness, it won't be by an indeterminist causal power of the self, and as a result it won't be an achievement in as robust a way as one might have believed, but it will be the agent's achievement is an appreciable sense nonetheless.

It could be argued that the intransigent response is more thoroughly mistaken than we have suggested so far. Life-hopes, one might contend, involve an aspiration for praiseworthiness, which determinism undermines. Since life-hopes are aspirations for achievement, and it is impossible to have achievements for which one is not also praiseworthy, the loss of praiseworthiness undermines life-hopes altogether. In response to an objection of this sort, Honderich remarks that the significance for life-hopes of the loss of praiseworthiness is tempered by the fact that actions can still have the "credit of rational action, or action in accordance with desires that serve my fundamental end . . . or the credit of strong character, or sensitivity, or judgment, or decency, or of rising over mere conventionality."[9] But this response is misleading. If determinism undermines praiseworthiness, then it rules out fundamental desert of any sort. We are then not creditworthy for moral actions, nor for rational actions, nor for traits such as sensitivity and judgment.

Achievement and life-hopes are not obviously tied to praiseworthiness in the strong way assumed by the objection. If one hopes for a certain outcome, then if one succeeds in acquiring what one hoped for, intuitively this outcome can be one's achievement, albeit in a diminished sense, even if one is not praiseworthy for it. For example, if an agent hopes that her efforts as a parent will result in happy and well-adjusted children, and they do, it seems clear that she can have an accurate perception of having achieved what she hoped for, even if because hard incompatibilism is true she does not deserve praise for her efforts. Consequently, this last objection to intransigence is not clearly correct.

But how significant is the aspect of our life-hopes that we must forgo if hard determinism or hard incompatibilism is true? Smilansky argues that although determinism leaves room for a limited foundation for the sense of self-worth that derives from achievement or virtue, the hard deterministic perspective can nevertheless be "extremely damaging to our view of ourselves, to our sense of achievement, worth, and self-

---

9. Honderich, *A Theory of Determinism*, p. 513.

respect." In his conception, "if any virtue that one has exhibited, if all that one has achieved, was 'in the cards,' just an unfolding of what one has been made out to be, one's view of oneself (or important others) cannot stay the same."[10] He contends that the foundation for self-respect provided by a sense of moral accomplishment is especially vulnerable:

> Even after admitting the compatibilist claim that on one level we have, say, reason to be morally proud of ourselves because we are honest (after all, we chose to be), when we reflect on life as a whole, it matters when we realize that we lack libertarian free will. We begin to see ourselves in a new light: what we choose . . . is the unfolding of what we are, the choices result from that which is not under our control (and ultimately is luck). We are honest, and we are honest despite the fact that (compatibilistically) we were able not to be. We chose to be honest because we are moral. But that we are this person (who chose freely as she did because she was moral) is not our doing. We deserve respect as morally worthy (not just useful) people, but not ultimately for being such people.[11]

Smilanksy argues that losing the grounds for incompatibilist moral worth may be beneficial in some respects. We have already examined one of his claims to this effect, that hard determinists are able to pursue moral goals purified of the concern for this kind of moral worth. He also contends that hard determinism yields the claim that in a sense we are all ultimately equal; "this realization presents the anti-luck 'here but for the grace of God' thought overwhelmingly."[12] Nevertheless, in his view, the potential damage to the incompatibilist sort of self-respect would be so severe that as an antidote we would be well-advised to maintain the illusion of free will.[13]

I agree with Smilansky that there is a kind of self-respect that has incompatibilist presuppositions, whose foundations would be undermined if hard determinism (or hard incompatibilism) were true. I do question whether he is right about how damaging it would be for us to find that we must relinquish this kind of self-respect, and thus whether the radical move to illusionism is warranted. Questions also arise as to how an illusionist program could be put into practice. Is it

---

10. Smilansky, "Can a Determinist Respect Herself?", p. 94.
11. Ibid., pp. 92–3.
12. Ibid., p. 95.
13. Ibid., pp. 96–8.

psychologically possible for convinced hard determinists to produce or maintain this illusion? Should the truth of hard determinism (if it is indeed true) actively be concealed? But I will set these issues aside.

First, one should not underestimate the degree to which our sense of self-worth, our sense that we are valuable and that are lives are worth living, is due to factors that are not even produced by voluntary endeavor, let alone by free will. Smilansky quotes an especially pithy expression of this thought from George Santayana:

> Even now, who of us in his heart would not be a rake rather than a hunchback, a villain rather than a fool? In spite of all the moralizing, we cannot admire desert or merit as much as the gifts of nature and fortune. There is nothing of which we are so proud as of a good family, a handsome face, a strong body, a ready wit – all of those things indeed, for which we are not responsible.[14]

Without going so far as to endorse Santayana's sentiments completely, it is clear that people place immense value, both in others and in themselves, on good looks, athletic ability, and native intelligence, none of which is produced voluntarily. However, we also place great value on voluntary efforts and their results – on hard work and the achievements it yields, on moral resolve and the character it produces. But how much does it matter to most of us that these voluntary efforts also be freely willed? Less than Smilansky supposes, I think.

Consider his example of moral character. The belief that morally impressive character is largely a function of upbringing is widespread in our society. Many people commonly think of themselves as having failed if their children turn out to have immoral dispositions, and many take great care to raise their children well in order to prevent this sort of tragedy. In accord with this conception, the following realization is not at all uncommon: "I turned out O.K. because of the way I was raised – because of the love my parents had for me as I was growing up, and the skill with which they nurtured me." Now, of the many people who have this thought, I suspect that for at most a scant few it is accompanied by a sense of dismay occasioned by coming to understand that to a large extent their moral character is not their own doing, and that they deserve at best diminished respect for having this char-

---

14. George Santayana, "A Junior Forensic," *The Daily Crimson* vol. 7, no. 15 (February 25, 1885) Supp., p. 3; quoted in Smilansky, "Can a Determinist Respect Herself?" p. 87.

acter. Rather, those who come to this conclusion tend to feel fortunate and thankful for the upbringing they received, and not to experience any sense of loss at all. Moreover, I don't think that people typically react with dismay when they realize the extent to which achievement in a career, or financial success, is dependent on upbringing, the opportunities that society presents, the help of colleagues, and plain luck. Again, I suspect that these thoughts frequently engender thankfulness and a sense of being fortunate, and virtually never dismay. Why then should we suppose that people will generally be overcome with dismay when they come to believe that because hard determinism is true, we do not shape our character and produce our achievements by free will, and that thus we do not for this reason deserve respect?

Undoubtedly there are some people who would react with dismay on having such thoughts. Then would it be warranted or advisable for these people to produce or maintain the illusion that they do deserve respect for originating their moral character and achievements? I think that most people would be capable of facing the truth without incurring much loss, and that those for whom it is painful will typically have the psychological resources to pull through. Smilansky, in my view, overreacts when he claims that such thoughts can be extremely damaging to our view of ourselves, and I believe that in the last analysis, the intransigent response to his claims is almost exactly right.

CAN BELIEF IN FREE WILL BE JUSTIFIED PRAGMATICALLY?

In Smilansky's illusionism, belief in free will is justified pragmatically, a feature of his position that invites further comment. A pragmatist view of this sort was first developed by Kant. Now, in several respects, Kant's views about free will are similar to my own. Like him, I maintain that incompatibilism is true, and that agent-causal libertarianism is required for moral responsibility. Moreover, I endorse his claim that although agent-causal libertarianism is a logically coherent position, we have no (theoretical) evidence that it is true. Kant does contend, however, that it is nevertheless legitimate to believe that we are free and morally responsible. He justifies this claim on two sorts of pragmatic and ethical grounds. First, the truth of moral "ought" principles requires that we have free will in a sense incompatible with determinism, and hence without this sort of free will there can be no moral law. Second, moral responsibility is too central to morality for the moral life to survive without it.[15]

In the Kantian conception, it is sometimes acceptable to believe a proposition for which we have little or no evidence. For instance, belief in such a proposition can be legitimate if it is required for living a moral life, and if on the theoretical side the proposition features no internal contradiction, and it is consistent with any other proposition that it is epistemically rational for one to believe. Now, I agree with Kant that it can be practically rational to believe a proposition for which we have little or no evidence. In fact, I doubt that the practical rationality of a belief is constrained by Kant's consistency requirement. But I do think that in such cases, subjects still violate the canons of epistemic rationality, in particular the requirement that one should proportion one's degree of belief to the evidence.

Mele also argues that given the strengths and weaknesses of the relevant arguments, belief in the sort of free will required for moral responsibility is pragmatically justifiable. One relevant difference between his assessment of the epistemic situation and mine is that he believes that the arguments against compatibilism are weaker than I hold them to be.[16] But even if they were somewhat weaker, I think that Mele's pragmatism, as well as Kant's and Smilansky's, will not stand up to scrutiny.

First, as I have been arguing, hard incompatibilism leaves intact much of what in human life is especially important to us – morality, preventing human evil, the possibility of meaning and fulfillment in life through achievement – and there is more to come. If indeed the important things in life are not undermined by the belief that hard incompatibilism is true, this sort of pragmatic justification will be defeated. Moreover, if it is defeated in this way, the epistemic requirements should prevail (in normal cirumstances).

Furthermore, even if the arguments against compatibilism (and the arguments against libertarianism) were somewhat weaker than I judge them to be, the pragmatic justification of belief in free will nevertheless founders on the following challenge. Given this epistemic situation, will it be morally acceptable to hold a wrongdoer blameworthy for what he has done? Or to justify expressing one's anger toward him by the claim that he is blameworthy? Or, if he is a criminal, to deprive

---

15. Kant, *Critique of Pure Reason*, A533/B560–A558/B586.
16. Mele, *Autonomous Agents*, pp. 251–4.

him of his liberty or life on the ground that he deserves such treatment just by virtue of having done wrong? Holding an offender blameworthy, expressing one's anger toward him, and depriving him of life or liberty all tend to be harmful to the offender. As I argued in the context of criminal punishment, if one aims to harm another, then one's justification must meet a high epistemic standard. If it is significantly probable that one's justification for the harmful behavior is unsound, then prima facie that behavior is wrong and one must refrain from engaging in it. For example, if one's justification for harmful behavior depended on an expectation, for which we have no evidence, that certain patterns of physical events would occur that we would not expect given our best physical theories, then that harmful behavior is prima facie morally wrong. Or if one's justification depended on the sufficiency for moral responsibility of a compatibilist condition that, given our best assessments, could well be false, then again that behavior is prima facie wrong.

Even if one is not disposed to accept hard incompatibilism, the strength of the arguments against libertarianism and compatibilism nevertheless provide a sound moral reason to treat wrongdoers as if hard incompatibilism were true. For even if these arguments are not forceful enough to confirm hard incompatibilism decisively, they could nevertheless be sufficiently powerful to show that the moral and epistemic standard for justifying harmful behavior has not been met. These considerations seriously jeopardize any pragmatic justification for believing in free will.

REACTIVE ATTITUDES AND INTERPERSONAL RELATIONSHIPS

As we have seen, P.F. Strawson contends that the justification for claims of blameworthiness and praiseworthiness ends in the system of human reactive attitudes, and because moral responsibility has this kind of footing, the truth or falsity of determinism is irrelevant to whether we legitimately hold agents to be morally responsible. Moral responsibility is founded in the reactive attitudes required for the kinds of relationships that make our lives meaningful. On the other hand, if the thesis of universal determinism did imperil the reactive attitudes, we would then face the prospect of a certain "objectivity of attitude," a stance that undermines the possibility of good interpersonal relationships.[17] I think

17. Strawson, "Freedom and Resentment," p. 66.

that Strawson is right to believe that objectivity of attitude would destroy interpersonal relationships, but that he is mistaken to hold that it would result or be appropriate if determinism did pose a genuine threat to the reactive attitudes.

In my view, first, some ordinary reactive attitudes, although they would be undermined by hard determinism, or more broadly by hard incompatibilism, are not obviously required for good interpersonal relationships. Indignation and moral resentment, for example, might be theoretically irrational given hard incompatibilism, but all things considered do more harm than good. Second, the reactive attitudes that we would want to retain either are not undermined by hard incompatibilism or else have analogs that would not have false presuppositions. The attitudes and analogs that would survive do not amount to Strawson's objectivity of attitude, and are sufficient to sustain good interpersonal relationships.

In Strawson's conception, some of the attitudes most important for interpersonal relationships are indignation, moral resentment, forgiveness, gratitude, and mature love. A certain measure of indignation and resentment is likely to be beyond our power to affect, and thus even supposing that one is committed to doing what is right and rational, one would still be unable to eradicate these attitudes. As hard incompatibilists, we might expect that indignation, for example, would occur in certain situations, and we might regard it as inevitable and exempt from blame when it does. But we sometimes have the ability to prevent, alter, or eliminate indignation, and given a belief in hard incompatibilism, we might well do so for the sake of morality and rationality. Modification of this attitude, aided by a hard incompatibilist conviction, could well be a good thing for relationships.

One might object that indignation plays an important communicative role in relationships with others, and if one were to strive to modify or eliminate this attitude, relationships might well be damaged. However, when one is wronged in a relationship, there are other emotions typically present that are not threatened by hard incompatibilism, whose expression can also communicate the relevant information. These emotions include feeling hurt or shocked about what the other has done, and moral sadness or concern for the other. These attitudes are not aggressive in the way that indignation can be, and all by themselves they do not typically have indignation's intimidating effect. But if aggressiveness or intimidation is required, a strongly worded threat, for instance, might be appropriate. It is not clear, therefore, that indignation is required for communication in interpersonal relationships.

The attitude of forgiveness would appear to presuppose that the person being forgiven deserves blame, and thus forgiveness would indeed be imperiled by hard incompatibilism. But there are certain features of forgiveness that are not threatened by this view, and these features can adequately take the place this attitude usually has in relationships. Suppose a friend has wronged you in similar fashion a number of times, and you find yourself unhappy, angry, and resolved to loosen the ties of your relationship. Subsequently, however, he apologizes to you, which, consistent with hard incompatibilism, signifies his recognition of the wrongness of his behavior, his wish that he had not wronged you, and his genuine commitment to improvement. As a result, you change your mind and decide to continue the relationship. In this case, the feature of forgiveness that is consistent with hard incompatibilism is the willingness to cease to regard past wrongful behavior as a reason to weaken or dissolve one's relationship. In another type of case, you might, independently of the offender's repentance, simply choose to disregard the wrong as a reason to alter the character of your relationship. This attitude is in no sense undermined by hard incompatibilism. The sole aspect of forgiveness that is jeopardized by a hard incompatibilist conviction is the willingness to overlook deserved blame or punishment. But if one has given up belief in deserved blame and punishment, then the willingness to overlook them is no longer needed for good relationships.

Gratitude might well require the supposition that the person to whom one is grateful is morally responsible for an other-regarding act, and therefore hard incompatibilism might well undermine gratitude.[18] However, certain aspects of this attitude would be left untouched, aspects that can play the role gratitude commonly has in interpersonal relationships. First, gratitude includes an element of thankfulness toward those who have benefited us. Sometimes, being thankful involves the belief that the object of one's attitude is praiseworthy for some action. But one can also be thankful to a pet or a small child for some favor, even if one does not believe that he is morally responsible. Perhaps one can even be thankful for the sun or the rain even if one does not believe that these elements are backed by morally responsible agency. In general, if one believed hard incompatibilism, one's thankfulness might lack

18. Cf. Honderich's discussion of gratitude, *A Theory of Determinism*, pp. 518–19.

201

features that it would have if one did not, but nevertheless, this aspect of gratitude can survive.

Gratitude involves an aspect of joy upon being benefited by another. But no feature of the hard incompatibilist position conflicts with one's being joyful and expressing joy when people are especially considerate, generous, or courageous in one's behalf. Such expressions of joy can produce the sense of mutual well-being and respect frequently brought about by gratitude. Moreover, when one expresses joy for what another person has done, one can do so with the intention of developing a human relationship.

The thesis that love between mature persons would be subverted if hard incompatibilism were true requires more thorough argument than Strawson has provided. Is it plausible that loving another requires that she be free in the sense required for moral responsibility? One might note that parents love their children rarely, if ever, because these children possess this sort of freedom, or because they freely (in this sense) choose the good, or because they deserve to be loved. Moreover, when adults love each other, it is also seldom, if at all, for these kinds of reasons. Explaining love is a complex enterprise. Besides moral character and action, factors such as one's relation to the other, her appearance, manner, intelligence, and her affinities with persons or events in one's history all might have a part. But suppose we assume that moral character and action are of paramount importance in producing and maintaining love. Even if there is an important aspect of love that is essentially a deserved response to moral character and action, it is unlikely that one's love would be undermined if one were to believe that these moral qualities do not come about through free and responsible choice. For moral character and action are loveable whether or not they merit praise. Love of another involves, most fundamentally, wishing well for the other, taking on many of the aims and desires of the other as one's own, and a desire to be together with the other. Hard incompatibilism threatens none of this.

One might argue that we nevertheless desire to be loved by others as a result of their free will. Against this, it is clear that parents' love for their children – a paradigmatic sort of love – is often produced independently of the parents' will. Kane endorses this last claim, and a similar view about romantic love, but he nevertheless argues that a certain type of love we want would be endangered if we knew that there were factors beyond the lover's control that determined it.

There is a *kind* of love we desire from others – parents, children (when they are old enough), spouses, lovers and friends – whose significance is diminished . . . by the thought that they are determined to love us entirely by instinct or circumstances beyond their control or not entirely up to them . . . To be loved by others in this desired sense requires that the ultimate source of others' love lies in their own wills.[19]

The plausibility of Kane's view might perhaps be enhanced by reflecting on how you would react were you to discover that someone you love was causally determined by a benevolent manipulator to have the love she has for you.

Leaving aside free will for a moment, in which sorts of cases does the will intuitively play a role in generating love for another at all? When the intensity of an intimate relationship is waning, people sometimes make a decision to try to make it work, and to attempt to regain the type of relationship they once had. When a student is placed in a dormitory suite and is not immediately disposed to friendship with one of the suitemates, he may make the decision to attempt nevertheless to form an emotional bond. Or when one's marriage is arranged by parents, one may decide to do whatever one can to love one's spouse.

But, first, in such situations we might desire that another person make a decision to love, but it is not clear that we have reason to want the decision to be *freely* willed in the sense required for moral responsibility. A decision to love on the part of another might greatly enhance one's personal life, but it is not at all obvious what value the decision's being free and thus praiseworthy would add. Second, although in circumstances of these kinds we might desire that someone else make a decision to love, we would typically prefer the situation in which the love was not mediated by a decision. This is true not only for romantic attachments, but also for friendships and for relationships between parents and children.

Perhaps the will plays a significant role in maintaining love over an extended period. Kierkegaard suggests that a marital relationship ideally involves a commitment that is continuously renewed.[20] Such a commitment involves a decision to devote oneself to another, and thus, in

19. Kane, *The Significance of Free Will*, p. 88.
20. Søren Kierkegaard, *Either/Or*, vol. 2, tr. Walter Lowrie (Princeton: Princeton University Press, 1971).

his view, a marital relationship ideally involves a continuously repeated decision. A decision of this kind may include a choice not to pursue intimate relationships with others. Indeed, many of us might very much desire a relationship with this sort of voluntary aspect. Again, it is difficult to see what is to be added by these continuously repeated decisions being freely willed in the sense required for moral responsibility. It might well be desirable for each participant that the other make these decisions. But that the participants should in addition be praiseworthy for these choices seems hardly relevant.

Suppose Kane's view could be defended, and we do have a desire for love that is freely willed, or free in the sense required for moral responsibility. If we indeed desire freely willed love, then we desire a kind of love whose possibility hard incompatibilism denies. Still, the possibilities for love that remain are surely sufficient for good interpersonal relationships. If we can aspire to the sort of love parents typically have toward children, or the kind romantic lovers ideally have toward one another, or the type shared by friends who are immediately attracted to one another, and whose relationship is deepened by their interactions, then the possibility of fulfillment in interpersonal relationships is far from undermined. Finally, of all the attitudes that Strawson thinks might be imperiled by a belief in universal determinism, love is surely the most crucial for our relationships. If the types of love important for mature human relationships can survive, as I have argued, then universal determinism's threat to such relationships has been largely defused.

GUILT AND REPENTANCE

It might be argued that the self-directed attitudes of guilt and repentance are also threatened by hard incompatibilism. There is much at stake here, one might claim, for these attitudes are not only essential to good interpersonal relationships for agents prone to wrongdoing, but are also required for the moral development and integrity of an agent of this sort. Deprived of the attitudes of guilt and repentance, such an agent would not only be incapable of reestablishing relationships damaged because he has done wrong, but he would also be barred from a restoration of his own moral integrity in these situations. For in the absence of the attitudes of guilt and repentance, there are no human psychological mechanisms that can generate a restoration of this sort. Hard incompatibilism would appear to undermine guilt because this attitude essentially involves a sense that one is blameworthy for what one has done. Plausibly, if one did not feel blameworthy for an offense, one would also not feel guilty for it. Moreover, one might argue that because feeling guilty is undermined by hard incompatibilism, feeling repentant is also no longer an option. For as a matter of psychological fact, feeling guilty is required for motivating an attitude of repentance.

However, suppose that you do wrong, but because you believe that hard incompatibilism is true, you reject the claim that you are blameworthy. Instead, you accept that you have done wrong, you feel deeply sad that you were the agent of wrongdoing, or as Waller advocates, you thoroughly regret what you have done:

> It is reasonable for one who denies moral responsibility to feel profound sorrow and regret for an act. If in a fit of anger I strike a friend, I shall be appalled at my behavior, and profoundly distressed that I have in me the capacity for such behavior. If the act occurs under minimum provocation, and with an opportunity for some brief reflection before the assault, then I shall be even more disturbed and disappointed by my behavior: I find in myself the capacity for a vicious and despicable act, and the act emerges more from my own character than from the immediate stimuli (thus it may be more likely to recur in many different settings), and my capacity to control such vicious behavior is demonstrably inadequate. Certainly, I shall have good reason to regret my character – its capacity for vicious acts and its lack of capacity to control anger.[21]

Also, because you have a commitment to doing what is right, and to personal moral progress, you might resolve not to perform an immoral action of this kind again, and seek out therapeutic procedures to help treat one's character problems. None of this is undermined by hard incompatibilism.

Since such sadness and regret for one's actions and character do not involve considering oneself blameworthy, one might not then have the attitude of guilt. But even this supposition can be challenged. Given what is ordinarily meant by "feeling guilty," it may be that feeling intensely sad and regretful that you are the agent of wrongdoing is sufficient for having this attitude. Bok eloquently advocates a position of this sort:

---

21. Waller, *Freedom Without Responsibility*, pp. 165–6, cf. 164–9.

The relation between the recognition that one has done something wrong and the guilt one suffers as a result . . . is like the relation between the recognition that one's relationship with someone one truly loves has collapsed and the pain of heartbreak. Heartbreak is not a pain one inflicts on oneself as a punishment for loss of love; it is not something we undergo because we deserve it . . . Similarly, the recognition that one has done something wrong causes pain. But this pain is not a form of suffering that we inflict on ourselves as a punishment but an entirely appropriate response to the recognition of what we have done, for two reasons. First, our standards define the kind of life we think we should lead and what we regard as valuable in the world, in our lives, and in the lives of others. They articulate what matters to us, and living by them is therefore by definition of concern to us. If we have indeed violated them, we have slighted what we take to be of value, disregarded principles we sincerely think we should live by, and failed to be the sorts of people we think we should be. The knowledge that we have done these things must be painful to us.[22]

But even if in the final analysis merely feeling sad or regretful or pained does not constitute feeling guilty, it can nevertheless generate a repentant attitude, a resolution not to perform the immoral action again. One might object that a feeling of moral sadness and regret is an insufficiently strong motivation to an attitude of repentance, but this claim is not obviously true.

Hard incompatibilism therefore endangers neither relationships with others or personal integrity. It might well undermine certain attitudes that typically have a role in these domains. Indignation, gratitude, and guilt would likely be theoretically irrational for a hard incompatibilist. But these attitudes are either not essential to good relationships, or they have analogs that could play the same role they typically have. Moreover, some of the most crucial reactive attitudes, such as forgiveness, love, and repentance, are not clearly threatened by hard incompatibilism at all.

We can now see that the hard incompatibilist need not adopt the objectivity of attitude so destructive to interpersonal relationships. The specter of this outlook arises from the sense that she is forced to regard other human beings as mere mechanical devices, to be used and not respected. She is not, however, constrained to view others in this way. The hard incompatibilist need not deny that human beings are rational and responsive to reasons, and no feature of her view threatens the respect she has for them because of their rational capacities. Moreover,

---

22. Bok, *Freedom and Responsibility*, pp. 168–9. I find the view she develops in the section "Excursus on Guilt" (pp. 167–79) very attractive.

thinking and acting in harmony with her hard incompatibilist convictions would not endanger her relationships. She would resist anger, blame, and resentment, but she would not be exempt from pain, sadness, or regret upon being wronged. When hurt by another, she might admonish, and upon acknowledgment of wrongdoing on the part of the other, cease to regard it as a hindrance to the relationship. She could be thankful and express joy toward others for the good things they provide for her. Her convictions pose no obstacle to love. Only if she also had an unappealing tendency to control another would she see him "as an object of social policy; as a subject for what, in a wide range of sense, might be called treatment; as something certainly to be taken account, perhaps precautionary account, of; to be managed or handled or cured or trained; perhaps simply to be avoided . . ."[23] But she would not be compelled to take on this objectivity of attitude by her hard incompatibilist beliefs.

THE ADVANTAGES OF HARD INCOMPATIBILISM

Hard incompatibilism holds out the promise of substantial benefits for human life. Philosophers in the Stoic tradition have argued that determinism allows for an increased degree of equanimity in the face of the bad things that happen. We find this view developed by the ancient Stoics themselves, in a similar way by Descartes, and also in Spinoza.[24] The central idea of this position is that if determinism is true, then everything that happens can ultimately be attributed to something encompassing – God, perhaps, or something more impersonal, such as nature or the universe. Then, by psychological identification with this entity, perhaps by taking on its perspective, one can achieve a sort of acceptance of whatever happens. Libertarian freedom would rule out this route to equanimity, because if human beings have freedom of this type, their free decisions could not be attributed to this encompassing entity, and then identifying with it would not serve as a route to acceptance of these decisions.

The hard incompatibilist might explore the possibilities of a view of this sort. But although its promised benefits are substantial, this

23. Strawson, *Freedom and Resentment*, p. 66.
24. The material that follows is derived from my "Stoic Psychotherapy in Descartes and Spinoza," *Faith and Philosophy*, October 1994, pp. 592–625. For an account of the Stoic view, see Brad Inwood, *Ethics and Human Action in Early Stoicism*, Oxford: Clarendon Press, 1985, pp. 42–101.

position nevertheless faces daunting problems. Many would regard the Stoic strategy as too ambitious because of its controversial theological and psychological assumptions. Moreover, this strategy recommends assuming a perspective from which things that ordinarily seem bad, do not seem as bad, or even bad at all, and one might argue that the diminished degree of sadness and concern it advocates is morally inappropriate.

Hard incompatibilism nevertheless undergirds a less comprehensive equanimity, of a sort that is grounded in the propensity of this view to diminish anger. Indeed, of all the attitudes associated with moral responsibility, it is anger that seems most closely connected with it. It is telling that debates about moral responsibility typically focus not on how we should regard morally exemplary agents, but rather on how we should consider those that are morally offensive. The kinds of cases most often employed in producing a strong conviction of moral responsibility involve especially malevolent actions, and the sense of moral responsibility evoked typically involves sympathetic anger. Perhaps our attachment to moral responsibility derives partly from the role anger plays in our emotional lives, and it could be that hard incompatibilism is especially threatening because it challenges its rationality.

The type of anger at issue is the sort that is directed toward someone who is represented as having done wrong (sometimes the representation is accurate, sometimes not). Let us call this attitude *moral anger*. Perhaps moral anger, as I have characterized it, is closely related to indignation. Not all anger is moral anger. One type of non-moral anger is directed at someone because his abilities in some respect are scant or because he performs poorly in some particular circumstance. We are on occasion angry with inanimate machines for malfunctioning. Sometimes we are just angry without any target. However, by far most human anger is moral anger.

Moral anger forms an important part of the ethical life as it is ordinarily conceived. It motivates us to resist oppression, injustice, and abuse. But often expressions of moral anger have harmful effects. They may fail to contribute to the well-being of those to whom they are directed. Frequently, expressions of moral anger are intended to cause physical or emotional pain. Partly as a result of these problems, moral anger often has a tendency to damage or destroy relationships. In extreme cases, it can provide motivation to take very harmful and even lethal action against another.

The sense that expressions of moral anger are damaging gives rise to a robust demand that they be morally justified when they occur. The call to produce a moral justification for behavior that is harmful to others is always strong, and expressions of moral anger are typically harmful to others. Moreover, this demand is made more acute by the fact that we are often attached to moral anger; we often in a sense enjoy displaying it, and this is partly why we want these displays to be morally justifiable. We most commonly justify expressions of moral anger by way of the claim that wrongdoers fundamentally deserve to experience them. From the hard incompatibilist perspective this claim is illusory. But even if it is in fact illusory, we might still retain a strong interest in preserving the belief in moral responsibility to satisfy the pressing need to justify these expressions of moral anger.

Other schemes of false beliefs have arguably been maintained to rationalize expressions of various types of anger. The beliefs associated with the once widespread practice of human sacrifice provide an interesting example. René Girard argues that life in human communities gives rise to angry tensions – largely born of envy, in his view – that threaten to fracture the community.[25] These groups would then vent their angry tensions on victims in ways that would preserve the integrity of the community. This had to be done in accordance with strict rules and in controlled circumstances, in order to prevent the violence from destroying the community itself. The victims of sacrifice were typically not "central" members of society: children, slaves, or captives. These sacrificial practices were always associated with beliefs that provided a moral or religious justification for violence. Similar violence against human beings was typically regarded as wrong absent such a justification. The permission or the demand for sacrifice was usually believed to derive from a higher authority – a god. Often, a sacrificial practice incorporated the belief that the god would require or enjoy the offering, and would reward it with blessings of various sorts. Thus, by means of a system of false religious belief, violent but controlled expression of anger was justified.

It is unlikely that the sole explanation for human sacrificial practice is that it allowed community anger to be vented in a controlled way. But it is also plausibly part of the explanation for this practice. By grounding sacrifice in theistic religious belief, expressions of anger

25. René Girard, *Violence and the Sacred* (Baltimore: Johns Hopkins University Press, 1977).

receive a kind of rationalization not readily available for such expressions in their own right. Moreover, other currently more common schemes of false beliefs have been devised that serve to rationalize expressions of anger. Countless atrocities have been rationalized by the false belief that an ethnic or religious group is out to destroy one's culture and society. Rationalizing expressions of anger by false beliefs is not an unusual practice for human beings.

Girard argues that modern societies have replaced sacrificial with legal systems as a strategy for controlled venting of anger. Legal systems also include beliefs that justify the violence they carry out. One of the most prominent of these is the belief that people are typically blameworthy for wrongdoing, and when the wrongdoing is serious enough, they deserve pain and deprivation as a result. Furthermore, not only the violence of the legal system would stand in need of such a justification, but also the violence of our more commonplace moral anger. The claim that agents, by virtue of wrongdoing, deserve to have these attitudes directed toward them plays a central role in the attempt to justify expressions of this attitude.

The hard incompatibilist proposal is that our tendency to express moral anger, along with our strong desire for such behavior to be legitimate in the typical case, is a factor that gives rise to the false belief that people are free in the sense that they are morally responsible for their actions. In *On Liberty*, John Stuart Mill makes a similar suggestion. About Robert Owen's claim that "it is unjust to punish at all, for the criminal did not make his own character," he remarks that as a refuge from this view, "men imagined what they called the freedom of the will – fancying that they could not justify punishing a man whose will is in a thoroughly hateful state unless it be supposed to have come into that state through no influence of anterior circumstances."[26] Moreover, the near inevitability of moral anger and our attachment to this attitude can explain the tenacity with which we maintain our belief in freedom and moral responsibility.

Acceptance of hard incompatibilism is quite unlikely to alter human psychology so that anger is no longer a problem for us. Nevertheless, much of our anger feeds on the presupposition that its object deserves blame for a moral offense. Destructive anger in relationships is nourished by the belief that the other is blameworthy for having done wrong. The anger that fuels many ethnic conflicts results partly from

26. John Stuart Mill, *Utilitarianism* (Indianapolis: Hackett, 1979), chapter 5, p. 55.

the belief that a group of people deserves blame for some large-scale evil. Hard incompatibilism advocates retracting such beliefs because they are false, and as a result the associated anger could be diminished, and its expressions curtailed.

In addressing these sorts of issues, Watson provides a striking quotation of Albert Einstein's:

I do not at all believe in human freedom in the philosophical sense. Everybody acts not only under external compulsion but also in accordance with inner necessity. Schopenhauer's saying, "A man can do what he wants, but not want what he wants," has been a very real inspiration to me since my youth; it has been a continual consolation in the face of life's hardships, my own and others', and an unfailing well-spring of tolerance. This realization mercifully mitigates the easily paralysing sense of responsibility and prevents us from taking ourselves and other people too seriously; it is conducive to a view of life which, in particular, gives humor its due.[27]

In Einstein's estimation, what appears to be a hard determinist conviction provides him with tolerance toward others and consolation in the hardships in life. What makes these benefits possible, I believe, is that this view can release us from false beliefs that rationalize expressions of moral anger, and thereby diminish such anger and its harmful expressions.

One might respond by claiming that this conception would also tend to reduce the benefits provided by moral anger and, more generally, by the reactive attitudes that this view undermines. Watson points out that Einstein in the same place speaks of himself as having a "pronounced lack of need for direct contact with other human beings and human communities," and as someone who has

never belonged to my country, my home, my friends, or even my immediate family, with my whole heart; in the face of all these ties, I have never lost a sense of distance and a need for solitude – feelings which increase with the years.[28]

This reflection might inspire the thought that even if a resolute hard incompatibilist conviction does not eliminate the possibility of good

27.   Albert Einstein, *Ideas and Opinions* (New York: Crown Publishers, 1982), pp. 8–9; quoted in Gary Watson, "Responsibility and the Limits of Evil," p. 284.
28.   Einstein, *Ideas and Opinions*, pp. 8–9; quoted in Gary Watson, "Responsibility and the Limits of Evil," p. 284.

interpersonal relationships, it would nevertheless tend to diminish the intensity of one's personal connections with others. I find this claim dubious for reasons that we have now examined. But other benefits could more plausibly be put at risk by this conviction, in particular because it might diminish moral anger. They include protecting ourselves and others in times of danger, providing motivation for eliminating injustice, and communicating problems in relationships with others. For example, anger against foreign oppressors stimulates people to drive them out, anger with tyrannical regimes incites salutary political reform, and anger in personal relationships discourages abuse. To the degree that hard incompatibilism diminishes anger, it could also decrease the intensity of the motivation to realize these goals, and thus the extent to which these goals are achieved.

Would the losses resulting from a hard incompatibilist conviction outweigh its benefits? This is an empirical issue that cannot easily be resolved. But perhaps the hard incompatibilist can typically retain the benefits while engaging different motivational resources to replace any decrease in instrumentally advantageous anger. When the assumption that wrongdoers are blameworthy is withdrawn for hard incompatibilist reasons, the conviction that they have in fact done wrong could legitimately survive. Not implausibly, such a moral conviction could lead to a firm resolve to resist oppression, injustice, and abuse. As a result, hard incompatibilism might allow for the benefits that moral anger may also produce, while avoiding its destructive consequences.

———————

Living without a conception of our choices and actions as freely willed in the sense required for moral responsibility does not come naturally to us. Our psychologies and our patterns of behavior presuppose that our choices and actions are free in this sense. Nevertheless, not only are there good arguments against this belief, but also, despite our initially apprehensive reactions to hard incompatibilism, believing it would not have disastrous consequences, and indeed it promises significant benefits for human life. Hard incompatibilism would not undermine the purpose in life that our projects can provide. Neither would it hinder the possibility of the good interpersonal relationships fundamental to our happiness. Acceptance of hard incompatibilism rather holds out the promise of greater equanimity by reducing the anger that hinders fulfillment. Far from threatening meaning in life, hard incompatibilism can help us achieve the conditions required for flourishing, for it can assist in releasing us from the harmful passions that contribute so much to human distress. If we did in fact relinquish our presumption of free will and moral responsibility, then, perhaps surprisingly, our lives might well be better for it.

Bibliography

Adams, Marilyn. "The Structure of Ockham's Moral Theory," *Franciscan Studies* 24 (1986), 1–35.

——"Duns Scotus on the Will as Rational Power," *Via Scoti: Methodologica ad Mentem Joannis Duns Scoti*, ed. Leonardo Sileo (Rome: PAA Edizioni Antonianum, 1995), pp. 839–54.

Alexander J.F., and B.V. Parsons. *Functional Family Therapy* (Monterrey: Brooks/Cole, 1982).

Allen, Francis A. "Criminal Justice, Legal Values, and the Rehabilitative Ideal," *Journal of Criminal Law, Criminology, and Police Science* 50 (1959), pp. 226–32.

Anscombe G.E.M. *Causality and Determinism* (Cambridge: Cambridge University Press, 1971).

Austin J.L. "Ifs and Cans," in *Free Will and Determinism*, ed. Bernard Berofsky (New York: Harper and Row, 1966), pp. 295–321.

Ayer, Alfred J. "Freedom and Necessity," in Alfred J. Ayer, *Philosophical Essays* (London: Macmillan, 1954), reprinted in *Free Will*, ed. Gary Watson (Oxford: Oxford University Press, 1982), pp. 15–23.

Bennett, Jonathan. "Accountability," in ed. Zak van Straaten, *Philosophical Subjects* (Oxford: Oxford University Press, 1980), pp. 74–91.

Bentham, Jeremy. *An Introduction to the Principles of Morals and Legislation* (1823) (New York: Macmillan, 1948).

Berofsky, Bernard, ed. *Free Will and Determinism* (New York: Harper and Row, 1966).

——*Freedom from Necessity: The Metaphysical Basis of Responsibility* (New York: Routledge and Kegan Paul, 1987).

Bernstein, Mark. "Kanean Libertarianism," *Southwest Philosophy Review* 11 (1995), pp. 151–7.

Bok, Hilary. *Freedom and Responsibility* (Princeton: Princeton University Press, 1998).

Braithwaite, John, and Philip Pettit. *Not Just Deserts* (Oxford: Oxford University Press, 1990).

Broad C.D. "Determinism, Indeterminism, and Libertarianism," in his *Ethics and the History of Philosophy* (London: Routledge and Kegan Paul, 1952), pp. 195–217, reprinted in *Determinism, Free Will, and Moral Responsibility*, ed. Gerald Dworkin (Englewood Cliffs: Prentice-Hall, 1970), pp. 149–71.

Castañeda, Hector-Neri. *Thinking and Doing* (Dordrecht: D. Reidel, 1975).

Chisholm, Roderick. "Reflections on Human Agency," *Idealistic Studies* 1 (1971), pp. 33–46.

——"Human Freedom and the Self," The Lindley Lecture, Department of Philosophy, University of Kansas, 1964, reprinted in *Free Will*, ed. Gary Watson (Oxford: Oxford University Press, 1982).

——*Person and Object* (La Salle: Open Court, 1976).

Clarke, Randolph. "A Principle of Rational Explanation," *The Southern Journal of Philosophy* 30 (1992), pp. 1–12.

——"Toward a Credible Agent-Causal Account of Free Will," *Noûs* 27 (1993), pp. 191–203, reprinted in *Agents, Causes, and Events*, ed. Timothy O'Connor (Oxford: Oxford University Press, 1995).

——"Indeterminism and Control," *American Philosophical Quarterly* (1995), pp. 125–38.

——"Contrastive Rational Explanations of Free Choice," *Philosophical Quarterly* 46 (1996), pp. 185–201.

——"Agent Causation and Event Causation in the Production of Free Action," *Philosophical Topics* 24 (1996), pp. 19–48; a shorter version appears in *Free Will*, ed. Derk Pereboom (Indianapolis: Hackett, 1997), pp. 273–300.

——"On the Possibility of Rational Free Action," *Philosophical Studies* 88 (1997), pp. 37–57.

——"Modest Libertarianism," *Philosophical Perspectives*, 14, 2000.

De Rose, Keith. "Review of William Rowe's *Thomas Reid on Freedom and Morality*," *Philosophy and Phenomenological Research* 53 (1993), pp. 945–9.

Della Rocca, Michael. "Frankfurt, Fischer, and Flickers," *Noûs* 32 (1996), pp. 99–105.

Dennett, Daniel. "Giving Libertarians What They Say They Want," in his *Brainstorms* (Montgomery, VT: Bradford Books, 1978), pp. 286–99.

——*Elbow Room: Varieties of Free Will Worth Wanting* (Cambridge: MIT Press, 1984).

Double, Richard. *The Non-Reality of Free Will* (New York: Oxford University Press, 1991).

——"The Principle of Rational Explanation Defended," *Southern Journal of Philosophy* 31 (1993), pp. 431–9.

——*Metaphilosophy and Free Will* (New York: Oxford University Press, 1996).

——"Honderich on the Consequences of Determinism," *Philosophy and Phenomenological Research* 56 (1996), pp. 847–54.

Dupré, John. *The Disorder of Things* (Cambridge: Harvard University Press, 1993).

——"The Solution to the Problem of the Freedom of the Will," *Philosophical Perspectives* 10 (Oxford: Blackwell Publishers, 1996), pp. 385–402.

Einstein, Albert. *Ideas and Opinions* (New York: Crown, 1982).

Farrell, Daniel M. "The Justification of General Deterrence," *The Philosophical Review* 104 (1985), pp. 367–94; reprinted in *Punishment and Rehabilitation*, third edition, ed. Jeffrie E. Murphy (Belmont, CA: Wadsworth, 1995), pp. 38–60.

Feldman, Fred. *Doing the Best We Can* (Dordrecht: D. Reidel, 1986).

Fischer, John Martin. "Responsibility and Control," in *Moral Responsibility*, ed. John Martin Fischer (Ithaca: Cornell University Press, 1986), pp. 174–90.

——ed. *Moral Responsibility* (Ithaca: Cornell University Press, 1986).

——"Responsiveness and Moral Responsibility," in *Responsibility, Character, and the*

Emotions, ed. Ferdinand Schoeman (Cambridge: Cambridge University Press, 1987), pp. 81–106.

——*The Metaphysics of Free Will* (Oxford: Blackwell, 1994).

——and Mark Ravizza. *Responsibility and Control a Theory of Moral Responsibility* (New York: Cambridge University Press, 1998).

——"Recent Work on Moral Responsibility," *Ethics* 110 (1999), pp. 93–139.

——Review of Richard Double, *Metaphilosophy and Free Will*, *Philosophy and Phenomenological Research* 59 (1999), pp. 1083–6.

Fodor, Jerry. "Special Sciences," *Synthese* 28 (1974), pp. 97–115, reprinted in *Readings in the Philosophy of Psychology*, ed. Ned Block (Cambridge: Harvard University Press, 1980), pp. 120–33.

——"Making Mind Matter More," in his *A Theory of Content and Other Essays* (Cambridge: MIT Press, 1992), pp. 137–60.

Foot, Philippa. "Free Will as Involving Determinism," *The Philosophical Review* 66 (1957), reprinted in her *Virtues and Vices* (Berkeley and Los Angeles: University of California Press, 1978), pp. 62–73.

Frankfurt, Harry G. "Alternate Possibilities and Moral Responsibility," *Journal of Philosophy* 66 (1969), pp. 829–39.

——"Freedom of the Will and the Concept of a Person," *Journal of Philosophy* 68 (1971), pp. 5–20, reprinted in *Free Will* ed. Gary Watson (Oxford: Oxford University Press, 1982), pp. 81–95.

——"Three Concepts of Free Action: II," *Proceedings of the Aristotelian Society* (1975), pp. 113–25, reprinted in *Moral Responsibility*, ed. John Martin Fischer (Ithaca: Cornell University Press, 1986), pp. 113–23.

——"Identification and Wholeheartedness, in *Responsibility, Character, and the Emotions*, ed. Ferdinand Schoeman (Cambridge: Cambridge University Press, 1987), pp. 27–45.

Gendreau, Paul, and Robert Ross. "Effective Correctional Treatment: Bibliography for Cynics," *Crime and Delinquency* 25 (1979), pp. 463–89.

——"Revivification of Rehabilitation: Evidence for the 1980's," *Justice Quarterly* 4 (1987), pp. 349–407.

Gert, Bernard, and Timothy J. Duggan. "Free Will as the Ability to Will," *Noûs* 13 (May 1979), pp. 197–217, reprinted in *Moral Responsibility*, ed. John Martin Fischer (Ithaca: Cornell University Press, 1986), pp. 205–24.

Ginet, Carl. "Might We Have No Choice," in *Freedom and Determinism*, ed. Keith Lehrer (New York: Random House, 1966), pp. 87–104.

——"Reasons Explanation of Action: An Incompatibilist Account," in *Agents, Causes, and Events*, ed. Timothy O'Connor (Oxford: Oxford University Press, 1995), pp. 69–94.

——"In Defense of the Principle of Alternative Possibilities: Why I Don't Find Frankfurt's Arguments Convincing," *Philosophical Perspectives* 10 (1996), pp. 403–17.

——"Freedom, Responsibility, and Agency," *The Journal of Ethics* 1 (1997), pp. 85–98.

Girard, René. *Violence and the Sacred* (Baltimore: Johns Hopkins University Press, 1977).

Goetz, Stewart. "Stumping for Widerker," *Faith and Philosophy* 16 (1999), pp. 83–9.

Greenwood P., and F. Zimring. *One More Chance: The Pursuit of Promising Intervention Strategies for Chronic Juvenile Offenders* (Santa Monica: RAND, 1985).

Haji, Ishtiyaque. *Moral Accountability* (New York: Oxford University Press, 1998).

——"Moral Anchors and Control," *Canadian Journal of Philosophy* 29 (1999), pp. 175–203.

Hampton, Jean. "The Moral Education Theory of Punishment," *Philosophy and Public Affairs* (1984), pp. 208–38.

Heinaman, Robert. "Incompatibilism without the Principle of Alternative Possibilities, *Australasian Journal of Philosophy* 64 (1986), pp. 266–76.

Henning, Kris R., and B. Christopher Frueh. "Cognitive-Behavioral Treatment of Incarcerated Offenders," *Criminal Justice and Behavior* 23 (1996), pp. 523–41.

Hill, Thomas E. Jr. "Humanity as an End in Itself," *Ethics* 91 (1980), pp. 84–90, reprinted in his *Dignity and Practical Reason* (Ithaca: Cornell University Press, 1993), pp. 38–57.

——"The Kantian Conception of Autonomy," in his *Dignity and Practical Reason* (Ithaca: Cornell University Press, 1993), pp. 76–96.

Hobart R. "Free Will as Involving Determinism and Inconceivable without It," *Mind* 43 (1934), pp. 1–27.

Holbach, Paul. *Système de la Nature* (Amsterdam, 1770).

Honderich, Ted. *A Theory of Determinism* (Oxford: Oxford University Press, 1988).

——"Compatibilism, Incompatibilism, and the Smart Aleck," *Philosophy and Phenomenological Research* 56 (1996), pp. 855–62.

Hume, David. *A Treatise of Human Nature*, ed. L.A. Selby-Bigge (Oxford: Oxford University Press, 1978).

——*An Enquiry Concerning Human Understanding*, ed. Eric Steinberg (Indianapolis: Hackett, 1981).

——*An Enquiry Concerning the Principles of Morals*, J.B. Schneewind, ed. (Indianapolis: Hackett, 1983).

Hunt, David. "Moral Responsibility and Avoidable Action," *Philosophical Studies* 97 (2000), pp. 195–227.

Inwood, Brad. *Ethics and Human Action in Early Stoicism* (Oxford: Clarendon Press, 1985).

James, William. "The Dilemma of Determinism," in *The Will to Believe* (New York: Dover, 1956), pp. 145–83.

Kane, Robert. *Free Will and Values* (Albany: SUNY Press, 1985).

——"Two Kinds of Incompatibilism," in *Agents, Causes, and Events*, Timothy O'Connor, ed. (Oxford: Oxford University Press, 1995), pp. 115–50. Originally published in *Philosophy and Phenomenological Research* 50 (1989), pp. 219–54.

——*The Significance of Free Will* (New York: Oxford University Press, 1996).

——"Responsibility, Luck, and Chance: Reflections on Free Will and Indeterminism," *Journal of Philosophy* 96 (1999), pp. 217–40.

——"Responses to Bernard Berofsky, John Martin Fischer, and Galen Strawson," *Philosophy and Phenomenological Research* 60 (2000), pp. 159–67.

Kant, Immanuel. *Critique of Pure Reason*, tr. Paul Guyer and Allen Wood (Cambridge: Cambridge University Press, 1997).

———*Groundwork of the Metaphysics of Morals*, tr. Mary Gregor (Cambridge: Cambridge University Press, 1997).

———*The Metaphysical Elements of Justice*, tr. John Ladd (New York: Bobbs-Merrill, 1965).

Kapitan, Tomis. "Deliberation and the Presumption of Open Alternatives," *The Philosophical Quarterly* 36 (1986), pp. 230–51.

Kierkegaard, Søren. *Either/Or*, vol. 2, tr. Walter Lowrie (Princeton: Princeton University Press, 1971).

Kim, Jaegwon. "Multiple Realizability and the Metaphysics of Reduction," in his *Supervenience and Mind* (New York: Cambridge University Press, 1993), pp. 309–35.

———"The Myth of Nonreductive Materialism," in his *Supervenience and Mind* (New York: Cambridge University Press, 1993), pp. 265–84.

Lehrer, Keith, ed. *Freedom and Determinism* (New York: Random House, 1966).

Levin, Yakir, and David Widerker. "Review of Richard Double, *Metaphilosophy and Free Will*," *The Philosophical Review* 107 (1998), pp. 630–4.

Lewis, David. *Philosophical Papers*, Volume II (New York: Oxford University Press, 1986).

Loewer, Barry. "Freedom from Physics: Quantum Mechanics and Free Will," *Philosophical Topics* 24 (1996), pp. 91–112.

Lucretius. *De Rerum Natura*, tr. W.H.D. Rouse, Loeb Classical Library (Cambridge: Harvard University Press, 1982).

Lycan, William G. *Consciousness* (Cambridge: MIT Press, 1987).

Mackie J.L. *Ethics: Inventing Right and Wrong* (Harmondsworth, England: Penguin, 1977).

Maletzky B.M. "Assisted Court Sensitization," in D.J. Cox and R.J. Daitzman, eds. *Exhibitionism: Description, Assessment, and Treatment* (New York: Garland, 1980).

Martinson, Robert. "What Works? – Questions and answers about prison reform," *The Public Interest* 35 (1974), pp. 22–54.

———"New Findings, New Views: A Note of Caution Regarding Sentencing Reform," *Hofstra Law Review* 7 (1979), pp. 242–58.

McCloskey H.J. "A Non-utilitarian Approach to Punishment," *Inquiry* 8 (1965), pp. 239–55.

McIntyre, Alison. "Compatibilists Could Have Done Otherwise: Responsibility and Negative Agency" *The Philosophical Review* 103 (1994), pp. 453–88.

McKenna, Michael. "Alternative Possibilities and the Failure of the Counterexample Strategy," *Journal of Social Philosophy* 28 (1997), pp. 71–85.

———"The Limits of Evil and the Role of Moral Address: A Defense of Strawsonian Compatibilism," *The Journal of Ethics* 2 (1998), pp. 123–42.

———"Assessing Reasons-Responsive Compatibilism," *International Journal of Philosophical Studies* 8 (2000).

McLaughlin, Brian. "The Rise and Fall of British Emergentism," in *Emergence or Reduction? Essays on The Prospects of Nonreductive Physicalism*, eds. A. Beckerman, H. Flohr, and J. Kim (New York: Walter de Gruyter, 1992).

Mele, Alfred. *Autonomous Agents* (New York: Oxford University Press, 1995).

———"Soft Libertarianism and Frankfurt-Style Scenarios," *Philosophical Topics* 24 (1996), pp. 123–41.

———and David Robb, "Rescuing Frankfurt-Style Cases," *The Philosophical Review* 107 (1998), pp. 97–112.

———"Review of Kane's *Significance of Free Will*," *Journal of Philosophy* 95 (1998), pp. 581–4.

———"Ultimate Responsibility and Dumb Luck," *Social Philosophy and Policy* 16 (1999), pp. 274–93.

Menninger, Karl. "Verdict Guilty, Now What?" *Harper's Magazine*, August 1959, pp. 60–4.

———*The Crime of Punishment* (New York: Viking Press, 1968).

Meyer, Robert G. *Abnormal Behavior and the Criminal Justice System* (New York: Macmillan, 1992), pp. 102–3.

Mill, John Stuart. *Utilitarianism* (Indianapolis: Hackett, 1979).

Montague, Philip. *Punishment as Societal Defense* (Lanham, MD: Rowman and Littlefield, 1995).

Moore, Michael. "The Moral Worth of Retribution," in *Responsibility, Character, and the Emotions*, ed. Ferdinand Schoeman (Cambridge: Cambridge University Press, 1987), pp. 179–219, reprinted in *Punishment and Rehabilitation*, third edition, ed. Jeffrie E. Murphy (Belmont, CA: Wadsworth, 1995), pp. 94–130.

Morris, Herbert. "Persons and Punishment," *The Monist* 52 (1968), pp. 475–501, reprinted in *Punishment and Rehabilitation*, third edition, ed. Jeffrie E. Murphy, pp. 74–93.

———"A Paternalistic Theory of Punishment," *American Philosophical Quarterly* 18 (1981);" reprinted in *Punishment and Rehabilitation*, third edition, Jeffrie E. Murphy, ed., pp. 154–68.

Murphy, Jeffrie E., ed. *Punishment and Rehabilitation*, third edition (Belmont, CA: Wadsworth, 1995).

Nagel, Thomas. *The View From Nowhere* (Oxford: Oxford University Press, 1986).

Nowell-Smith P.H. "Free Will and Moral Responsibility," *Mind* 57, pp. 45–65.

Nozick, Robert. *Philosophical Explanations* (Cambridge: Harvard University Press, 1981).

O'Connor, Timothy. "Indeterminacy and Free Agency: Three Recent Views," *Philosophy and Phenomenological Research* 53 (1993), pp. 499–526.

———"Emergent Properties," *American Philosophical Quarterly* 31 (1994), pp. 91–104.

———"Agent Causation," in *Agents, Causes, and Events*, ed. Timothy O'Connor (Oxford: Oxford University Press, 1995), pp. 170–200.

———ed. *Agents, Causes, and Events* (Oxford: Oxford University Press, 1995).

Otsuka, Michael. "Killing the Innocent in Self-Defense," *Philosophy and Public Affairs* 23 (1994), pp. 74–93.

———"Incompatibilism and the Avoidability of Blame," *Ethics* 108 (1998), pp. 685–701.

Palmer T. "The 'Effectiveness' Issue Today," *Federal Probation* 46 (1983), pp. 3–10.

Patterson G.R. *A Social Learning Approach: Coercive Family Process 3* (Eugene, OR: Catalia, 1982).

Patterson G.R., P. Chamberlain, and J. Reid. "A comparative evaluation of a parent training program," *Behavior Therapy* 13 (1982), pp. 638–50.

Pereboom, Derk, and Hilary Kornblith. "The Metaphysics of Irreducibility," *Philosophical Studies* 63 (1991), pp. 125–46.

Pereboom, Derk. "Stoic Psychotherapy in Descartes and Spinoza," *Faith and Philosophy* 12 (1994), pp. 592–625.

——"Determinism *Al Dente*," *Noûs* 29, March 1995, pp. 21–45.

——ed. *Free Will* (Indianapolis: Hackett, 1997).

——"Alternative Possibilities and Causal Histories," *Philosophical Perspectives* 14, 2000, pp. 119–37.

——Review of Robert Kane, *The Significance of Free Will*, *Ethics* 111 (2000), pp. 426–9.

Pettit, Philip. "Determinism with Deliberation," *Analysis* 49 (1989), pp. 42–4.

Pietroski, Paul, and Georges Rey. "When Other Things Aren't Equal: Saving *Ceteris Paribus* Laws from Vacuity," *British Journal for the Philosophy of Science* 46 (1995), pp. 80–110.

Priestley, Joseph. *A Free Discussion of the Doctrines of Materialism and Philosophical Necessity, In a Correspondence between Dr. Price and Dr. Priestley* (1788), Part III, pp. 147–52, reprinted in Joseph Priestley, *Priestley's Writings on Philosophy, Science, and Politics*, ed. John Passmore (New York: Collier, 1965).

Quinn, Warren. "The Right to Threaten and the Right to Punish," *Philosophy and Public Affairs* 14 (1985), pp. 327–73.

Ravizza, Mark. "Semi-Compatibilism and the Transfer of Non-Responsibility," *Philosophical Studies* 75 (1994), pp. 61–93.

Rawls, John. "Two Concepts of Rules," *The Philosophical Review* 64 (1955), pp. 3–32.

Reid, Thomas. *The Works of Thomas Reid, D.D.*, eighth edition, ed. Sir William Hamilton (Edinburgh, 1895). Reprinted with an introduction by H.M. Bracken (Hildesheim: Georg Olms Verlag, 1967).

Rowe, William. *Thomas Reid on Freedom and Morality* (Ithaca: Cornell University Press, 1991).

——"Two Concepts of Freedom," in *Agents, Causes, and Events*, O'Connor, ed. (Oxford: Oxford University Press, 1995), pp. 151–71.

Russell, Paul. *Freedom and Moral Sentiment* (New York: Oxford University Press, 1995).

Santayana, George. "A Junior Forensic," *The Daily Crimson* v. 7, no. 15 (February 25, 1885).

Sartre, Jean-Paul. *Being and Nothingness* (New York: Philosophical Library, 1956).

——"The Humanism of Existentialism," in *Existentialism and the Human Emotions*, tr. Bernard Frechtman (New York: Philosophical Library, 1957).

Schlick, Moritz. "When is a Man Responsible?" in *Problems of Ethics*, tr. David Rynin (New York: Prentice-Hall, 1939), pp. 143–56; reprinted in *Free Will and Determinism*, ed. Bernard Berofsky (New York: Harper and Rowe, 1966), pp. 54–63.

Schoeman, Ferdinand D. "On Incapacitating the Dangerous," *American Philosophical Quarterly* 16 (1979), pp. 27–35.

——ed. *Responsibility, Character and the Emotions* (Cambridge: Cambridge University Press, 1987).

Shatz, David. "Free Will and the Structure of Values," *Midwest Studies in Philosophy* 10 (1985), pp. 451–82.

Sinnott-Armstrong, Walter. "'Ought' Conversationally Implies 'Can'," *The Philosophical Review* 93 (1984), pp. 249–61.

———"'Ought To Have' and 'Could Have'," *Analysis* 45 (1985), pp. 44–8.

Skinner, B.F. *Beyond Freedom and Dignity* (New York: Vintage Books, 1970).

Slote, Michael. "Ethics Without Free Will," *Social Theory and Practice* 16 (1990), pp. 369–83.

Smart J.J.C. "Free Will, Praise, and Blame," *Mind* 70 (1961), pp. 291–306.

Smilansky, Saul. "Does the Free Will Debate Rest on a Mistake?" *Philosophical Papers* 22 (1993), pp. 173–88.

———"The Ethical Advantages of Hard Determinism," *Philosophy and Phenomenological Research* 54 (1994), pp. 355–63.

———"Can a Determinist Help Herself?" in C.H. Manekin and M. Kellner, eds. *Freedom and Moral Responsibility: General and Jewish Perspectives* (College Park: University of Maryland Press, 1997), pp. 85–98.

Sobel, Jordan Howard. *Puzzles for the Will* (Toronto: University of Toronto Press, 1998).

Spinoza, Baruch. *Ethics*, in *The Collected Works of Spinoza*, ed. and tr. Edwin Curley (Princeton: Princeton University Press, 1985).

Strawson, Galen. *Freedom and Belief* (Oxford: Oxford University Press, 1986).

———"The Impossibility of Moral Responsibility," *Philosophical Studies* 75 (1994), pp. 5–24.

Strawson, Peter F. "Freedom and Resentment," in ed. Gary Watson, *Free Will* (Oxford: Oxford University Press, 1982), pp. 59–80, originally published in *Proceedings of the British Academy* 48 (1962), pp. 1–25.

Stump, Eleonore. "Intellect, Will, and the Principle of Alternate Possibilities," in *Christian Theism and the Problems of Philosophy*, ed. Michael Beaty (University of Notre Dame Press, 1990), pp. 254–85. Reprinted in *Moral Responsibility*, eds. John Martin Fischer and Mark Ravizza (Ithaca, NY: Cornell University Press, 1993), pp. 237–62.

———"Persons: Identification and Freedom," *Philosophical Topics* 24 (1996), pp. 183–214.

———"Libertarian Freedom and the Principle of Alternative Possibilities," in *Faith, Freedom, and Rationality*, eds. Jeff Jordan and Daniel Howard Snyder (Lanham, MD: Rowman and Littlefield, 1996), pp. 73–88.

———"Dust, Determinism and Frankfurt: A Reply to Goetz," in *Faith and Philosophy* 16 (1999), pp. 413–22.

Taylor, Richard. *Metaphysics*, fourth edition (Englewood Cliffs: Prentice-Hall, 1974).

———*Action and Purpose* (Englewood Cliffs: Prentice-Hall, 1966).

Ten C.L. *Crime, Guilt, and Punishment* (Oxford: Oxford University Press, 1987).

Thorp, John. *Free Will* (London: Routledge & Kegan Paul, 1980).

Van Inwagen, Peter. "The Incompatibility of Free Will and Determinism, *Philosophical Studies* 27 (1975), pp. 185–9, reprinted in *Free Will*, ed. Gary Watson (Oxford: Oxford University Press, 1982), pp. 46–58.

———*An Essay On Free Will* (Oxford: Oxford University Press, 1983).

Wallace, R. Jay. *Responsibility and the Moral Sentiments* (Cambridge: Harvard University Press, 1994).

Waller, Bruce. "Free Will Gone Out of Control," *Behaviorism* 16 (1988), pp. 149–67.

——*Freedom Without Responsibility* (Philadelphia: Temple University Press, 1990).

Walters, Glenn D. *Foundations of Criminal Science* (New York: Praeger, 1992).

Wasserstrom, Richard. "Punishment," in *Philosophy and Social Issues* (Notre Dame: University of Notre Dame Press, 1980).

Watson, Gary. "Free Agency," in ed. Gary Watson, *Free Will* (Oxford: Oxford University Press, 1982), pp. 96–110, originally published in *Journal of Philosophy* 72 (1975), pp. 205–20.

——ed. *Free Will* (Oxford: Oxford University Press, 1982).

——"Responsibility and the Limits of Evil," in *Responsibility, Character, and the Emotions*, ed. Ferdinand Schoeman (Cambridge: Cambridge University Press, 1987), pp. 256–86.

Widerker, David. "Libertarianism and Frankfurt's Attack on the Principle of Alternative Possibilities," *The Philosophical Review* 104 (1995), pp. 247–61.

——"Libertarian Freedom and the Avoidability of Decisions," *Faith and Philosophy* 12 (1995), pp. 113–18.

Wiggins, David. "Towards a Reasonable Libertarianism," in *Essays on Freedom of Action*, ed. T. Honderich (London: Routledge & Kegan Paul, 1973).

Wolf, Susan. "Asymmetrical Freedom," *Journal of Philosophy* 77 (1980), pp. 151–66.

——*Freedom Within Reason* (Oxford: Oxford University Press, 1990).

Wyma, Keith D. "Moral Responsibility and Leeway for Action," *American Philosophical Quarterly* 34 (1997), pp. 57–70.

Yochelson S., and S. Samenow. *The Criminal Personality: A Profile for Change* (New York: Aronson, 1976).

——*The Criminal Personality: The Change Process* (New York: Aronson, 1977).

Zagzebski, Linda. *The Dilemma of Freedom and Foreknowledge* (New York: Oxford University Press, 1991).

——"Does Libertarian Freedom Require Alternate Possibilities?" *Philosophical Perspectives* 14 (2000).

Zimmerman, David. "Hierarchical Motivation and the Freedom of the Will," *Pacific Philosophical Quarterly* 62 (1981), pp. 354–68.

Zimmerman, Michael. *The Concept of Moral Obligation* (New York: Cambridge University Press, 1996).

Index

Broad, C.D., xx, 59, 63-5, 142n.40
Buddhism, xxv
"BW" (blameworthy-wrong) principle,
145-7

Castañeda, Hector-Neri, 136
causal determinism. *See* determinism
causal history incompatibilism. *See*
incompatibilism
Causal History Principle, 54, 111, 126,
128
causation. *See* agent causation,
determinism, indeterminism
ceteris paribus laws, 86-8
Chamberlain, P., 182n.36
Chisholm, Roderick, xvii, 40, 57-9,
85-6
choice. *See* decision, responsibility for
Christensen, David, 83n.20, 86n.23
Clarke, Randolph, xvii, 13n.29, 39-40,
46, 52n.28, 60-4, 65-6n.29,
66n.50, 68n.52, 81-5, 129n.5
Clockwork Orange, 179
coercion, xix, 101-6, 124-5, 110-20,
189
cognitive therapy for criminals, 183-5
compatibilism, xvi-xx, 89-128, 130-5,
198-9
definition of, xvi-xviii, 130-1, 134-
5
P.F. Strawson's, xix, 90-100, 123-5
Hume's, 90-103, 110-17, 123-5
Ayer's, 101-3, 110-17
Frankfurt's, 103-6, 110-17
Fischer and Ravizza's, 106-22
Wallace's, 109-20, 123-5
Haji's, 117-20
generalization arguments against, 95,
98-100, 110-20, 123-8, 133
manipulation arguments against,
110-28, 133
consequence argument, 36-7, 133
consequentialism, 148-52
constraint, xix, 101-6, 110-20, 124-5,
189
control, xv, xxiii, 4-6, 13, 38-128
volitional, 118-20

could-have done-otherwise, *See*
alternative possibilities
criminal behavior and treatment, xv,
xxi-xxii, 155-86, 198-9, 210
Curtis, Robert Lee, 175

decision, responsibility for, xxiii, 43
deliberation, 131, 136-8
Della Rocca, Michael, 2n.1, 6n.11
Dennett, Daniel, xxiv, 13n.28, 81n.16,
138, 156-8, 184
De Rose, Keith, 55-6n.30
Descartes, René, 192, 207-8
desert, xxii, 134, 159-61, 170-2, 186,
194. *See also* responsibility,
blameworthiness, praiseworthiness
desires, first- and second-order, 103-6,
110-17
irresistible, 102-6, 108, 110-20, 124-5
determinism, 1-37, 48-50, 54-7, 70-3,
79-81, 89-128, 187-213. *See also*
hard determinism, hard
incompatibilism
dignity, 151-2
direct argument for incompatibilism,
33-6
dismay, 190-7
definition of, 190
Double, Richard, xx, 39n.2, 50-1, 65-
6n.49, 131-2
dualism (mind-body), 70, 79-86
Duggan, Timothy J., 107n.35
Dupré, John, 72-3

Einstein, Albert, 211-12
emergence, 70, 73-88. *See also* strong
emergentism
emotions. *See* reactive attitudes
Epicureanism, xvii, 40n.5
epistemic conditions on responsibility,
25-7, 29-31
error theory, meta-ethical, 132-3
ethics, xxi, 131-5, 139-57
event-causal libertarianism, xvii, 40-54,
127-8
definition of, xvii, 40-1
and explanation of action, 39

226

and rationality of action, 39
  Humean challenge to, 41-54
  luck objection to, 50-4
  rollback argument against, 50-1n.23
  randomizing manipulator argument
    against, 50-4
excuses, 92-3, 123-5
exemptions from responsibility, 92-100,
  123-5
explanation
  causal, 38-9, 59-65, 74-9
  rational, 65-8
  of responsibility, 1-37
explanatory exclusion, 74-9

Farrell, Daniel M., 168-74
Feldman, Fred, 144n.43
Fischer, John Martin, xix, 2-10, 23, 34-
  6, 37n.58, 100, 106n.34, 106-22,
  133, 140-1, 151
flickers of freedom, 6-28
Fodor, Jerry, 76-7, 87
Foot, Philippa, 43n.12
forgiveness, 92, 201
Frankfurt, Harry G., xix, 2, 100, 103-
  6, 110-17, 124
Frankfurt-style cases and arguments,
  xvii, 2-36, 133, 140-1
  Fischer's, 2-3, 7-10
  Ginet's, 28-33
  Haji's, 13
  Hunt's, 15-18
  McIntyre's, 5n.9
  Mele and Robb's, 14-18, 35
  Pereboom's (Tax Evasion), 18-23
  Ravizza's (Avalanche), 34-6
  Stump's, 11-12
free will, *passim*
  compatibilist, 100-9
  incompatibilist, 1-37
  event-causal libertarian, 40-54
  agent-causal libertarian, 55-68
  phenomenology of, 41, 44-6, 136-7
freedom, xxv, 129. *See also* free will
  political, xxv
  religious, xxv
Frueh, B. Christopher, 183-5

"GR" (good-right) principle, 145-7
Gendreau, Paul, 181-3
generalization arguments against
  compatibilism, 95, 98-100, 110-
  20, 123-5, 133
Gert, Bernard, 107n.35
Ginet, Carl, xvii, 8, 28-33, 35n.53, 54,
  36n.56, 39-54, 56-9, 63-5, 84,
  193n.8
Girard, René, 209
Goetz, Stewart, 12
gratitude, xix, 92, 201-2
Greenwood, P., 181n.35
guilt, xix, 204-7

Haji, Ishtiyaque, 9n.17, 11, 13, 28n.46,
  106n.34, 111n.48, 117-20, 141-8
Hampton, Jean, 162-4, 178n.25
hard determinism, xvi, xx, 128-31,
  135-9, 142, 148-54, 187-9, 211-
  12. *See also* determinism, hard
  incompatibilism
  definition of, xvi
hard incompatibilism, xx-xxv, 1-213
  definition of, xx-xxi, 127-8
  argument for, 1-128, summary, 127-8
  and agency, 135-9
  and rationality, 138-9
  and morality, 139-57, 195-213
  and moral worth, 152-4, 195-7
  and non-consequentialism, 148-52
  and wrongdoing, 154-6, 198-200,
    204-13
  and treatment of criminals, 155-86,
    198-9
  and meaning in life, 187-213
  and self-respect, 195-7
  and relationships, 199-213
  and reactive attitudes, 199-213
  advantages of, 200-1, 207-13
  disadvantages of, 139-47, 152-4,
    159-61, 172
Heinaman, Robert, 2n.1
Henning, Kris R., 181n.34, 183-5
Hill, Thomas E. Jr., 151-2
Hobart, R., xix, 39n.1
Holbach, Paul, xx, 129

microphysical constraints, 70-9
Mill, John Stuart, 210
Montague, Philip, 160n.2, 166n.15
Moore, Michael, 159n.1, 160n.3
moral accountability. *See* accountability
moral anger, 208-13
moral luck, xxiii
moral responsibility. *See* responsibility
moral worth, 152-4, 195
morality, xxi, 130-5, 139-57
Morris, Herbert, 162-6, 178-86

Nagel, Thomas, 65-6n.49, 137-8
no-free-will-either-way theory, xx,
    129-33
non-cognitivism, meta-ethical, xxii,
    132-5
non-consequentialism, 148-52, 159
non-physicalism, 69-70, 73-88
nonreductive materialism, 69-88
Nowell-Smith, P.H., 39n.1
Nozick, Robert, 40n.5

"O" (origination) principle, 4-7, 47, 54
obligation, 143-8
Ockham, William of, xvii, 27-8
O'Connor, Timothy, xvii, 39-40, 41n.6,
    57-9, 64, 69-88
omissions, xviii
ordinary nonreductive materialism, 70-
    3
    definition, 70
Oregon Learning Center, 182
origination, 4-6, 47, 54, 134-5, 189-
    90
Otsuka, Michael, 23-7, 172n.21
ought, 143-8, 197
overdetermination, 34-6
overriding strategy, 79, 85-8
"OW" (ought-wrong) principle, 143-
    8

Palmer, T., 181n.35
Parsons, B.V., 182n.36
partially random events, 48-50, 54-7,
    71-2, 89-90, 126-8, 135-6, 140,
    143

definition of, 48
Patterson G.R., 182n.36
Pereboom, Derk, 2n.1, 19n.39, 77,
    207n.24
Pettit, Philip, 137n.26, 160n.2
phenomenology of free will, 41, 44-6,
    136-7
physics, xxi, 41-2, 69-88. *See also* laws
    of physics, quantum physics
Pietroski, Paul, 87
power for alternative possibilities, 23-8
powers of reflective self control
    (Wallace), 110-17, 123-5, 139
pragmatic arguments and responsibility,
    197-9
praiseworthiness, xxii, 139-40. *See also*
    responsibility
Priestley, Joseph, xx, 129, 148-9
principle of alternative possibilities.
    See alternative possibility
    conditions
probabilistic causation. *See*
    indeterminism, laws of physics
probabilistic explanation, 65-6n.49
punishment, 134, 158–186
    deterrence theory of, 166-86
    moral education theory of, 161-6,
        186
    retribution theory of, 134, 159-61,
        170-2, 186

quantum physics, 41-2, 71-2, 83-5
quarantine and criminal detention,
    174-86
Quinn, Warren, 168-74

random events. *See* partially random
    events, truly random events
rationality, 7, 55-6, 65-8, 107-22, 131,
    138-9, 179-86, 189, 197-213. *See*
    also accountability, autonomy,
    reasons-responsiveness
Ravizza, Mark, 34-6, 100, 106-22
Rawls, John, 167-8
reactive attitudes, xix, xxii-xxiii, 90-
    100, 109-10, 187-8, 199-213
reasons, 65-8, 106-26, 138-41, 180

van Inwagen, Peter, 7, 33-7, 50n.23, 52n.27, 82, 136
volitional control, 118-20
voluntary, 134-5, 196-7, 203-4

Wallace, R. Jay, 95, 98-100, 109-20, 123-5, 139
Waller, Bruce, xx, 50-1, 129, 150, 156, 205
Walters, Glenn D., 181n.32, 182n.36
"WAP" (wrong-alternative-possibilities) principle, 144-8
Wasserstrom, Richard, 180n.30
Watson, Gary, xix, 5n.8, 95-6, 106n.34, 211-12

Wertheimer, Rachel, 155n.64
Widerker, David, 8-22, 133n.17
Wiggins, David, 40n.2
will. *See* free will, voluntary
Wolf, Susan, xix, 140-1
wrongdoing, 154-86, 198-200, 204-13
wrongness, 141-8
Wyma, Keith D., 8n.16, 23-7

Yochelson, S., 183-5

Zagzebski, Linda, 2n.1
Zimmerman, David, 106n.34
Zimmerman, Michael, 144n.43
Zimring, F., 181n.35